Strengthening Ethical Wisdom

This publication is designed to provide accurate and authoritative information in regard to the subject matter covered. It is sold with the understanding that neither the author nor the publisher are engaged in rendering legal, accounting, or other professional services. If legal advice or other expert assistance is required, the services of a competent professional should be sought.

The views expressed in this publication are strictly those of the author and do not represent the official positions of the American Hospital Association.

Printed in the United States of America - *01/12*

ISBN: 978-0-8401-0799-2

Strengthening Ethical Wisdom

Tools for Transforming Your Health Care Organization

Jack A. Gilbert

Health Forum, Inc.
An American Hospital Association Company
CHICAGO

AHA press

For all those who strive
to do the right thing every day,
and
for my children,
Julian, Jonathan, and Naomi

I long to accomplish a great and noble task,
but it is my chief duty to accomplish humble tasks
as though they were great and noble.
The world is moved along not only by the mighty shoves
of its heroes, but also by the aggregate
of the tiny pushes of each honest worker.

—Helen Keller

Contents

List of Figures

About the Author

Jack Gilbert, Ed.D., is a consultant, presenter, and award-winning author. His work is focused on issues of leadership, organizational and personal integrity, and large-scale change.

His book *Productivity Management: A Step-By-Step Guide for Health Care Professionals*, published by AHA Press, was named Book of the Year by the Healthcare Information and Management Systems Society and was used widely by health care managers.

Jack Gilbert is a fellow of the American College of Healthcare Executives, a member of the San Diego Organization of Healthcare Leaders, and a member of the National Speakers Association. He holds his doctorate from The George Washington University in Washington, DC, where his dissertation focused on the role of ethics in decision making.

Preface

THE PURPOSE of this book is to affirm the belief that when health care organizations and those who work in them can more fully express their passion for caring by doing the right thing every day, the result is stronger organizational performance, including improved safety and care, and higher personal satisfaction.

I have written this book to give leaders, managers, and individual contributors in health care organizations effective and practical ways to strengthen everyday ethical behaviors and ethical decision making. The book looks beyond compliance programs to provide a blueprint for success for organizations and individuals committed to achieving exceptional performance while aspiring to the highest levels of organizational and personal integrity. In fact, it demonstrates that high levels of integrity are critical to reaching and sustaining higher levels of organizational performance in safety, care, patient and employee satisfaction, retention, and financial health. This is a practical book full of ways to assess where the organization and individuals stand in their relative strengths and weaknesses regarding everyday ethical decision making. It provides guidance for actions needed to build strengths and to lessen weaknesses.

My intention is that this book will also support people who struggle with reconciling their personal values with organizational actions at odds with those values by offering ways to resolve this conflict—and that it will support those who experience a match between their own values and the values of the organization by showing ways for them to further strengthen that match.

This book is research based. My doctoral dissertation focused on the role of ethics in decision making. From that and other research, and from my own work and life experiences, I have observed the dynamic of ethical erosion. Research shows that it is the small steps and small decisions that lead even well-meaning individuals and their organizations into ethical conflicts—a slippery slope that can ultimately undermine the organization's viability. The antidote to ethical erosion is ethical wisdom. Tapping the latent individual and collective ethical wisdom of staff and other stakeholders is crucial in stopping ethical erosion and in strengthening organizational and personal integrity. How to avoid ethical erosion and foster ethical wisdom is an important focus of the book.

I have made mistakes and, at times, have failed in my personal ethics. I know what it is like to park some of my values at the door at work in order to keep a job to pay the mortgage and to support my family. I also know I was less than fully effective, not much fun to be around, and not a great dad or husband during those times. Like so many others, I strive to do what is right even when there are pressures to do otherwise. My hope is that this book supports you and your organization in doing the same.

Part I of this book defines what doing the right thing means for health care organizations and for those who work in them. It shows the linkage between ethical behavior and sustainable performance and explores the negative dynamic of ethical erosion and the opposing positive dynamic of ethical wisdom.

The rest of the book focuses in depth on the four ethical pathways through which an organization produces exceptional results by doing the right thing, and it discusses the disciplines (or practices) that are essential to the health of each of those pathways: Part II focuses on culture and the disciplines of mindfulness, voice, respect, tenacity, and legacy. Part III focuses on leadership and governance; the leadership disciplines of noble purpose, ceaseless ambition, candor, and passion; and the governance disciplines of noble purpose, independent engagement, ethical board culture, and ethical succession. Part IV focuses on infrastructure and the disciplines of ethical engagement, accountability, and management by facts. Part V focuses on personal integrity and the disciplines of personal legacy, mindfulness, and choice.

Each part of the book discussing an ethical pathway includes a "vital signs" diagnostic to help you assess the strength of that pathway and its disciplines. Each part also provides ways to use the diagnostic to create needed change. Appendix 1 brings together those diagnostics in a comprehensive ethical health survey that is also available for completion on-line. Appendix 2 contains the key needed to evaluate your responses to "The Approaches to Ethical Decision Making Diagnostic," which is included with the permission of Brian O'Toole, vice president, mission and ethics, Sisters of Mercy Health System, and is presented in chapter 15.

Acknowledgments

SO MANY PEOPLE have made this book possible. To anyone I have omitted, I apologize.

I want first to acknowledge Jo Anne Kellert, my coach and friend, for her tireless support in helping me find my own voice; Richard Hill, my editor at AHA Press, for his consistent and patient encouragement and direction; Richard Howells, my friend and colleague, for his thoughtful insights about the diagnostics; Brian O'Toole for his generosity and permission to include "The Approaches to Ethical Decision Making Diagnostic" in this book; and the many colleagues and friends who have supported and encouraged me over many years, including Dave Butts, Jeanne Cherbeneau, Merrili Escue, Christine Gaunt, Faith Gibson, Nancy Golden, Benn Greenspan, Glenda Hanna, Chip Hardt, Carolyn Hendrickson, Paul Hofmann, Cathy Holmquist, Kate Howells, Jan Lawrence, Miles Kierson, Mark Millemann, Pat Millemann, Ruth Reiner, Diana Stonis, and Kay Zurn.

Thanks to the following people who have enriched this book by giving so freely of their time and insights: Bob Akins, Cindy Banta, Vic Buzachero, Charley Corace, Doug Cropper, Jeff Dutton, Richard Esgate, Olive Gallagher, Marshall Goldsmith, Peter Hursh, Steve Ivy, Tom Jensen, Rod Lanthorne, Carol Miltner, Glen Mueller, Mike Murphy, Jim Neal, Barbro Owens-Kirkpatrick, Robbie Pearl, Marilyn Potgiesser, Howard Putnam, Robert Quinn, Garry Ridge, Nicholas Rosseinsky, Frank Sardone, Greg Schaffer, Jay Shutter, Becky Siegel, Al Stubblefield, Judy Thompson, Chris Van Gorder, Susan Watts, and the wonderful employees I met at Baptist Health Care in Pensacola, Florida, and at Bronson Healthcare Group in Kalamazoo, Michigan.

And I give a final thank-you to the many baristas in Encinitas, California, who gave me sustenance as I worked on this book.

1

Ethics, Integrity, and "Doing the Right Thing"

Man is born a predestined idealist, for he is born to act.
To act is to affirm the worth of an end,
and to persist in affirming the worth of an end
is to make an ideal.

—Oliver Wendell Holmes

THERE ARE enough different definitions of what constitutes ethical behavior to stock a few shelves in a bookstore. And if you search through them long enough, you are sure to find a definition to suit any point of view that appeals to you, whether you believe that ethics is relative and depends on the culture of your times or specific circumstances; you believe that ethical behavior is absolute and transcends any time, place, or circumstance; you believe that ethics is what is best for the greatest number; or you believe that ethics is what is best for you. What is common to those definitions is that they seek to explain which behaviors and practices are right and which are wrong in deciding how we treat others as individuals, as groups, as organizations, and as a society.

The definitions you are about to read have been created for this book for the purpose of illuminating what it means to do the right thing in health care organizations, which have both social and business commitments and which are full of people with a passion for healing and caring, and for the health of the individuals, families, and communities they serve.

This interdependence of the organization and the individuals who work in it is amplified in health care organizations in which the organization and those who work within it share the calling to service.

A Partnership of Goodwill

It is very difficult for an individual or small group of employees to make a substantial impact in having their organization do the right thing when the leadership, culture, and work processes give them insufficient support in making that impact. In such cases an employee may see an unethical act, or a common practice that is unsafe, and decide to withhold information, often for fear of retaliation or because he or she assumes management will not act on the information. In rare cases whistle blowing may follow, driven by current or ex-employees who, having failed to make a difference working within the organization, go public to be heard and to create change. Or a whistle blower may act for personal gain by reporting unethical practices to a third party in order to receive a financial reward.

By the same token, it is discouraging to any leadership trying to make changes and to do the right thing when employees defeat their efforts by debating the leadership's sincerity and, finding it lacking, then decide to sit on the sidelines. On the other hand, doubters who are concerned about the future of the organization, who are willing to share their questions about change in constructive ways, and who are open to being participants in change are contributors to finding ways to do the right thing. But employees who are immoveable in their cynicism about the value and possibility of positive change are persistent obstacles to progress of any kind.

For the organization and those who work within it to succeed in doing the right thing requires a partnership of goodwill, each engaged by the other in strengthening ethical behavior (figure 1-1). For that reason, this book consistently looks at ethical behavior and decision making from the perspective of the organization and of the individual employee, starting with defining ethical behavior.

Personal Integrity Defined

Part V of this book, "The Ethical Pathway of Personal Integrity," examines in detail the role of personal integrity in sustaining high ethical standards. The purpose of defining personal integrity here is to provide a way to think about individual action and accountability throughout the book.

For us as individuals, doing the right thing consists of demonstrating through our actions those values we hold most dear. When we act in full harmony with those cherished values, we experience personal integrity—a

Figure 1-1. A Partnership of Goodwill

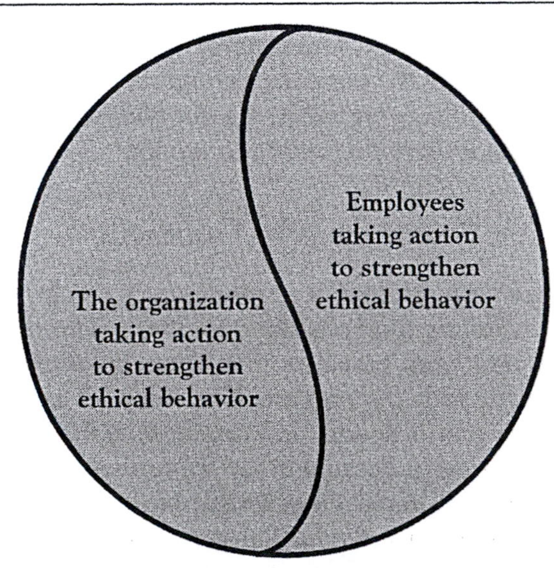

sense of wholeness and peace. When we act in ways inconsistent with them, we often experience an internal dissonance and uncomfortable emotions, among them disappointment, frustration, and blame of ourselves and others in the organization, or of the organization itself. The realization of this dissonance brings the opportunity to be "truer" to ourselves, to enhance our personal integrity. This "truing" is a life-long process that brings us closer to an ideal of ourselves, and our work provides important and continual opportunities for this process. We define personal integrity as:

> **A state of wholeness and peace experienced when our goals, actions, and decisions are consistent with our most cherished values**

Organizational Integrity Defined

Organizations also have an ideal of themselves that is expressed through their vision, mission, and values. Organizational dynamics are more complex than individual dynamics given the diversity of individuals, groups of employees, and stakeholders that influence an organization's actions and performance. Nevertheless, the goal is organizational integrity, which we define as:

> **The means of producing stronger, sustainable performance through ethical pathways consistent with the vision, mission, and values of the organization**

Implicit in this definition is a belief that the vision, mission, and values of a health care organization speak to the best aspirations of the organization and those who work within it. This is reasonable. The calling to care for and enrich the quality of life for patients, to support their families in times of stress, and to enhance the wellness of communities served by the organization, is implicitly or explicitly stated in vision, mission, and value statements, and is at the heart of what draws many to health care, whether in for-profit or in not-for-profit environments. It is also a reason why so many react negatively when health care is talked about as a business or the term *health care industry* is used. For many, these terms discredit the avocation of working in health care.

An organization experiences its own integrity when its behavior and decision making are consistent with its vision, mission, and values. In addition, an organization experiences dissonance and stress when its behavior and decision making are at odds with them.

Dissonance occurs when the vision, mission, and values are not integrated into the everyday life of the organization. Sometimes an organization and its leadership become preoccupied with the financial condition of the organization to the exclusion of its vision, mission, and values. This preoccupation can look like a tolerance of behaviors and decisions that conflict with the organization's values. For example, a results-producing member of the management team, a long-term employee, or an influential physician is tolerated even while their treatment of others in the organization is completely at odds with the values of the organization. The message heard loud and clear by staff is: "Yes, our values matter, but sometimes we need to downplay them to get the results we need." In such an organization, values are a contingent commitment; their day-to-day importance depends on the circumstances the organization faces. It is a slippery slope. The management of Enron, a company with a 64-page code of ethics, asked its board of directors to waive a part of the code, which opened the door for some executives to engage in activities that were a clear conflict of interest, all supposedly in service of the company's financial health. This contributed to the eventual collapse of the company.[1]

Another version of values as contingent commitment is maintaining a pretense of their importance rather than demonstrating their importance by continually seeking to strengthen them in a variety of ways. For example, some leaders may express satisfaction that high ethical standards are ensured in their organization because there was a leadership workshop on values 12 months ago, because the values are prominently posted, and because every employee has received training in ethical compliance sometime in the past few years and signed that they understand the organization's code of conduct. Part III of this book, "The Ethical Pathway of Leadership and Governance," and part IV, "The Ethical Pathway of Infrastructure," show that health care organizations committed to living their vision, mission, and values are relentlessly creative in finding ways to focus on them every day—ways that include events and trainings but go far beyond them.

It is essential that doing the right thing is an unwavering commitment if the vision, mission, and values are to be strengthened. As long as ethical behavior is seen as a "nice to have" and not a "need to have," it will quickly lose its place as a priority in decision making, especially when times are tough or when a decision poses a choice between organizational values and financial results. And lack of uncompromising adherence to ethical pathways will accelerate the erosion of ethical behavior and decision making. These concerns are discussed more fully in chapter 2.

Intentions, Performance, and Ethical Pathways

In this book we take the point of view that (1) all performance, including financial performance, is strengthened through a consistent focus on vision, mission, and values, and (2) that the realization of the organization's vision, mission, and values is attained through diligent attention to the ethical pathways used to create high, sustained performance. These ethical pathways are introduced in chapter 3 and discussed in more detail throughout the book. Figure 1-2 shows ethical pathways as the vehicle to transform the organization's intentions into performance.

Intentions include not only the vision, mission, and values, but also the strategies and goals of the organization, not just at the highest level but throughout the organization. For example, these intentions include departmental, team, and individual goals.

Figure 1-2. From Intentions to Performance through Ethical Pathways

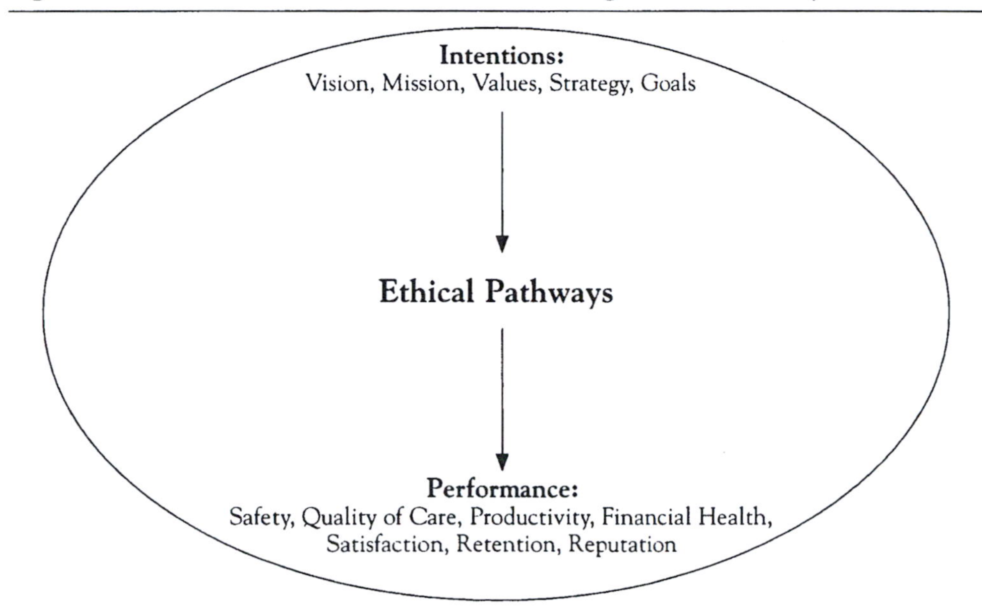

Performance refers to a wide range of outcomes vital to the health and welfare of patients and their families, to the communities served, and to the sustainability of the organization. They include:

- Stronger performance in patient safety
- Improved quality of care
- Higher productivity
- Sound financial health
- Increased patient and employee satisfaction
- Improved retention of staff
- Strong community reputation

Clearly, the scope of organizational and personal integrity extends far beyond risk management or compliance issues. Integrity is about more than avoiding exposure. It is about instilling the vision, mission, and values the organization and those who work in it aspire to in everyday work. As Lynn Paine, a Harvard Business School professor, points out, "Risk management is only part of the story and the benefits of positive values go well beyond problem avoidance."[2]

Survival is a powerful motivator. Leaders can jolt their organization out of the status quo by convincing employees that only immediate dramatic action will avoid dire results, including the possible failure of the organization. That works, but only in the short term. A sole focus on survival over time becomes wearying, discouraging, and exhausting, which is to say that leadership's persistent and narrow focus on doing more with less will lead to fatigue, burnout, turnover, and more and more difficulty in producing results.

But when a call to action even in difficult times is accompanied by the possibility of a compelling future for the organization and its workers, then both the work itself as well as those involved in it are enriched. After all, work is about far more than earning money. It is an access to self-identity, self-esteem, contribution, independence, social relationships, and a sense of accomplishment.[3] This is not to say the way is easy, but this book presents examples of the results of this approach.

Values and Profit

More than three quarters of hospitals in the United States fall under the definition of not-for-profit.[4] It is clear that, whether investor-owned or not-for-profit, any hospital needs to operate on sound business principles to ensure economic viability. This has created ongoing debate, especially in the not-for-profit community, about whether the adoption of business principles has come at the expense of the treasured vision, mission, and values of health care organizations—that it is a devil's bargain selling the soul of health care for financial benefit, which has become the end and not the means. The fear is of the old maxim, "no margin, no mission," becoming the new maxim, "more margin, more margin."

For those working in health care, this is not a philosophical debate but a day-to-day reality. Doing more with less can become a primary goal as measures of organizational effectiveness such as patient safety and quality of care can take a back seat to financial measures of success. By far the top issue confronting hospital CEOs is financial challenges. In a survey in which they were asked to identify the top three issues currently confronting their hospital, 67 percent of CEOs cited financial issues. Other major issues trailed. Quality was cited by 23 percent, and 20 percent cited patient safety.[5]

We run the risk of being trapped and led by a false choice. Living values and making a profit or surplus is not an either/or proposition. There is no reason why one should be subordinate to the other. In fact, there is strong evidence that a key to long-term organizational success is the capacity to focus on the organization's vision, mission, and values, while also having a clear focus on all parameters of performance, including financial health. The authors of the book *Built to Last* conducted rigorous research in comparing the performance of visionary companies with other companies that were primarily driven by profit. They found that:

> Contrary to business school doctrine "maximizing shareholder wealth" or "profit maximization" has not been the dominant driving force or primary objective through the history of the visionary companies. Visionary companies pursue a cluster of objectives of which making money is only one—and not necessarily the primary one. Yes, they seek profits, but they are equally guided by a core ideology—core values and a sense of purpose beyond just making money. Yet, paradoxically, the visionary companies make more money than the more purely profit-driven comparison companies.[6]

Following are two examples of successful companies with very different products and histories, which have followed these principles, Johnson & Johnson and Kyocera.

The Story of Johnson & Johnson

Johnson & Johnson was organized in New Jersey in 1887. Today, it is a family of companies employing more than 115,000 worldwide. It has had 73 consecutive years of sales increases and 44 years of dividend increases for its shareholders.[7,8] It is committed to the health and well-being of people and to financial success.

The company was founded by Robert Wood Johnson and his two brothers, James Wood Johnson and Edward Mead Johnson. Of the three brothers Robert Wood Johnson was the driving force of the company and its direction. He had a commitment to creating a profitable enterprise that would reduce unnecessary death and increase health. He was convinced of the validity of Joseph Lister's principle of asepsis at a time when support for it was mixed and attacks on Louis Pasteur's theory of germs (on which this principle was based) were frequent. He partnered with a pharmacist, Fred Kilmer, who became a lifetime colleague and friend. Kilmer would come to be called the most revered pharmaceutical chemist in the country by *Time* magazine.

Both Johnson and Kilmer had a thirst for knowledge and innovation, and they also shared a yearning to explore the frontiers of medicine and health. Their business and research collaboration created a range of products consistent with Lister's principles of antiseptic surgery. Their experiments in product development yielded products that would have an important impact on the practice of health care and the health of society.

Good medicine and good business went hand in hand. In 1888, based on Kilmer's extensive research, the company published a manual titled *Modern Methods of Antiseptic Wound Treatment*. This scientific contribution was coupled with business promotion. At the back of the manual, the reader could find surgical products available from the company. The manual's compilation of wide-ranging notes from eminent surgeons was hailed as the most authoritative discussion of aseptic wound treatment ever published. Demand was overwhelming and the manual became an influential argument for Lister's principles. Sales of Johnson & Johnson products soared.

The company continued to develop innovations that responded to unmet medical needs. For example, on a train ride with the Denver & Rio Railway's chief surgeon, Robert Wood Johnson learned of the growing number of railroad accidents and lack of medical expertise and supplies, which increased the adverse consequences to those injured. This conversation resulted in publication of the first manual on first aid accompanied, naturally, by the first set of first aid products.

After his death in 1910, Robert Wood Johnson was lionized as a great humanitarian and businessman. Twenty-two years later his son General Robert Wood Johnson took the helm of the company. It was this Johnson who created the Johnson & Johnson credo. First conceived in 1935 as a broad statement of corporate responsibility for fellow industrialists, it was published as a Johnson & Johnson document in 1943. It contained a set of guiding values that codified the company's balance of service and financial responsibility. In 1957, at an event celebrating the 70-year anniversary of the founding of the company, which had by then become profoundly successful, Johnson said, "[W]e are dedicated to the success of this business, and it will continue to succeed if we adhere to the principles of our credo—first, the serving of our customers, then to the people in the plant, and then the management, and then the community, and, finally and last, to the stockholders."[9]

What made the credo famous was the company's reaction to the Tylenol tampering events of 1982 and 1986. Seven people died in 1982 when cyanide was introduced into this Johnson & Johnson product. Guided by the credo, "We believe our first responsibility is to the doctors, nurses, hospitals, mothers,[10] and all others who use our products,"[11] and at a $100 million charge against its earnings, the company immediately pulled every Tylenol product from the shelves, not to be replaced until the company could ensure the products' safety. Another person died in a similar event in 1986, and the company decided to stop selling Tylenol in capsule form. It was these quick and clear decisions, driven by values and not by financial concerns, that elevated the company's reputation.

Johnson & Johnson, like any organization cited as a positive example in this book, is not a perfect company. There have been times in the company's history when the focus on its credo has wavered. But the credo represents an ideal to strive for. The inevitable gap between the ideal and the real can either be taken as a reason to throw up one's hands in resignation to the current circumstances, or it can be used to bring attention to the ideal and fuel action to close the gap. This is true of both organizations and individuals. We continue to strive to close the gap between our ideal of ourselves as a spouse, partner, friend, parent, child, employee, or other role important to us, even though we realize perfection is not at hand.

The Story of Kyocera

Kyocera is a company started in a different era than Johnson & Johnson, in a different country, and with very different products. Yet it shares important characteristics with Johnson & Johnson and other visionary companies.

In 1959 Kyocera was founded in Japan by Kazuo Inamori. It had a staff of 28. The company first established its presence in the United States in 1969. Kyocera initially focused on the production of fine ceramics to support the emergent semi-conductor industry. Its initial product was a ceramic insulator critical to that industry. Today Kyocera is a global company with more than 12,000 employees. It also has 170 subsidiary companies employing over 60,000 people.[12,13]

Profits are important to Kyocera. During the past five years, for example, net sales, net income, and earnings per share have all grown. But for a company rooted in science and engineering, with an eagle eye on profit, its vision may surprise you. "Respect the divine and love people" means "to preserve the spirit and work fairly and honorably, respecting people, our work, our company, and our global community."

Kyocera's management rationale is to provide opportunities for the material and intellectual growth of all its employees, and through their joint effort, to contribute to the advancement of society and humankind. Kyocera's management philosophy is to coexist harmoniously with nature and society—harmonious coexistence being the underlying foundation of all its business activities as the company works to create a world of abundance and peace.

Inamori never saw a conflict between making a profit and doing the right thing. Indeed, he wrote a book titled *For Profit and For People*.[14] However, he did see a problem if a decision maker's view was limited to the issue of profit. He wrote: "It isn't what is good for Kyocera or what is good for me as an individual that matters. . . . [W]e have to carry out the right decision, which you as a human being can be proud of, surpassing shallow ideas about profit and loss to the corporation—or to any one individual. This is the most fundamental standard of conduct for all employees, including myself."[15]

This vision and these philosophies are rooted in the personal values of Inamori, who today is chairman emeritus of Kyocera and is a celebrated and much honored figure in Japan. Early on in the history of the company, after Inamori had taken a huge risk in leaving his job and starting his own company, he was weighed down by the responsibility he had assumed not only for himself, but also for those who had committed themselves to his company. He wrote: "[A] bad decision on my part could send the company into the gutter almost immediately. This pressure to make correct judgments gave me many sleepless nights. . . . I realized that business decisions must be made on fundamental truths and principles. . . . I made a firm resolution: 'From now on I will base my management decisions on whether or not they are the right thing to do as a human being.'"[16] This philosophy has been a constant touchstone for the company in making decisions large and small.

Is it a challenge for Kyocera to hold to these principles? Absolutely. Pressure on profit targets and personal agendas at odds with core values can erode a focus on values. But the company continually strives to lead and to make decisions based on its values. Indeed, currently there is a great deal of discussion and a focus on how to preserve the essence of the value system as the workers and leaders who have grown the company pass the baton to the next generation.[17]

In Short

A partnership of personal integrity and organizational integrity is essential for a health care organization to strive every day to realize its intentions. Behaviors and actions consistent with the vision, mission, and values of the organization and expressed through ethical pathways transform those intentions into sustainable performance over a wide range of parameters. The vision and mission may never be fully attained and the values may not be demonstrated perfectly every day. But a consistent focus on closing the gap between the current reality and the ideal yields positive results.

The impact of the dynamic of ethical erosion, which draws an organization and those within it away from the ideal, and its counterweight, the impact of the dynamic of ethical wisdom on the health of ethical pathways, are discussed in chapter 2.

References

1. Eichenwald, K. 2005. *Conspiracy of Fools*. New York: Broadway Books.
2. Harvard Business School. 2002. Where morals and profits meet: the corporate value shift. *The Carbon Report*.
3. Manion, J. 2005. *Create a Positive Health Care Workplace!* Chicago: Health Forum.
4. Weckwerth, V.E. 2006. Is there a future for the not-for-profit hospital? *Frontiers of Health Services Management*, Summer.
5. [No author cited.] 2006. Top issues confronting hospitals: 2005. *Chief Executive Officer*, Winter.
6. Collins, J., and Porras, J. 1994. *Built to Last*. New York: Harper Collins, p. 8.
7. Foster, L. 1999. *Robert Wood Johnson: The Gentleman Rebel*. State College, PA: Lillian Press.
8. www.jnj.com [Johnson & Johnson Web site]. 2006.
9. Foster, *Robert Wood Johnson: The Gentleman Rebel*, p. 424.
10. The phrase "and fathers" was added in a later version.
11. Foster, *Robert Wood Johnson: The Gentleman Rebel*, p. 454.
12. Inamori, K. 2000. *Respect the Divine and Love People*. San Diego: Joan Kroc Center for Peace and Justice.
13. www.global.kyocera.com [Kyocera Web site]. 2006.
14. Inamori, K. 1994. *For People and For Profit*. Tokyo: Kadonsha.
15. Inamori, *Respect the Divine and Love People*, p. 77.
16. Inamori, *Respect the Divine and Love People*, p. 31.
17. Lanthorne, R. [President, Kyocera International] 2006. Interview with author, San Diego, February 17.

2

Ethical Erosion and Ethical Wisdom

What is truth? A difficult question;
but I have solved it for myself by saying that
it is what the "voice within" tells you.
—Mahatma Gandhi

THIS CHAPTER looks at the implications of two dynamics that exist in any organization and that have a profound impact on personal and organizational integrity. They are ethical erosion and its counterweight, ethical wisdom. These dynamics impact the degree to which an organization expresses its intentions, the health of its ethical pathways, and its performance (figure 2-1).

Ethical erosion is a pervasive and subtle, negative dynamic to which we are all vulnerable, organizationally and personally. You can find it everywhere, even among those organizations and individuals who care deeply about their values and the values of the organization.

Ethical wisdom is its counterweight. It is the sum total of individual and collective experience, knowledge, and good sense, which is already resident in an organization. When that wisdom is leveraged to strengthen everyday behaviors and decision making consistent with the vision, mission,

Figure 2-1. Two Opposing Forces: Ethical Erosion and Ethical Wisdom

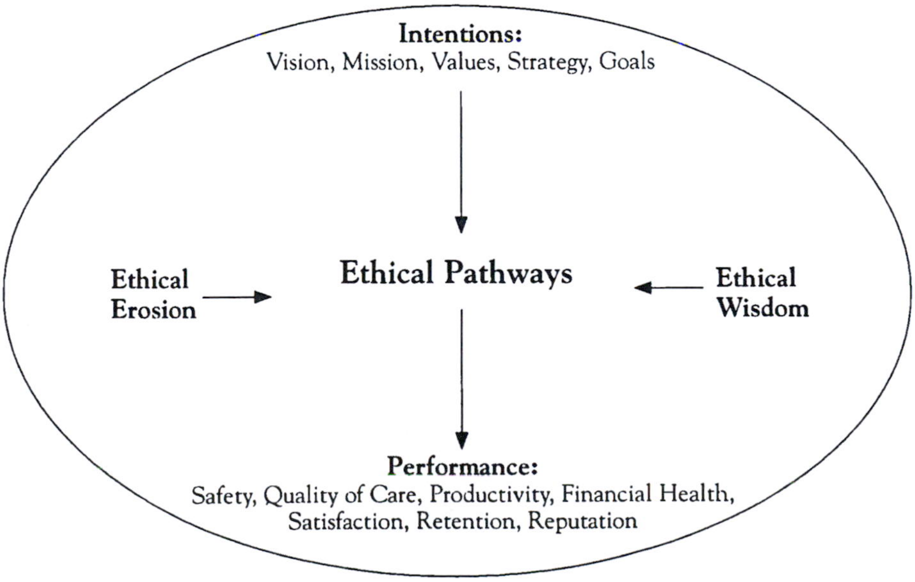

and values, it offsets and reverses ethical erosion and promotes doing the right thing.

Ethical Erosion

The following quotation speaks to the heart of ethical erosion. It is from a senior executive in a very large consulting firm who is talking about what happened during hard times for his company:

> This was two years of hell. And so I witnessed a slow erosion of focus on values. . . . If you looked at them without regard to their magnitude, and you asked, was this right or wrong? The answer would be wrong and you know it. Okay. But it's only a little bit wrong and I think in your head, the more you let these little wrongs build up, you start setting these mental precedents that make it easier to slide into doing more and more little things or slightly bigger and then bigger and bigger things.[1]

Yes, we need to be vigilant in stopping big unethical acts from occurring, but we have to be even more vigilant in stopping ethical erosion—the very small, almost unnoticeable slippages that provide the basis for more slippage, then even more, until we find ourselves surprised by events and in the deep weeds. No part of an organization's life is immune to erosion; its reach extends beyond financial integrity to patient and employee safety and to quality of care. One lesson from the space shuttle Challenger disaster is that people can die even when everyone involved is well intentioned and has no thought of causing harm. In her analysis of the events surrounding the space shuttle's explosion, Diane Vaughan noted how:

> small changes regarding [quality and safety standards]—new behaviors that were slight deviations from the normal course of events—gradually became the norm, providing the basis for accepting additional deviance. . . . The responsible organizations proceeded as if nothing was wrong in the face of evidence that something was wrong.[2]

Ethical Erosion and Medication Errors

Medication errors are among the most common health care errors. They are a prime example of where profit and values intertwine. Medication errors are estimated to injure 1.5 million people each year in the United States at an annual cost of more than $4 billion.[3] Every health care organization and every right-minded person within them do not seek to harm patients. But harm occurs. Look at the MEDMARX[sm] data for total reported medication errors categorized by severity (figure 2-2).[4] The figure shows sentinel events (where the error may have resulted in permanent patient harm, required intervention to sustain life, or may have contributed or resulted in patient death), harmful errors excluding sentinel events (where the error may have contributed or resulted in temporary harm and required intervention, or required initial or prolonged hospitalization), and nonharmful events (where an error did not reach the patient, or reached the patient but did not cause harm, or required monitoring to confirm no harm, or required intervention to preclude harm).

The sentinel events are underlaid, like an iceberg, by a greater mass of harmful events, and an even greater mass of nonharmful events. For every sentinel event there were about 24 harmful, nonsentinel, events and more than 1,900 nonharmful events. It is likely that there is at least another level of events below the nonharmful events that never rise to a recordable level in the data base, such as those "new behaviors," in Diane Vaughan's words, "that were slight deviations from the normal course of events . . . [that] gradually became the norm."

The natural inclination and an appropriate response to these data are to focus on the most serious events and to seek their root causes. But looking through the lens of erosion and seeing how small slippages lead to bigger and bigger slippages, a powerful complementary approach is to focus on preventing nonharmful events, which means exposing the previously unnoticed events that underlay them, thus reducing the source of harmful and sentinel events (see figure 2-3)—an approach taken by Six Sigma, for example.

Figure 2-2. MEDMARX℠ Total Medication Errors, 2004

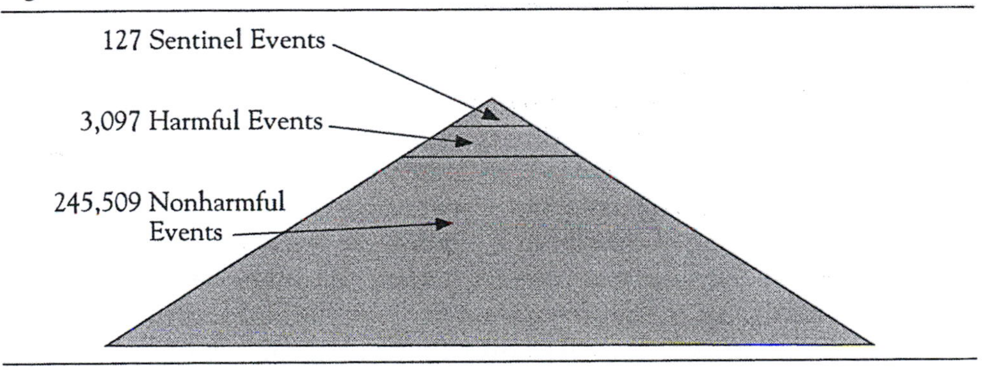

Figure 2-3. The Possible Impact on Focusing on Nonharmful Events and Reducing Them by 25 Percent Using MEDMARX℠ Medication Errors, 2004, as Source Data

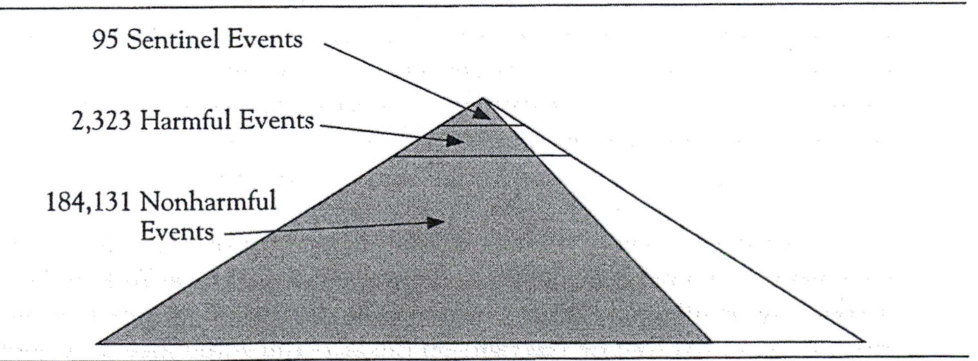

Patient and employee safety are important performance criteria. The lesson in thinking of the analogy of the iceberg, where so much mass is hidden, is that it is essential to expose and avoid the very small, even unnoticed, events that eventually can build into a situation that causes harm. Using ethical pathways is in part about finding ways to identify, stop, and reverse erosion—to do the right thing consistent with the vision, mission, and values of the organization.

Ethical Erosion and Common Practice

At its worst, ethical erosion can become so complete that unethical behavior becomes accepted practice. We often do a disservice to new employees or others who question common practice. They may see new ways of doing things or have questions about current practices and, rather than using their questioning as a way to reexamine our own patterns of behavior and decision making, we straighten them out for their own good, explaining "the way we do things around here." But common practice is not the same as ethical practice. Consider the following case.

The Chicago Way

In 2003 the University of Illinois agreed to pay a total of $2 million to the federal government and to the state of Illinois to settle a lawsuit accusing the university's medical center in Chicago of improperly diagnosing the condition of certain patients to make them eligible sooner for liver transplants. The University of Illinois admitted no liability.[5]

Dr. Ray Pollak, who used to run the abdominal transplant program at the University of Illinois Medical Center, had drawn attention through a series of letters and internal university memos voicing his concerns about suspected fudging of cases by exaggerating the severity of the condition of candidates for a liver transplant. According to his lawsuit, he was invited to discuss the issue with a lawyer and five senior medical center administrators. Pollak said they wanted to know what was the downside of fudging. In a second meeting with many of the same attendees, Pollack was asked, "What's the downside of doing things the Chicago way?" Later the dean of the College of Medicine sent Pollak a disciplinary letter, accusing him of "virtual insubordination." Pollak was demoted, his salary was more than halved, and he was transferred to another of the university's hospital operations in Peoria, more than 150 miles from Chicago. According to Pollak, clinical decisions were driven by concerns for revenue and profit. In 2004 the dean of the College of Medicine and the vice chancellor of health affairs resigned in a reorganization of roles.[6]

The "Not as Bad" Defense

Here is another example when common practice is not the same as ethical practice. When Eliot Spitzer, as attorney general of New York, indicted a company on illegal business practices, the company's lawyers met with him and admitted that he was right on the facts (meaning they were guilty as charged), but they argued in their defense that "we aren't as bad as our competitors."[7]

These vivid examples have their roots in the subtle dynamic of ethical erosion's producing systemic, unethical, illegal, but fully justified, behaviors and decisions. Before we point fingers elsewhere, it is worthwhile asking ourselves this question: "What over time has become common practice where I work that is a result of ethical erosion that has gone unnoticed and unchecked?" It is easier than we might think to fall into habitual behavior and, in a way, go to sleep in a bed of long-held and unquestioned assumptions, which allow unethical behaviors and decisions to hide in plain sight. That is why Diane Vaughan could observe in the space shuttle Challenger case that "responsible organizations proceeded as if nothing was wrong in the face of evidence that something was wrong."

Ethical erosion is both an organizational and a personal accountability. The *village honest man* is a term used by the philosopher Mencius to describe persons who find their values in common practice without worrying whether it may be ethical or not. Such a person is considered the enemy of virtue because he or she operates from what is expected to get along in the world and not make waves, and not by self-generated ethical action.[8]

To sum up, ethical erosion is characterized by a series of small, even unnoticed acts that erode ethical standards. Each act provides a foundation for the next more erosive act, leading eventually to situations where common unethical practices are accepted as the appropriate standard for behavior and action—all of which can lead to significant, even disastrous, adverse organizational and personal consequences.

Ethical Wisdom

In his book *Blink*, Malcolm Gladwell writes about "adaptive unconsciousness" in situations where we do not think through things analytically—we may not have time—but instead make very quick, even instantaneous, judgments on very little information. He cites the example of the sixth century Greek statue purchased by the J. Paul Getty Museum for many millions of dollars after exhaustive research into its validity. In spite of extensive supportive documentation, there were doubts voiced about the authenticity of the piece by some experts in Greek sculpture. Their comments did not center on the documentation, nor were they the result of thoughtful analysis. They were instinctive. On his first sight of the statue, one expert said the word that came to mind was "fresh." After viewing the statue, another expert said he felt a wave of "intuitive revulsion." They could say no more. Many months after it was purchased, the statue was proved to be a fraud.[9]

Ethical Know-How and Ethical Know-What

The experience of these experts in the case above mirrors what happens to each of us in our chosen area of expertise in health care, or in any area of life, even sometimes those new to us, where we can bring to bear our experience, knowledge, and good sense. When we can, seemingly without thought or analysis, size up a situation and sense or feel if it is "on" or "off," we are accessing our ethical wisdom. In these cases we feel something intuitive rather than logical. This is very different from following an ethical decision process. This intuition is ethical know-how.[10]

Certainly many ethical issues (bioethical decisions or employee issues, for example) need to pass through an orderly process before coming to the chosen course of action. This reasoning is ethical know-what. But this and similar processes and compliance programs alone cannot create high ethical standards. Truly ethical behavior needs both the intuitiveness of ethical know-how and the reasoning of ethical know-what.

This book stresses ethical know-how, not because it is better than ethical know-what, but because its essential role as a counterweight to ethical erosion needs to be stressed. For this book, we are calling this know-how *ethical wisdom*, which is the individual and collective knowledge, experience, and good sense to make sound ethical decisions and judgments everywhere, every day.

Know-How as Ethical Wisdom

Ethical wisdom does not exist in every person to the same degree or in the same manner. It is most common where a person's depth of experience is greatest. For example, a physician or nurse may have an intuition about a patient even before beginning a physical examination or running any tests. Nor is ethical wisdom limited to any one area of expertise. A laboratory technician might have a sense of something's being "off" when he or she is on a unit or in a department other than his or her own. Because wisdom may be of value to an area beyond a person's expertise, it is useful to encourage input on an issue beyond those with deep expertise in a given area. Valuable insights may come from those unencumbered by unquestioned assumptions that can calcify thinking.

Because ethical wisdom is already resident in the organization and in enough quantity collectively to guide ethical behavior and ethical decision making, the focus for strengthening ethics needs to look beyond compliance programs and ethical training to include how to access and leverage latent ethical wisdom into an asset that will strengthen personal and organizational integrity every day, everywhere in the organization.

To do so is critical if we are to arrest and reverse ethical erosion. Because ethical erosion is subtle in its impact and growth, we need responses that are equally subtle to identify and deal with it. Ethical wisdom is often experienced through what have been called weak or faint signals, such as discomfort, a gut reaction, or other reaction signaling that something is "off." Many people at the J. Paul Getty Museum wanted to believe the Greek sculpture was authentic; it was their first major buy, and it would put the museum on the map. If the intuitive responses of those experts had been taken seriously, the museum may have spared itself great loss and embarrassment.

In the case of liver transplants at the University of Illinois Medical Center, following Dr. Pollak's demotion, all 65 surgery residents signed a letter "imploring" the president of the University of Illinois to reinstate Dr. Pollak, describing him as "one of the most dedicated, moral, and honest mentors we have." In addition, nurses on the transplant unit sent a letter to the university's board of trustees complaining of a "cover up . . . [that] will do serious damage to the reputation of the medical center and its administration."[11] We can only speculate what pain and suffering would have been avoided if these voices of ethical wisdom had been heard, and what faint signals on the practices of the program went ignored and for how long.

A word of caution: earlier we said that a faint signal "can be" ethical wisdom. It is important that we are aware of the source of our response. Sometimes our wisdom may be colored or distorted by preconceptions, prejudices, or fears about people, groups, or situations. For example, if we have an unfavorable view of a group or individual at work, we may jump to an immediate conclusion about a situation, which is more like a well-worn pattern of reaction than an intuition about the issue at hand. We could say the difference is that preconceptions or prejudices are mindless and ethical wisdom is mindful. Preconceptions provide a knee-jerk response to a situation, but ethical wisdom provides a full awareness of a situation and our intuitions about it. If we are mindful, we can distinguish between wisdom and preconceptions. The ethical pathways introduced in chapter 3 focus in part on that mindfulness.

In Short

In every organization and every individual are two subtle and opposing dynamics: ethical erosion and ethical wisdom. Ethical erosion is the subtle, even unnoticed slippage of ethical standards. The first time we notice this erosion may be when we find ourselves in the deep weeds. At worst it is so pervasive that it becomes an unthinking acceptance in the name of "the way it is" or "everybody does it that way."

Ethical wisdom is the sum of experience, knowledge, and good sense, which provides equally subtle signals that alert us to the possibility that something is "off" and worth checking on, and which is driven more by intuition than by an assembly of facts. This wisdom expresses itself differently for different people in an organization. For example, some may most often size up a situation without analysis, drawing on a wisdom rooted in their work experience. Or others may most often tap their internal sense of when something is "off," even in unfamiliar situations where work experience is lacking. Some employees may be more in tune with their wisdom than others, although there is usually enough collective wisdom in the organization to prevent ethical erosion.

The four ethical pathways are the vehicles for stopping and reversing ethical erosion, leveraging ethical wisdom, and translating intentions into performance. These are discussed more fully in chapter 3.

References

1. Gilbert, J. 2004. *The Role of Ethics in Decision-Making for Senior Management Consultants in Large Consulting Firms* [Doctoral Dissertation]. Washington: George Washington University, p. 123.
2. Vaughan, D. 1996. *The Challenger Launch Decision: Risky Technology, Culture and Deviance at NASA*. Chicago: University of Chicago Press, p. 409.
3. Institute of Medicine. 2006. Preventing medication errors [report]. Washington: Institute of Medicine.
4. Santell, J.P., Hicks, R.W., and Cousins, D.D. 2005. MEDMARX[sm] data report: a chartbook of 2000–2004 findings from intensive care units and radiological services. Rockville, MD: U.S. Pharmacopeia Center for the Advancement of Patient Safety, p. 113.
5. Illinois Attorney General. 2003. UIC Medical Center pays $2 million to United States and State of Illinois to settle liver transplant fraud suit. Press release, November 17.
6. Schoenberg, N. 2005. A man of principle. *Chicago Tribune Magazine*, January 25.
7. Spitzer, E. 2005. Speech to the Corporate Directors Forum, San Diego, December 6.
8. Varela, F. 1992. *Ethical Know-How*. Stanford, CA: Stanford University Press.
9. Gladwell, M. 2005. *Blink*. New York: Little, Brown & Co.
10. Varela, *Ethical Know-How*, p. 38.
11. Schoenberg. A man of principle.

3

Ethical Pathways, Disciplines, and Diagnostics

Vision without action is a daydream.
Action without vision is a nightmare.
—Japanese proverb

FOR AN ORGANIZATION to be ethical, both the ends (the intentions) and the means (the pathways to performance) need to be ethical. There are many pathways through which an organization can transform intentions into performance. Some of them are not ethical or legal. Some, as we have seen, rationalize the use of unethical pathways to achieve short-term results for the sake of some greater, long-term good. Given the dynamic of ethical erosion, such actions are unlikely to be isolated acts but will instead become the precedent for even more ethically compromised acts, with potentially dire consequences. For example, the future of Alvarado Hospital Medical Center in San Diego was placed in jeopardy after its leadership was accused of making inappropriate relocation payments to doctors that, according to prosecutors, amounted to illegal kickbacks for patient referrals. After spending $30 million defending itself against these allegations over three years, Alvarado's owner, Tenet Healthcare, settled the matter for $21 million and was forced to close or sell the hospital[1]; all this because of the unethical pathways chosen to achieve financial results. Fortunately, a sale occurred and the hospital still provides essential services to the community it serves. We have also presented strong evidence that great and enduring companies that hold an absolute commitment to ethical pathways can enjoy the best of all worlds. They can achieve sustained high performance (including financial performance) by doing the right thing, and they can reduce their organization's exposure both to unethical acts and to the consequences of those acts.

The Four Ethical Pathways

There are four ethical pathways through which intentions are transformed into performance by doing the right thing (figure 3-1). They achieve results by leveraging ethical wisdom and by stopping ethical erosion. These four ethical pathways are:

1. Culture
2. Leadership and governance
3. Infrastructure
4. Personal integrity

Figure 3-1. The Four Interdependent Ethical Pathways

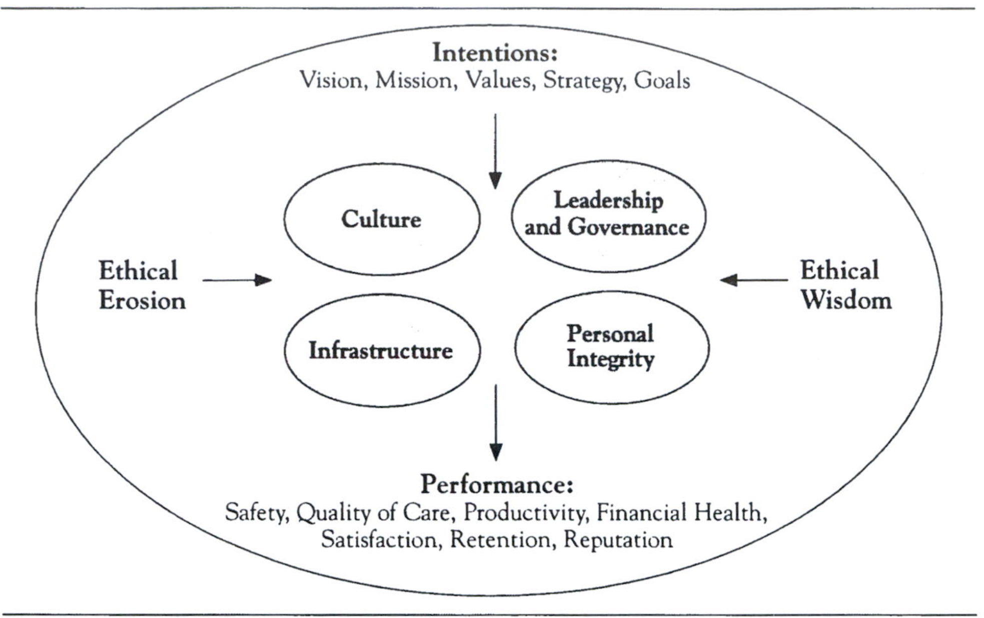

These pathways are interdependent, and the good health of every one is essential to an organization committed to fulfilling its vision, mission, values, and other intentions everywhere in the organization, every day. For example, behavioral values that encourage employees to speak up when they have ethical concerns (culture) must be supported by vehicles that are available to hear those concerns, such as employee forums and recognition systems that acknowledge individuals when they do speak up (infrastructure), by leaders who not only encourage employees to speak up but who model the candor they demand (leadership), and by the initiative of individual employees who recognize the value of speaking up to their own peace of mind (personal integrity).

Ethical Pathways and Disciplines

Each ethical pathway has a small set of disciplines, or practices, that are the keys to the health of the pathway. Just as the ethical pathways are interdependent, so also are these disciplines. For example, two disciplines discussed in the ethical pathway of culture are mindfulness and voice. Mindfulness, as we will see, is the private voice of ethical wisdom, while voice is mindfulness made public. When we are sensitive (mindful) to faint signals that suggest ethical concerns, but do not believe we are safe in sharing those concerns (have no voice), the pathway cannot be healthy.

Part II of this book, "The Ethical Pathway of Culture," discusses the underlying patterns of behavior and action that promote an ethically strong culture. It presents the five disciplines of an ethically healthy culture: mindfulness, voice, respect, tenacity, and legacy.

Part III, "The Ethical Pathway of Leadership and Governance," discusses the role of the organization's leaders and of the board of directors or trustees in creating and sustaining an organization that has an unqualified commitment to ethical behavior and decision making. It presents the four disciplines that leaders must embrace to strengthen and sustain an organization high in integrity: noble purpose (a discipline shared with the board), ceaseless ambition, candor, and passion. It then presents the four disciplines the board must embrace to strengthen and to sustain an organization high in integrity: noble purpose (shared with the leadership), independent engagement, ethical culture, and ethical succession.

Part IV, "The Ethical Pathway of Infrastructure," discusses the systems and processes in the organization that can either support or thwart ethical behavior. Here we examine the role of mission statements and codes of ethics, ethics training, performance appraisals, incentives, hiring and disciplinary action, and policies and procedures within three disciplines necessary to support high ethical standards: ethical engagement, accountability, and management by facts.

Part V, "The Ethical Pathway of Personal Integrity," discusses the impact of every individual's actions on their environment and on themselves through three disciplines: personal legacy, mindfulness, and choice.

Diagnostics for Assessment of Vital Signs of Ethical Health

For each ethical pathway in parts II through V, a simple to complete high-level diagnostic is provided to help you assess the vital signs of the health of each pathway for your organization. In part III, "The Ethical Pathway of Leadership and Governance," there are two diagnostics provided in separate chapters, one for leadership and one for the board or directors or trustees. In part V, "The Ethical Pathway of Personal Integrity," two diagnostics are provided in separate chapters, each offering a different perspective on individual action in sustaining personal and organizational integrity. All diagnostics, together with their associated suggestions for action, are designed (1) to identify areas of relative strength and weakness, and (2) to frame discussions that are focused on areas of concern by offering observations, questions for discussion, and possible actions.

A comprehensive ethical health survey that covers all four ethical pathways can be found in appendix 1, including a link to where you can complete the survey on-line.

In Short

The four interdependent ethical pathways of culture, leadership and governance, infrastructure, and personal integrity and their associated disciplines, when healthy, maximize organizational and personal integrity. The following parts of this book discuss each pathway and its associated disciplines in detail and provide a high-level diagnostic for each with its possible actions. These begin in the next chapter with the ethical pathway of culture.

Reference

1. Darce, K. 2006. Alvarado's owner agrees to sell or close hospital. *San Diego Union-Tribune*, May 18, p. A-1.

II

The Ethical Pathway of Culture

4

The Five Disciplines of an Ethical Culture

Let us not be content to wait and see what will happen,
but give us the determination to make the right things happen.
—Peter Marshall

CULTURE IS A critical ethical pathway in transforming the organization's intentions into performance. The culture of an organization goes a long way in determining whether ethical wisdom will be leveraged and whether ethical erosion will be stopped.

The Importance of an Ethical Culture

Since 1994 the Ethics Resource Center has conducted the National Business Ethics Survey (NBES), a study of employees across for-profit, not-for-profit, and governmental sectors in the United States. The 2005 report shows

Figure 4-1. The Five Disciplines of an Ethical Culture

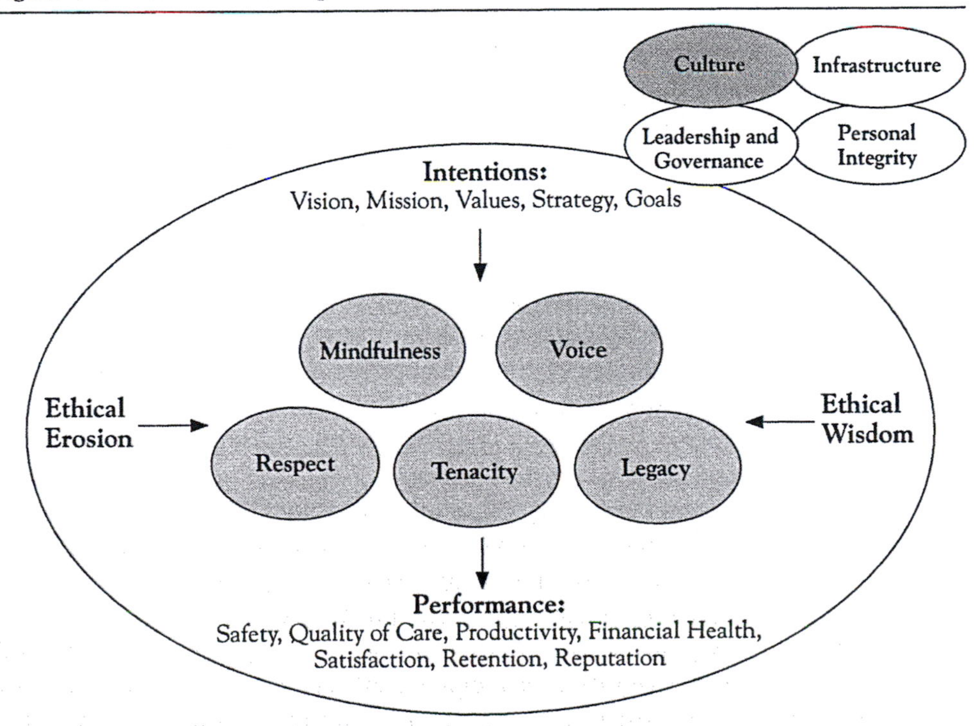

important findings.[1] On a national level, attention to many formal ethics programs—written standards of conduct, training on ethics, mechanisms through which to seek ethics advice or information, means of reporting misconduct anonymously, and discipline of employees who violate ethical standards—has increased. But this rise in formal ethics and compliance programs has not produced the positive outcomes expected. In fact, there is little change in the extent to which employees have observed misconduct in the workplace since 1994. The 2005 NBES finds that organizational culture is more influential in determining outcomes than formal programs. As a legal report published by the Society for Human Resources Management pointed out: "[I]t is irrational to implement any compliance or ethics program without first considering the company culture."[2] Revised federal sentencing guidelines, which govern the severity of sentences handed down following convictions for ethical misconduct, direct in part that companies must promote both an organizational culture that encourages ethical conduct and a commitment to compliance to the law.[3]

These findings all make sense. Think of new employees. They do not get fully trained in how their new organization works through orientation, nor by signing that they have read and understand the organization's values or code of ethics, nor by vision and value statements posted on the walls. They are fully trained on the job. More than trained, new employees are indoctrinated in common practice and common beliefs. Co-workers teach what the organization truly values, what actions can and cannot be made without risking their future, with whom they can be honest and with whom they should keep quiet, who really cares about patients and who doesn't, and what the organization and its leadership say they value and what they really do. After indoctrination over time, new employees become trainers themselves, and thus, the culture, sometimes for better and sometimes for worse, is perpetuated.

The Five Disciplines: An Overview

How do we know whether the culture fosters organizational and personal integrity? Because an ethical culture is expressed through the health of five disciplines (or everyday practices). When these disciplines are strong, the ethical pathway of culture is strong, supporting the transformation of intentions into performance by doing the right thing. Ethical wisdom is leveraged and ethical erosion is stopped. These five ethical disciplines are mindfulness, voice, respect, tenacity, and legacy.

Mindfulness is the private voice of ethical wisdom. It is the self-awareness that brings ethical dilemmas and issues to our awareness, such as a sense of calm or comfort with a decision, a gut reaction or discomfort, or a nagging doubt that something may be "off" with a decision.

Voice is the public expression of ethical wisdom. It brings mindfulness into open conversation and enables ethical issues to be revealed and explored in a constructive spirit in many forums, such as in meetings, informal conversations, everyday work, employee surveys, or other forms of communication. Voice is shared mindfulness, which leverages collective ethical wisdom.

Respect is the practice of listening to others with generosity rather than suspicion, with a commitment to understand and value differing views. It strengthens our ability to work on ethical issues as colleagues, not critics, irrespective of different views.

Tenacity is the quality of being unstoppable in the quest for ethical behavior and ethical decision making. It is the shared commitment to see difficult conversations through to their resolution no matter what—harnessing, not avoiding, problems, addressing fundamental issues, and grappling with ambiguous situations.

Legacy is the practice of making ethical decisions in a spirit of stewardship, understanding the implications and the consequences of our behaviors and decisions for those who follow, including fellow employees, patients and their families, our own families, our community, and our society. It is acting in keeping with the long view, personally and organizationally, consistent with vision, mission, and values.

These disciplines are intertwined. If an employee becomes *mindful* of an ethical concern, *voice* is needed to share that concern. The concern can only be shared freely when there is a spirit of *respect*, which allows many views and commitments to be included in conversation. Because difficult issues may be raised, *tenacity* is needed to take effective action, and that action needs to embrace the *legacy* being created—that it is consistent with the vision, mission, and values of the organization and not driven by short-term expediency at odds with these intentions.

The following is a fuller discussion of each of these disciplines.

The Discipline of Mindfulness

Malcolm Gladwell writes about an experiment at the University of Iowa in which subjects acting as gamblers were asked to play a card game with decks of red and blue cards.[4] The subjects did not know it, but even though the red cards produced bigger payoffs, the subjects could only win in the long run by betting the blue cards. Generally, the gamblers reported that after playing about 50 cards, they came to believe that the blue cards were a better choice, although they could not say exactly why. After playing 80 cards, they had deciphered the logic of the game and could explain with facts why the blue cards were a better choice.

But these findings were not the "punch line" of the experiment. The experimenters placed monitors on the subjects' palm, which measured sweat gland activity (a stress response). In many cases, the gamblers' stress response to the red cards began by the tenth card, and they began to move away from gambling with the red cards a full 40 cards before they could articulate their preference for the blue cards, and 70 cards before they could offer a fact-based rationale for their decision making.

The implications of this experiment to the ethical health of an organization are huge, especially for a health care organization or any organization whose work is grounded in science. Such organizations are frequently dominated by a high regard for fact-based, procedural, decision-making processes while, at the same time, this regard is accompanied by a habitual discounting of views not supported by well-argued facts. Even in organizations not in the scientific field, the usual response to employees coming to managers with complaints has been to establish the now pervasive directive, "Don't come to me with a problem unless you have a solution."

Respecting the Voice of Ethical Wisdom

Fact-based decision making is critical to success. But the demand for all the facts before being willing to hear an ethical concern is counterproductive and exposes the organization to undue risk. The gamblers in the University of Iowa experiment could only provide a fact-based response when they were deep into playing the game. Had they been more sensitive to their own wisdom, even though not fact-based, they would have played the game more efficiently and with far greater success. Similarly, if we can identify and intervene in ethical concerns at an early stage, we too can have the opportunity to be more effective and to enjoy greater success—to smooth the transformation of intentions into performance by doing the right thing. An unwillingness to hear an ethical problem without its accompanying solution can result in not hearing it in good time, if at all. This concern is reinforced when we appreciate that ethical erosion frequently operates under the radar. In the discussion of the disciplines of voice and respect that follows, we shall see that the challenge is not only to be mindful of our ethical wisdom, but also to give it (and the ethical wisdom of others) the hearing it deserves.

Mindfulness is the attentiveness to clues of whether actions we see or take, and decisions we hear about or are part of, are consistent with our personal and organizational integrity. To be mindful is to be self-aware—to recognize the early signal analogous to a sweat response like that demonstrated in the subjects in the University of Iowa experiment. As mentioned before, the signal can be a sense of calm and comfort with an action or decision when we know it is "on," or a more disturbing gut reaction or discomfort that something is "off." The organization can foster a higher probability of mindfulness, but it is a personal phenomenon—the private voice of ethical wisdom. Mindfulness is the foundation of a healthy ethical culture and the bridge from our personal values to our behaviors and decisions.

Mindfulness needs to be practiced every day because it is easy for us collectively and individually to stop thinking. We often cease to acknowledge, let alone question, our many assumptions and prejudices. When we cease to be mindful of our ethical choices and assumptions, we lose the ability to question them, and in so doing, we lose the ability to question the strength of organizational and personal integrity in everyday work. Common practice regarding behavior and decision making becomes mistaken for inevitable ways of operating. Opinions we have formed or have inherited about the capabilities and commitments of others, of the organization, and even of ourselves, turn into impregnable facts. Conscious choice becomes unthinking habit.

Organizational Support for Mindfulness

Mindfulness is an individual discipline. However, an ethically aware organization continuously seeks to inspire that mindfulness. The organization does it in two critical ways. The first is by making discussion of values focused, simple, and a constant part of everyday conversations. Part III, "The Ethical Pathway of Leadership and Governance," and part IV, "The Ethical Pathway of Infrastructure," discuss this more fully. However, for now, the following examples show how the organizational mindset drives mindfulness.

Johns Hopkins Bayview Medical Center in Baltimore is one of the Johns Hopkins health care institutions. Johns Hopkins has an unrelenting focus on safety, service excellence, and diversity. Bayview's CEO, Greg Schaffer, in talking about hiring and retention, says, "We talk about these values over and over and over. You had better be excited about them if you work here; if you aren't you will move on."[5]

Another way an organization inspires mindfulness is by building straightforward processes designed to put values front and center every day. The following example illustrates a process that fosters a daily focus by employees on values.

Baptist Health Care in Pensacola, Florida, a winner of the prestigious Malcolm Baldrige National Quality Award, has repeatedly been named to *Fortune* magazine's list of the "100 Best Companies to Work for." One thing you will find at Baptist is *The Daily*, a briefing document for all staff, which focuses on the values and standards that drive behavior. In a few paragraphs, *The Daily* covers an aspect of the organization's values and poses a question for discussion. For example, on one day, *The Daily* focused on ethical challenges, and the question for discussion on that day was, "Why is it important that we properly report our concerns regarding ethics?" You could say that this briefing document is making the same request of staff every day to be mindful of Baptist's vision and values today and to let them shape work and decisions.

The Discipline of Voice

The 2005 National Business Ethics Survey (NBES) reported that 52 percent of employees surveyed observed at least one instance of ethical misconduct at work in the past year.[6] That is not good news, but there is worse. Of the employees who observed ethical misconduct, 45 percent did not report the violation to management. The two primary reasons they gave for not reporting a violation were: (1) fear of retaliation, and (2) the belief that management would not act anyway.[7] Mindfulness, the private voice of ethical wisdom, is of no value to the individual or the organization without voice, the public expression of ethical wisdom. Evaluation of a situation and any change can only occur by bringing the issues into open discussion. Perceived or real organizational unwillingness to discuss ethical concerns openly leads to inattention, frustration, and ethical erosion.

Personal Voice

Has this ever happened to you? You are in a meeting where a decision is being made with which you are uncomfortable. You may experience a gut reaction, sweaty palms, or other discomfort. It just does not feel right. This feeling is an example of your mindfulness at work. It is a weak or faint signal because you may not be able to express it in any other way. However, the signal's faintness and lack of an organized set of facts to support it have nothing to do with its validity, even though we may question its validity and withhold our reaction.

For example, here is what has happened to me in meetings, more times than I would like to admit, when I have experienced such a faint signal or feeling. The first thing I do is try to talk myself out of it. Maybe I am the one who is "off." After all, as I look around at the faces of those in the meeting, everyone else seems to show no evidence of similar discomfort. Then, knowing that I have not thought through my discomfort, I feel reluctant to interrupt a meeting with a full agenda that nobody wants to be in anyway and cannot wait to be over. I want to be seen as a good team player, so perhaps the best thing to do is ignore my discomfort and go along with the decision. I do not want to look foolish when someone asks me to support my feeling with well-argued facts. But I am still uncomfortable. If this internal dialogue goes on long enough, by the time I may decide to speak, the meeting has moved on to the next topic and the moment to intervene is lost, often never to be recovered.

For an ethical culture to prosper, it is critical that an individual, and it usually starts with an individual, has the freedom to speak up and be heard, especially when he or she has no more than a feeling of discomfort—a nudge from his or her ethical wisdom. Because ethical erosion is subtle, we need to respond to it by honoring the faint signals that our mindfulness offers us, be they physical, emotional, or psychological. In addition, honoring those weak signals means speaking up as early as possible at a time and in a place where our intervention can be most productive.

Seeking out sympathetic colleagues after a decision is made and expressing our concerns to them is not sufficient. The best time to speak up is before or at the moment of decision. We do not have to be self-righteous by saying: "This decision is bad!" We only need to raise our concern to test whether others have resolved the concern for themselves, share the concern, or think it is worth considering. We can do this by saying, "I feel uncomfortable with this decision, although I cannot say exactly why, and I want to know how others stand with it." By voicing our concern, we provide the great service of evoking mindfulness and focusing the collective ethical wisdom in the group on the decision. Sometimes, intervening takes courage—we choose to act for the greater good in spite of our fears, discomfort, or vulnerabilities. These opportunities for intervention extend far beyond meetings to a myriad of everyday conversations at work with co-workers, superiors, and subordinates.

If we cannot claim our voice at work, we surrender our power and deny our ethical wisdom to both ourselves and the organization. If not claiming our voice led to higher satisfaction, less exposure to unethical acts, higher ethical standards, and stronger personal and organizational integrity and results, then silence would not be a problem. But it leads to the opposite—lower satisfaction, weakened ethics, less powerful results, greater exposure to unethical acts, and weakened personal and organizational integrity. This is a significant problem, especially in a field where harm can come to those in our trust when we do not act with the highest ethical standards. The personal choices we make at work, including whether to exercise our voice, are discussed more fully in part V, "The Ethical Pathway of Personal Integrity."

Organizational Voice and Ownership

We are not saying the responsibility of claiming voice falls only on the individual. Claiming voice is the shared accountability of the organization and its employees. It is part of the partnership of goodwill. The organization is accountable through its board, leadership, and management to foster a culture where the expression of concerns and ideas about ethics is appreciated, encouraged, and rewarded.

For example, one of this author's clients is building a code of ethics. The organization has more than 2,000 employees working at a single site. The board and the executive team had their ideas about what needed to be included in the code, but decided to put its development in the hands of a multi-level task force of 20 employees who would report to the board and the executive team at key points in the process for update, input, and needed approvals. The first time the task force came together the atmosphere could best be described as suspicious. Team members were unsure why they were being asked to do this work. Were they going to be able to raise issues important to employees? Would whatever they did make a difference in the end product? Was it a plot of some kind designed to give the appearance of valuing their opinion? But they proceeded in spite of their doubts. Since that rocky beginning, the task force has conducted more than 40 focus groups with more than 200 of their fellow employees seeking to understand what values at work mattered most. They went through a rigorous process of synthesizing the data and distilling it into six critical values with associated behaviors, a draft of which has been refined through further analysis and has received the approval of the board and the leadership. The task force is now developing an implementation plan for the ethics code.

The organization's board and leadership were impressed. They had not been convinced that the task force could make this kind of dramatic progress. But the task force had embraced the opportunity provided by the organization. They presented their work to executive management with passion. In the process they claimed their ethical wisdom, the wisdom of their colleagues, and their voice. Without leadership's willingness to trust their employees, this would never have happened.

Another clue to voice lies in the response rate to employee satisfaction surveys. For example, Johnson & Johnson works hard to live up to its credo. It knows that a reputation takes a lifetime to develop and can be lost very quickly. For the past three years, the company has conducted an annual worldwide values survey to see where it stands in the view of its 115,000 employees. Last year the response rate to the survey, which was sent to every employee, was 97 percent.[8] Irrespective of the data generated, this response rate shows a lot about the voice employees believe they have in the decisions made by the company. In health care organizations where the employees believe they have voice, the results are similar.

Personal and Organizational Voice: Rapid Response Teams

Rapid response teams (RRT) are one of six initiatives of the Institute for Healthcare Improvement 100,000 Lives Campaign, a campaign successful in saving more than 120,000 lives from unnecessary death in its 18-month pilot.[9] The teams are a great illustration of staff, patients, and their families using voice for the betterment of patient care. The initiative is also an example of a respect for faint signals acted on without need for factual justification.

Under the RRT approach, a health care worker can bypass the typical chain-of-command and call an RRT—essentially a medical SWAT team—to assess the condition of a patient quickly and intervene when life-saving care may be needed. Unlike the traditional "code" team, an RRT intervenes before the patient experiences a respiratory or cardiac arrest. The results have been impressive, with reductions in cardiac arrests, deaths, and lengths of stay. In addition, the teams and their use have been credited with higher unit staff satisfaction, a higher culture of patient safety and awareness, and improved family involvement and satisfaction.[10]

Many hospitals, including the University of Pittsburgh Medical Center in Shadyside, Pennsylvania, extended this team intervention to patients and family members by encouraging them to pick up any phone in the hospital to report a condition H (for *help*) if they fear something is seriously wrong with the patient. They can make the call if they experience a communication failure, become confused about the patient's care, need to know where to voice concerns, or feel something about the patient's condition is "just not right." Condition H is available around-the-clock. The call goes to the hospital operator, who pages the RRT. The team arrives at the patient's bedside within minutes, listens to the patient's or family member's concerns, assesses the condition of the patient, and responds with medical care or further investigation as needed.[11]

Voice and Whistle-Blowing

What is whistle-blowing? It occurs when (1) an individual performs an action or series of actions intended to make information public; (2) the information is made a matter of public record; (3) the information is about possible or actual, nontrivial wrongdoing in an organization; and (4) the whistle-blower is a member or a former member of the organization.[12]

Although greater financial incentives for bringing to light illegal acts have increased the possibility of doing it for the money rather than for the principle* or even for spite, most whistle-blowers act on principle and frustration. Many go public after not being taken seriously despite repeated attempts to right what they see as a wrong through normal organizational channels or even extraordinary ones, such as when Sherron Watkins, a vice president at Enron, went directly to Ken Lay, Enron's chairman, to alert him to her concerns about wrongdoing at the company.[13]

Whistle-blowers can be praised for illuminating illegal or unethical behavior. For example, three whistle-blowers were named *Time* magazine's 2002 Persons of the Year. On the other hand, whistle-blowers are also criticized for disloyalty and often are denounced as troublemakers. Retaliation against them is common, which is why protections have been strengthened. Remember the example in part I of this book about Dr. Pollak at the University of Illinois Medical Center. After persisting in raising concerns about the classification of liver transplant patients, Dr. Pollak was demoted and his salary halved, and he was moved to a position requiring a three-hour commute.

By not providing voice for ethical concerns, an organization increases its vulnerability to damage to its financial health, its reputation, and its organizational pride through whistle-blowing. In a case in which the eventual whistle-blower acted on principle and frustration, the organization will be portrayed not only as making errors, but also as disinterested in seeking out and addressing those errors. In a case in which the eventual whistle-blower acted for financial gain, secretly accumulating evidence of wrongdoing, the organization must face the question of whether others knew of the wrongdoing and, if so, why they did not speak up.

The organization may stress regulatory and legal compliance, set up hotlines to report wrongdoing, and take other measures to encourage those seeing wrongdoing to speak up. And there may be legal protections in place for those reporting wrongdoing, at least in the case of illegal acts. But the fact remains that, according to the findings of the NBES, nearly half of those who witness unethical misconduct do not report it, and those who do not cite fear of retaliation as a major reason for their inaction. Giving voice to those who see wrongdoing so the organization is alerted to it, and at an early stage, is critical to ethical health.

---

*A successful action brought for health care fraud under the *qui tam* stipulation of the 1986 Federal False Claims Act can return up to 30 percent of the amount of the fraud to the whistle-blower. [www.QuiTamFYI.com, 2006. Whistleblowers and the Federal False Claims Act.]

The Discipline of Respect

Too often in health care organizations, different groups of professionals or work groups pigeonhole others, collectively and individually, or cast doubt on the motives of other groups. For example, nurses may believe that they are the primary advocates for the interests of patients and their families, with a commitment to care that is not embraced as fully by others such as physicians or administrators. Physicians may feel thwarted in their freedom to deliver excellent care and look at administrators, for example, as being dominated by financial concerns at the cost of patient care. Those same administrators may consider physicians and nurses as insensitive to the constraints and demands the administrators face to keep the organization financially viable, and as having self-centered interests they promote under the banner of patient care. Those and similar situations are not a foundation on which it is possible to build an ethical culture. Long-standing grievances, well founded or not, deafen the ability to listen to the legitimate concerns of others and stifle voice and ethical wisdom. What these grievances foster instead is an environment of mutual distrust and blame in which issues may be hidden, positive action thwarted, communication limited, and significant problems unresolved.

There is too much at stake for this mindset to be tolerated in ourselves or in others. For example, there is growing evidence that communication breakdowns during patient transfers and staff turnover are the single largest source of medical error. For the first time, the Joint Commission requires hospitals to establish standards for hand-off communications. The Joint Commission seeks to "break down long-standing cultural barriers in the exchange of patient information between doctors and nurses."[14]

Yet underlying these sometimes disharmonious work relationships is a pervasive and profound shared commitment to patients, their families, and the communities the organization serves. Sometimes we need a crisis to remind us what immense collaborative power is available when those in health care join together in common cause.

Respect and Partnership under Stress

When the tsunami struck Southeast Asia in late December 2004, causing widespread destruction, injury, and loss of life, one of the 6,000 physicians in The Permanente Medical Group (TPMG) exercised his voice by e-mailing the executive director and CEO, Dr. Robert Pearl, to ask: "What are we going to do?" Deciding immediately that he would make it possible for interested physicians to volunteer, Dr. Pearl sent out an e-mail to every physician in the group, thinking he might get only a few responses, especially since this catastrophe occurred during the holidays. He made it clear that this was a situation for which neither TPMG nor Kaiser Permanente (of which it is part) could promise the safety of those who would volunteer, their access to basic needs such as food or water, or an environment conducive to the practice of medicine. Dr. Pearl had 300 volunteers within

48 hours. Multiple teams of physicians and other health care professionals went to the region. Many of these volunteers would later describe this time of service in extreme conditions as their most wonderful experience in health care.[15] Why? Because they were able to come together to express the fundamental values of caring that they shared, irrespective of circumstances, irrespective of background, irrespective of role, and irrespective of status. They did what needed to be done to care for those in need.

In another example, a team made up of more than 70 nursing staff, physicians, physician assistants, and administrators from Scripps Health Care in San Diego went to New Orleans as part of the Hurricane Katrina relief mission. You might think that those who did not go would feel left out, even resentful of having to shoulder the added work that came from the absence of colleagues. This was far from the case. The regular updates from the team in New Orleans evoked many e-mails from all levels of the organization, such as the following: "Thank you so much for these updates. The caring and compassion are so beautiful it is really hard to put into words how I feel. There are many more people who feel the same way by reading these updates"; and "Thanks for sharing these amazing stories. At a meeting today, I updated my staff. We are all proud to belong to such an organization. I told them they are the people who make Scripps great."[16]

The responses to both the Asian tsunami and Hurricane Katrina are great examples of events permeated with respect. Respect is critical to an ethical culture. Mindfulness brings ethical concerns to our awareness and voice makes concerns available for conversation. But for the conversation to bear fruit, it must be characterized by respect. In the book of the same name, "crucial conversations" are defined as a discussion between two or more people where (1) the stakes are high, (2) opinions vary, and (3) emotions run strong.[17] This describes well many of the conversations that take place every day at every level in every health care organization. And why is respect important for these conversations to be productive? Again from *Crucial Conversations:*

> As people perceive that others don't respect them, the conversation immediately becomes unsafe and the dialogue comes to a screeching halt. Why? Because respect is like air. If you take it away, it's all people can think about. The instant people perceive disrespect in a conversation, the interaction is no longer about the original purpose—it is about defending personal dignity.[18]

What the authors of *Crucial Conversations* are talking about is creating an environment of dialogue[19] in which important, even intractable, issues large and small can be discussed so all participants experience the freedom to share their point of view and know that they are heard in a spirit of respect, without defensiveness, and with a willingness to revisit long-held positions. Only in this way can new levels of thinking and new avenues for action be co-created and owned by all.

The challenges of health care today, including elimination of medical errors, universal access to care, long-term financial viability of health care organizations, and employee satisfaction and retention, demand that we come together to create a powerful, committed, and coordinated force for positive change consistent with our highest values in spite of difficult circumstances—that we tap the immense collaborative power available in us as a community. So often we spend time focusing on the differences between us across silos, professions, functions, and levels in the organizational hierarchy. As stakeholders engaged in challenging crucial conversations, we need instead to stress the similarities of concerns and commitments that bind us. The examples of the medical responses to the Asian tsunami and Hurricane Katrina underscore how potent we can be working together in a partnership of goodwill for the good of those we serve.

Problem People

You may be thinking: "But what about the real jerks I have to deal with? What about the people who really should not be in health care to start with because, whatever their priorities, caring for patients and co-workers is not on the list?" The critical question is, "How do you know that you are right beyond having decided so?" After all, some people may be leveling the same criticisms against you, or against those with whom you feel an affinity. And you know they are wrong. But could you be wrong? Not in every case, but in some? Is it possible there are relationships you have long ago written off that are important to those you serve and are worth revisiting?

When one of my sons was very young, he was fascinated by how things worked, including his toys. Seeking to take things apart, but often lacking the appropriate tools or motor skills, he would sometimes use a hammer or some other blunt object in his attempts to disassemble them. We would find toys damaged beyond repair. One day I came home to find a small toy fire truck in the driveway. Clearly, it had received a blow and was much flatter than it should be. No one was home. I placed the truck carefully on the kitchen table and waited for my young son's arrival, stewing over yet another act of destruction. When he came through the door, I confronted him with typical parental outrage full of threats that there would be no toys in his future. When I finally stopped my tirade, he responded, "But, Daddy, Mommy drove over it in the driveway." And that is what actually happened. We can agree that had I withheld my preconception of what happened and listened before speaking, that crucial conversation would have gone a lot better.

It is worth the effort to enter into crucial conversations in a spirit of respect, no matter what our preconceptions. Sometimes we will be pleasantly surprised. Our ability to hear others, take their commitments and views into account, and explore issues without blame or preconception can make all the difference. It may also mean that we challenge our cherished but negative assumptions about individuals, groups, or the organization. This is no small thing. It could even be called a loving act. In the words of Paulo Friere, "Love is an act of courage, not fear; love is a commitment to others."[20] To which we could add: "for the sake of our patients, their families, the communities we serve, and in honor of our highest values of service." To take these courageous steps requires a faith in a new possibility; otherwise why would we bother? Nelson Mandela talked about his struggle against the great moral wrong of apartheid:

> I never lost hope that this great transformation would occur. . . . I knew deep down in every human heart there is mercy and generosity. No one is born hating another person because of the color of his skin, or his background, or his religion. People must learn to hate, and if they can learn to hate, they can be taught to love, for love comes more naturally to the human heart than its opposite. Even in the grimmest times in prison, when my comrades and I were pushed to our limits, I would see a glimmer of humanity in one of the guards, perhaps for a second, but it was enough to reassure me and keep me going. Man's goodness is a flame that can be hidden but never extinguished.[21]

The Discipline of Tenacity

Tenacity is important because, when an organization strives for a bold new future, the boldness of the challenge naturally encounters obstacles to success as it rubs up against business as usual. Sometimes the existing culture is tenacious as well in resisting new possibilities and new ways of operating.

Southwest Airlines: Tenacity in Taking Off

Southwest Airlines is one of America's great corporate success stories. In a volatile airline industry its track record is exceptional. It has consistently produced profitable results and is known for its engaged and valued employees. It has experienced remarkable growth since it began flying. From 1971 to 2006, Southwest Airlines grew from 108,554 customers to 88.4 million, from 195 employees to 32,000, and from a net loss of $3.7 million to a net profit of $548 million.[22]

But Southwest would not have even gotten off the ground, literally, without incredible tenacity. The story of Southwest's inception is a lesson in what is required to translate a vision and values into everyday reality. The airline began with the relatively modest aim of seeking approval to offer services between the three Texas cities of Dallas, Houston, and San Antonio. It received authority to fly in 1968, but 30 different legal actions launched by competitors kept the company grounded from 1967 to 1971.

As early legal decisions went against the company, the board of directors, fearing putting money and energy into a protracted and losing battle, was ready to shut down the enterprise. But tenacity won the day, and it was exemplified by Herb Kelleher. At that time, the now legendary chairman of Southwest Airlines was not even an employee; he was legal counsel to the corporation. As the fledgling company's prospects of getting off the ground foundered, he made a deal with the board. He would work for nothing and pay the legal costs himself as long as the board would keep fighting for as long as it took. Speaking of that time, Herb Kelleher touched on the vision and the values that fueled the fight: "I was enraged by the anti-competitive activities that the other carriers conducted against Southwest Airlines and in a sense it was a fairly high-flown thing. I wanted to vindicate the system, so that the system could produce the right results. All we wanted to provide was better service at lower fares. That's in the interests of the American people."[23] Kelleher continued, "If [our competitors] were successful it meant my vision for America was wrong."[24]

This story has all the critical elements of tenacity: (1) clear vision, mission, and values, which the organization had a strong hunger to realize; (2) the fire, heart, and even bull-headedness to fight for the realization of the vision, mission, and values; and (3) an uncompromising will to see the effort through to the end, even when success was uncertain. The following example demonstrates these same critical elements.

Baptist Health Care: Tenacity in Changing Course

In 1995 things were not well at Baptist Health Care in Pensacola, Florida. The previous few years had been spent with a leadership focus on external issues, in particular, looking for financial viability through mergers or acquisitions. When that effort proved unsuccessful, the leadership focus returned to the internal condition of the system. What they quickly faced was that Baptist was in bad shape. Employees were unhappy with senior management (surveys showed Baptist to be lower than average on 13 of 18 categories of employee satisfaction), patient satisfaction scores were in the 18th percentile (meaning more than 80 percent of hospitals surveyed were doing a better job satisfying patients than Baptist), overall morale across the system was low, and the viability of the organization was in doubt. The question on the table was not how to grow, but how to survive. Dramatic changes were needed. The board and leadership committed to providing the highest level of customer service possible, both as a vision for the future, a competitive strategy, and a way for survival.

Today, customer service ratings at Baptist are consistently in the 99th percentile, employee satisfaction is high, and the future of the organization is positive. It seems like a miracle, but it isn't. To get from the 18th percentile to the 99th percentile and to sustain that performance has required a tenacious belief in the chosen path, even when circumstances and objective data screamed out that it was impossible.[25] And it takes a continual striving to sustain success and to avoid the complacency that is an invitation to ethical erosion. Baptist, like other high performing vision- and value-driven health care organizations, is always raising the bar on its own performance. It has created a bolder vision that provides a continual challenge to strive for better performance and strengthened ethical pathways to success—to be the best hospital in the United States. In addition, continual improvement is fueled by a passion to succeed through ethical pathways.

Baptist's success has been accomplished by the unqualified commitment and passion for change in vision, mission, and values (a Malcolm Baldrige National Quality Award examiner called it "a maniacal consistency of purpose"[26]). Al Stubblefield, Baptist Health Care's president and CEO, put it this way: "Your senior managers must completely commit to the new culture; they must display a nonnegotiable, no-excuse determination that says we are going to do this—no matter what."[27] That is why some leaders and managers at Baptist never made the journey. A manager at Baptist was asked what was her turning point in the transformation. Her answer was "when two senior managers left," because their departure signaled that leadership really meant business and was willing to do what it would take to make the transformation happen.[28]

Tenacity does not guarantee the success of bold efforts to change, but without tenacity those efforts are doomed. In part I, we mentioned the Challenger disaster and the erosion of standards of quality and safety at NASA. In 2003 there was another shuttle disaster when Columbia was lost with its seven crew members on reentry into the earth's atmosphere. No one wanted to harm the astronauts, but they were nevertheless lost. These were not unrelated events, but they were reflections of negative elements of the NASA culture. Mike Mullane, a retired astronaut, wrote:

> Columbia's loss, just like Challenger's, wasn't an accident but rather a prediction. Cultural issues within the agency allowed intense schedule pressures . . . to overwhelm warnings of serious design flaws. The flaw that brought Challenger down was in the booster rocket O-ring design; for Columbia it was in the foam used to insulate the gas tank. In fact, in some of its findings, the Columbia Accident Investigation Board could have plagiarized the Challenger Rogers Commission report nearly word for word.[29]

The independent Columbia Accident Investigation Board pinned much of the blame for the accident on NASA's self-deception and overconfident culture, a culture that had persisted in spite of the Challenger disaster 17 years earlier. Constant, tenacious attention to an ethical culture and other ethical pathways is critical to sustain high ethical standards and stop ethical erosion.

Everyday Tenacity

When we hear of or read about these success stories or failures, it is worth bringing to mind another lesson they teach us. In his book *Good to Great*, Jim Collins, writing about high achieving companies, discusses what he calls the flywheel phenomenon of growth and change shared by successful companies:

> No matter how dramatic the end result, the good to great transformations never happened in one fell swoop. There was no single defining action, no grand program, no one killer innovation, no solitary lucky break, no miracle moment. Rather the process resembled relentlessly pushing a giant heavy flywheel in one direction, turn upon turn, building momentum until a point of breakthrough, and beyond.[30]

It takes a long time to change a culture. That change often begins with major interruption in the status quo. For Southwest Airlines the change was in refusing to capitulate to legal devices used by its competitors to keep them grounded. For Baptist the change came in taking on a new vision for the organization in order to survive. But it takes tenacity in everyday behaviors and decision making to sustain that change. We know this in our own case. For example, we may start a fitness program and get into a great rhythm with our fitness practices. Then some distraction occurs in our life, and before we know it, we are no longer in a fitness program, but anticipating being back in one very soon.

As we shall see in the following parts of this book, the ethical pathways of leadership and governance, infrastructure, and personal integrity are critical to sustaining change. The good news is that, to the degree doing the right thing becomes everyday practice, it becomes the culture. But old habits die hard, and everyday tenacity is needed because the organizational norms that are being altered are strongly rooted, employees are well-indoctrinated in them, and erosion always lurks. Without vigilance and tenacity, lasting change will not be accomplished, and ethical pathways will be compromised.

The Discipline of Legacy

Jonas Salk, discoverer of the polio vaccine that bears his name, in an article titled "Are We Being Good Ancestors," asked:

> Will we have the wisdom to perceive the long- as well as the short-term advantages in the choices we make so as to enhance the quality of our own lives and of the generations to follow? Will future generations speak of the wisdom of their ancestors as we are inclined to speak of the wisdom of ours? It is relevant and even part of wisdom to ask not only are we being good citizens of the world today, but are we being good ancestors?[31]

I never considered this question. Clearly, I had ancestors, and whether immediate or lost to history, they had provided the environment and the cultural and business norms into which I was born and socialized. To think of myself as an ancestor brought me up short. But I too am an ancestor in the making, as are we all. What we will leave as a personal legacy, and what the organizations in which we work will leave as a legacy, are profoundly important to the social and organizational culture others will inherit. The 2006 Josephson Institute Report Card on the Ethics of American Youth contained both good and sobering news that should encourage and concern us as ancestors. Of those surveyed, 98 percent said it was important to them to be a person of good character. What is more, 82 percent said that most adults in their lives consistently set a good example of ethics and character. The bad news is that 59 percent of the youths surveyed believe that, in the real world, successful people do what they have to do to win even if others consider it cheating, and 42 percent believe that a person has to lie and cheat sometimes in order to succeed.[32] This makes it imperative to create positive organizational and personal legacies (more about the latter can be found in part V, chapter 13), which will help shape the world of integrity we want for future generations.

But it can be hard to focus on our legacy. There is so much pressure to produce immediate results. If you work for a publicly owned health care organization, your reputation in the marketplace can rise and fall on the short-term promises you make, especially on the quarterly financial performance you delivered compared with the one you promised. If you work in a not-for-profit environment, you may exchange the label "surplus" for the label "profit," but that does not alter the need to make money to sustain the financial viability of the organization. The demand for short-term results and the urgency to act are fertile ground for ethical erosion. We may focus so much on financial concerns that the focus on our values may slip, especially in difficult times. Political and organizational pressure, not unlike the extreme reluctance to delay the launch of the space shuttle Challenger, can stifle concerns about the ethics of decisions. It is only by keeping our eye consistently on the long-term implications of today's decisions that we can remain true to our vision, mission, and values—to the legacy our organization will leave for others. When an organization chooses legacy and values over expedience, it provides a powerful signal of leadership priorities to the organization, which in turn will influence the everyday priorities of employees in their own decision making. The following are two examples of legacy-based decisions.

Cymer: A Commitment to Communication

Bob Akins and Rick Sanstrom founded Cymer, Inc., in a garage in San Diego more than 20 years ago. They had a dream of using innovative optical communication technology to create breakthroughs in the semiconductor equipment industry. Today they are the world's leading supplier of excimer light sources. You are unlikely to know their name, but their products are influential in how cell phones, computers, personal digital assistants or PDAs, and most modern electronic appliances and communication devices are made. Part of what has driven Akins and Sanstrom is a belief that communication is a vehicle for a more peaceful world—that people who can communicate freely with each other and understand each other's common concerns and commitments are more likely to talk than to fight. Although Akins and Sanstrom could have also made money working on defense applications, they focused their efforts on commercial applications of the technology. They had a firm belief in the beneficial impact of their technology on the world by creating communication breakthroughs.

There have been many ups and downs at Cymer, as in the life of any company. One down time occurred before the company had established itself. With bills and employees to pay, their own money and the welfare of families including their own at risk, and the future of the company in serious doubt, Akins and Sanstrom had an opportunity to take on a contract for work in the defense industry. They thought long and hard about what to do; and they decided that they would rather fail in a whole-hearted attempt to realize their vision than to compromise that vision, even for the sake of the company's short-term survival. They declined to pursue the defense industry contract. Things worked out for them. Even if they had not, Bob Akins today speculates that they would have walked away with heads held high, true to the vision they chose in those early days.[33]

Their decision was legacy driven, guided by Cymer's vision and values. Today Cymer still has a strong focus on its vision and values, which continue to be a guiding light for behavior and action. And Cymer's people work at keeping it that way. Bob Akins reflects, "Whenever we have taken a decision at odds with our values, we have paid the price for it."[34]

Bronson Healthcare: A Commitment to Mission

The Bronson Healthcare Group in Kalamazoo, Michigan, faced a similar decision that was influential to their legacy. In 2000 it became clear that Bronson Methodist Hospital, the flagship facility, had become outdated and a new facility was needed. Downtown Kalamazoo was not in strong economic health, and the most obvious solution was to build a new facility in a more affluent and attractive suburban setting, with an accompanying improvement in payer mix. But the board at Bronson chose another path. In a defining moment for the organization, the board members decided to honor three of their core values by committing to remain and build downtown: care and respect for all people, stewardship of resources, and commitment to community. Bronson Methodist Hospital has become a success story, now serving nearly double the inpatients it served in 2000 (and still including the most needy). The hospital is a Malcolm Baldrige National Quality Award recipient and is regularly cited in *Fortune* magazine's "100 Best Companies to Work for." What's more, the decision to stay in the city has been instrumental in the revitalization of downtown Kalamazoo.[35]

Legacy and the Short Term

Some organizations consider their values important but are willing to compromise them to achieve short-term results. Decisions inconsistent with their values are rationalized as necessary for the greater good. For example, a hospital's leadership, reluctant to anger a physician who provides an important stream of income to the hospital, but who does not treat hospital personnel with respect (a value of the institution), will tolerate that physician's behavior for the sake of financial viability, in itself a worthy goal. Or a manager who has organizing skills is similarly tolerated for the sake of performance, in itself a worthy goal, because he or she can be counted on to get the job done, even if his or her way of doing it is contrary to the values of the institution. Or a long-time employee whose interpersonal manner is at odds with the hospital's values is given a pass by superiors for the sake of showing appreciation for those who have given much to the hospital, in itself a worthy goal. Such decisions are rationalized as exceptions. But knowing what we know about ethical erosion, those decisions are not exceptions; they are precedents. As such, they lay the groundwork for further erosion of values. And the message that shouts out to employees trying to live the values is: these values are important, but they will be trumped by financial needs, by the importance of efficiency, or by the desire to not create turmoil, personal and organizational, by confronting difficult personnel issues.

Cindy Banta, director of patient care planning at Sutter Health in Sacramento, California, is one leader who knows the value of legacy. She is part of a multidisciplinary planning team working on a new hospital space. Whenever the team begins to get stuck in difficult issues or crucial conversations, the members return to their guiding principle, "patients and family first." In so doing, they rise above restrictive parochial interests and let that legacy-driven principle guide their decision making.[36]

Simply put, the many decisions that are made every day can be driven by habit (we always do it that way), expediency (what do we need to do to get through this moment?), or legacy (what is most consistent with the organization's vision, mission, and values?). Among the choices we make every day, it is the legacy-driven decisions that hold the most promise for realizing the values we hold dear, for achieving the legacy we want to leave, and for achieving the levels of performance we seek.

In Short

Culture is a critical ethical pathway because culture shapes ethical behavior and decision making far more profoundly than ethical training and compliance programs alone can do. An ethical culture is composed of five disciplines:

- Mindfulness—An individual discipline that an organization can support but not create. It is the private voice of ethical wisdom.
- Voice—The public voice of ethical wisdom, which can be supported or suppressed by individuals and the organization.
- Respect—A behavior that allows the ethical concerns of individuals and groups to be heard and issues to be openly and constructively discussed.
- Tenacity—The resolve to meet difficult situations and work through them to the best conclusion.
- Legacy—A quality that drives decisions based on their impact on the vision, mission, and values of the organization, and not based on short-term expediency that compromises the long term.

Chapter 5 provides a diagnostic you can use to measure the vital signs of the ethical pathway of your culture.

References

1. National Business Ethics Survey. 2005. How employees view ethics in their organizations 1994–2005. Washington: Ethics Resource Center.
2. Seidman, D. 2004. Compliance is not enough: law enforcement looks to a company's ethical culture. *SHRM Legal Report*, October-November.
3. Kaplan, J.M. 2004. The new corporate sentencing guidelines. *Ethikos Journal*, July/August.

4. Gladwell, M. 2005. *Blink*. New York: Little, Brown & Co.
5. Schaffer, G. [CEO, Johns Hopkins Bayview Medical Center] 2006. Interview with author, Baltimore, July 13.
6. National Business Ethics Survey. 2005.
7. National Business Ethics Survey. 2003. Washington: Ethics Resource Center.
8. Corace, C. [Director, Credo Survey and Organizational Analysis, Johnson & Johnson] 2006. Interview with author, New Brunswick, NJ, June 9.
9. Institute for Healthcare Improvement. 2006. IHI announces that hospitals participating in 100,00 Lives Campaign have saved an estimated 122,300 lives. Press release, June 14.
10. Ward, Jr., W. 2006. The business case for implementing rapid response teams. Baltimore: Johns Hopkins Bloomberg School of Public Health, May 17.
11. Institute of Safe Medication Practices. 2006. Rapid response team activation by patients can mitigate errors, June 1.
12. Elliston, F., Keenan, J., Lockhart, P., and van Schaick, J. 1985. *Whistleblowing Research: Methodological and Moral Issues*. New York: Praeger.
13. Eichenwald, K. 2005. *Conspiracy of Fools*. New York: Broadway Books.
14. Landro, L. 2006. Hospitals combat errors at the "hand off." *Wall Street Journal*, June 28.
15. Pearl, R. [CEO, The Permanente Medical Group, Kaiser Permanente] 2006. Interview with author, Oakland, CA, July 12.
16. [No author cited.] 2005. Special report: hurricane Katrina. San Diego: Scripps Health, September-October, pp. 32–33.
17. Patterson, K., Grenny, J., McMillan, R., and Switzler, A. 2002. *Crucial Conversations*. New York: McGraw-Hill, p. 3.
18. Patterson and others, *Crucial Conversations*, p. 71.
19. For more about dialogue, refer to the following: Bohm, D. 1996. *On Dialogue*. New York: Routledge; Friere, P. 2000. *Pedagogy of the Oppressed*, 30th anniversary ed. New York: Continuum, pp. 87–93; Isaacs, W. 1999. *Dialogue and the Art of Thinking Together*. New York: Currency; Senge, P., and others. 1994. *The Fifth Discipline Field Book*. New York: Currency.
20. Friere, P. 2000. *Pedagogy of the Oppressed*, p. 89.
21. Mandela, N. 1994. *Long Walk to Freedom*. Boston: Little Brown & Co., p. 622.
22. [No author cited.] 2006. Little giant. *Spirit Magazine*, June, p. 154.
23. Guinto, J. 2006. Wheels up. *Spirit Magazine*, June, p. 114.
24. Guinto, J. 2006. Rollin' on. *Spirit Magazine*, June, p. 140.
25. Stubblefield, A. 2004. *The Baptist Health Care Journey to Excellence*. Hoboken, NJ: John Wiley & Sons.
26. Stubblefield, *Baptist Health Care Journey to Excellence*, p. 34.
27. Stubblefield, *Baptist Health Care Journey to Excellence*, p. 38.
28. Baillie, S. [Diagnostic Imaging Supervisor, Baptist Health Care] 2006. Interview with author, Pensacola, FL, August 14.

29. Mullane, M. 2006. Challenger's lessons prove elusive. *USA Today*, January 26, p. 13A.
30. Collins, J. 2001. *Good to Great*. New York: HarperBusiness, p. 14.
31. Salk, J. 1992. Are we being good ancestors? *World Affairs*, December, p. 16.
32. Josephson Institute. 2006. 2006 Report card on the ethics of American youth: part one—integrity summary of data. Press release, October 15.
33. Akins, R. [Chairman and CEO, Cymer, Inc.] 2006. Interview with author, San Diego, May 24.
34. Akins, interview with author.
35. Sardone, F. [President and CEO, Bronson Healthcare Group] 2006. Interview with author, Kalamazoo, MI, July 21.
36. Banta, C. [Director of Patient Care Planning, Sutter Health] 2006. Interview with author, Sacramento, CA, August 22.

5

A Diagnostic for the Ethical Pathway of Culture

The permanent temptation of life is to confuse dreams with reality. The permanent defeat of life comes when dreams are surrendered to reality.

—James Michener

THIS CHAPTER provides a "vital signs" diagnostic to help you assess at a high level the health of the ethical pathway of culture for your organization, department, work group, or team, or for yourself. Although the area you assess is your choice, it might be best to start with your immediate area to become familiar with using the diagnostic and leading the discussions that encourage an open dialogue and positive change.

After you have scored the diagnostic, you can use the results to choose a discipline for your focus of action. Read more on this choice in the section on "Interpreting the Diagnostic." The following are some broad guidelines you should follow in conducting the diagnostic:

1. Be sure to introduce the use of the questionnaire by sharing why you think completing and discussing the results will be a valuable use of time, and also share its purpose, which is about gaining understanding and making improvements and is not about blame.
2. Assure those taking the diagnostic that it is safe to respond. Generally, the smaller the group completing the diagnostic, the more difficult it is to maintain anonymity, and the more important it is that those taking the diagnostic trust your good intent. If different departments or teams are being assessed, be clear how confidentiality will be maintained and how differences between areas will be managed. Be sure the diagnostic will not be used to place blame on the leader of a comparatively low scoring area, but will be used to expose opportunities for improvement.
3. If you are conducting the diagnostic across different areas of your organization or with different groups within an area, consider using a trusted facilitator to administer, tally, and present the findings. As mentioned later in this chapter, that facilitator could also be used to manage discussions and help build action plans.
4. Use the diagnostic and what you learn from it with caution. You would not make a diagnosis from a patient's vital signs, but you would use them as one input. This diagnostic and others in this book are best used in the same way, provoking questions, not answers, and opening up discussion and thinking, not closing them off.

Appendix 1 presents a comprehensive diagnostic survey to assess the health of all four ethical pathways. This is a better tool to gather a complete picture of ethical health. Instructions on how to complete an on-line version of the questionnaire can also be found in appendix 1.

The "From-To's" of an Ethical Culture

The disciplines of an ethical culture exist to some degree in all organizations. But unlike the light from an on-off switch, they are not completely present or completely absent. Their condition can be thought to occur on a continuum. Figure 5-1 shows some of the "from-to's" of the disciplines and gives a sense of the "cultural mood" we want to minimize and the one we want to instill.

The Ethical Culture Diagnostic

The questions in the following diagnostic are connected to a specific discipline. A short description of the discipline precedes the questions to remind you what discipline is being considered in the questions. Figure 5-2 is a score sheet to use in producing results for each discipline and a total score. There are three options for responding to each question:

- *Strongly Agree*—The behavior or point of view is a pervasive, common practice. **Score a 5.**
- *Sometimes Agree*—You see the behavior or point of view, but it is inconsistent, and you cannot count on its happening routinely. **Score a 3.**
- *Strongly Disagree*—The likelihood of the behavior or point of view occurring is much more unusual than usual. **Score a 1.**

Circle the number that applies for each question. Score the diagnostic as you go along.

Mindfulness is the private voice of ethical wisdom. It is the self-awareness that brings ethical dilemmas and issues to top of mind. It is an early signal, such as a sense of calm or comfort with a decision, a gut reaction, discomfort, nagging doubt, or a feeling that something could be "off" with a decision.

1. Leadership* is passionate about employees' living the organization's values every day.
2. Where I work, we take the time to talk about our ethics and values when making decisions.
3. I take the time to reflect on whether the decisions we make on a daily basis are consistent with the vision, mission, and values of the organization.
4. I think about whether or not my core values are consistent with the organization's values.

---

*Whom *leadership* refers to will vary depending on the scope of the diagnostic. For example, if the diagnostic is conducted for the organization, then leadership will refer to the executive team. If it is for a work team, then leadership will refer to the team leader.

Figure 5-1. The "From-To's" of the Disciplines of an Ethical Culture

Discipline	From	To
Mindfulness	I don't think about the ethics of what I am asked to do or about decisions being made.	I am sensitive to my emotional, mental, or physical reactions that signal to me something may be "off" ethically.
	I assume my superiors are fully aware of the consequences of their decisions.	My reactions to situations are important, and I have a lot to say about what is right and what is wrong.
	Our leadership rarely talks about living our values or about doing the right thing as a big priority.	Our leadership is always stressing that living our values and doing the right thing trump other priorities.
Voice	I am a team player, meaning that I keep my head down, do what I am told, and don't make waves.	I am accountable for speaking up when I feel something is "off" ethically.
	Saying something that disagrees with a superior is a good way to limit your career here.	This is a safe place to express differing points of view and to be heard; in fact, you get into trouble when you don't speak up.
Respect	We (my team, department, profession, or shift) are more committed to doing the right thing than a lot of others who work here.	Everywhere you look in the organization, people are committed to doing the right thing, even if we come at it from different viewpoints.
	I don't trust some other groups to behave ethically; I think they put their own agendas first.	Behaving ethically matters a lot to the vast majority of people in the organization, no matter in what area or at what level.
	The leadership operates from a silo mentality.	The leadership consistently acts as a team sharing the same priorities.
Tenacity	We gloss over ethical concerns and move on quickly.	When an ethical issue comes up, we stop to discuss it and really dig for the root cause.
	Problem solving around here mostly consists of finding someone to blame.	We stick with tough ethical problems and work through them together until we get to the best solutions we can find.
Legacy	If I get through it in one piece, I've had a good day.	I go home proud of my work and my organization, knowing I have lived my own values in my actions.
	Our focus around here is on short-term results; looking beyond the short term is a distraction we can't afford.	In our everyday actions and decisions, we always have our eyes on living our vision and values and doing the right thing.
	The leadership mantra here is that we need to focus on doing more with less so we can make our numbers and be around to serve our patients and our community.	The leadership mantra here is that the bottom line is important, but we need to focus on doing the right thing for our patients, our community, and our employees to sustain a healthy bottom line.

Figure 5-2. Ethical Culture Diagnostic Score Sheet

	Strongly Agree	Sometimes Agree	Strongly Disagree	Discipline Total	÷ Number of Questions	= Average Score
Mindfulness						
Question 1	5	3	1			
Question 2	5	3	1			
Question 3	5	3	1			
Question 4	5	3	1			
Score					4	
Voice						
Question 5	5	3	1			
Question 6	5	3	1			
Question 7	5	3	1			
Question 8	5	3	1			
Score					4	
Respect						
Question 9	5	3	1			
Question 10	5	3	1			
Question 11	5	3	1			
Question 12	5	3	1			
Score					4	
Tenacity						
Question 13	5	3	1			
Question 14	5	3	1			
Question 15	5	3	1			
Question 16	5	3	1			
Score					4	
Legacy						
Question 17	5	3	1			
Question 18	5	3	1			
Question 19	5	3	1			
Question 20	5	3	1			
Score					4	
		Total Score			20	

Voice is the public voice of ethical wisdom. It brings mindfulness into open conversation and enables ethical issues to be revealed and explored in a constructive spirit in many forums, such as meetings, informal conversations, employee surveys, or other forms of communication. Voice is shared mindfulness that leverages collective ethical wisdom.

5. Our organization is a safe place to express differing points of view about the ethics of a decision.
6. It is safe to speak up about ethical concerns without having a full set of facts.
7. I speak up when I think the organization's values are being ignored or discounted.
8. The organization encourages employees to express their opinions when they have something to say about our ethics.

Respect is listening to others with generosity rather than suspicion, with a commitment to understand and value differing views. It strengthens our ability to work on ethical issues as colleagues, not critics, irrespective of differences.

9. I can speak freely and directly about my ethical concerns with my boss.
10. I can speak freely and directly about my ethical concerns with my peers.
11. I can speak freely and directly about my ethical concerns with other departments or disciplines.
12. The organization values different points of view among employees.

Tenacity is being unstoppable in the quest for ethical behavior and ethical decision making. It is the shared commitment to see difficult conversations through to their resolution, no matter what. It is harnessing—not avoiding—problems, addressing fundamental issues, and grappling with ambiguous situations.

13. In this organization, we don't hide our ethical concerns.
14. We deal with ethical concerns until they are resolved, even when it requires having uncomfortable conversations.
15. We will delay a decision when there are unresolved ethical issues connected with that decision.
16. When our values clash with pressures to cut corners, we don't give up on our values.

Legacy is making ethical decisions in a spirit of stewardship, understanding the implications and the consequences of our behaviors and decisions for those who will follow, including fellow employees, patients, their families, and our own families. Legacy is acting in keeping with the long view, personally and organizationally, consistent with vision, mission, and values.

17. My actions and decisions are building a future here I will be proud of.
18. I am happy to recommend my organization to other people as a place where they can build a satisfying career.
19. Our vision and values drive both small and large decisions.
20. Our organization will let go valuable staff who don't respect our values rather than compromise our values for greater efficiency or revenue.

Scoring the Diagnostic

The following are steps to score the diagnostic to produce an average score for the questions for each discipline and an average score for all 20 questions. Figure 5-3 shows an example of a completed score sheet.

1. Go down the columns vertically and add the scores for each set of questions for a discipline.
2. Add the scores for each discipline across to produce a discipline total.
3. Divide the discipline total for each discipline by 4 (the number of questions) to find the average score for each discipline.
4. Total all the discipline totals vertically to produce the total score.
5. Divide the total score by 20 (the total number of questions) to find the average score for all of the disciplines combined.

Interpreting the Diagnostic

You can decide your own approach in interpreting the survey results, but consider the following questions and approaches in your interpretation.

Questions and Approaches to Interpretation

1. What is the total score average?
   Obviously, if the average score for an individual discipline or the total of all disciplines is 3 or below, it is a red flag. "Sometimes" may be an acceptable average for some surveys, but in the case of an ethical pathway, any lack of consistency in living values is an invitation to ethical erosion. In fact, any score is a basis for a conversation about how to improve. You may well see scores of 5 for individual questions; however, an average score of 5 is both an opportunity to acknowledge success and also to explore whether this perfect ethical condition holds up under scrutiny.
2. On what discipline would you focus for discussion and change?
   You can select a discipline on which to focus in at least three ways:
   - It can be the discipline with the lowest average score.

Figure 5-3. Example of a Completed Ethical Culture Diagnostic Score Sheet

	Strongly Agree	Sometimes Agree	Strongly Disagree	Discipline Total	÷ Number of Questions	= Average Score
Mindfulness						
Question 1	(5)	3	1			
Question 2	5	(3)	1			
Question 3	5	(3)	1			
Question 4	(5)	3	1			
Score	*10*	*6*		*16*	4	*4.0*
Voice						
Question 5	5	(3)	1			
Question 6	5	(3)	1			
Question 7	5	(3)	1			
Question 8	5	(3)	1			
Score		*12*		*12*	4	*3.0*
Respect						
Question 9	5	3	(1)			
Question 10	5	(3)	1			
Question 11	5	(3)	1			
Question 12	5	3	(1)			
Score		*6*	*2*	*8*	4	*2.0*
Tenacity						
Question 13	(5)	3	1			
Question 14	(5)	3	1			
Question 15	5	(3)	1			
Question 16	5	(3)	1			
Score	*10*	*6*		*16*	4	*4.0*
Legacy						
Question 17	(5)	3	1			
Question 18	5	(3)	1			
Question 19	5	(3)	1			
Question 20	5	(3)	1			
Score	*5*	*9*		*14*	4	*3.5*
		Total Score		*66*	20	*3.3*

- It can be the discipline with the most 1 scores.
- It can be the discipline that, if paid attention to, you decide will produce the best opportunity for change (this may or may not be the lowest scoring discipline).

Whatever discipline you choose to focus on, do not be surprised if discussion about it leads to discussion about one or more other disciplines. This is because the disciplines are related to each other.

3. To enrich a conversation about these results, you can choose the discipline with the best score and compare it to a weak-performing discipline. This comparison provides an opportunity to not only ask what is not working about a weak-performing discipline, but also to ask what we can learn from what we are doing right with a high-performing discipline.
4. Remember that this is a high-level diagnostic and, as such, should not be used to provide answers but to provoke focused questions and open discussion.

Thoughts for Each Discipline

Each discipline has its own characteristics. Ways to explore the implications of responses to the questions within each of the disciplines follow.

Mindfulness

Questions 1 and 2 ask about the organization's support for mindfulness. Questions 3 and 4 focus more on individual behavior. Do not be surprised if individuals score themselves higher than they do the organization (that is, questions 3 and 4 get a higher score than questions 1 and 2). For example, in a survey of an executive team with which this author once worked, every executive scored themselves higher on commitment to teamwork than they scored the team as a whole. The disparity in these responses did produce a useful conversation.

If this disparity occurs, to encourage mindfulness, look to see if there is in your view, and in the view of others, a partnership of goodwill between the organization and those who work in it; or whether there is a belief the organization does not support individual mindfulness; or whether, on the other hand, there is a belief that individuals do not support organizational efforts to promote mindfulness.

Voice

The key words in questions 5, 6, and 8 are *safe* and *encourages*. If safety and encouragement are deemed to be weak or inconsistent, or there is encouragement without safety, this discipline will not be healthy enough to influence ethical behavior and decision making. Question 7 asks, in spite of whether there is safety and encouragement, does the individual feel a duty to speak? When the response to questions 5, 6, and 8 are generally more positive than the response to question 7, or vice versa, this mismatch is worth exploring.

Respect

In comparing the responses to questions 9, 10, and 11, it is valuable to look for significant variances. The general tendency is for employees to feel most comfortable speaking freely with their peers, less comfortable with their boss, and even less comfortable with employees outside their department or discipline. The more uniformly positive the responses to these three questions, the more you are to be congratulated. Conversely, it is important to address what limits speaking freely and to what degree. Question 12 tests for diversity of views, a key element in bringing new ways of thinking to any conversation.

Tenacity

Taken as a whole, these question probe for whether values are kept front and center in everyday decision making. If the responses to these questions differ significantly one to another, then this is a reason to dig deeper to find out what is going on. On the surface, you could expect consistency of response. A low set of scores is a cause for concern because it implies an awareness of ethical issues but a discounting of their importance, or a reluctance to confront them.

Legacy

Just as the questions in "mindfulness" addressed both personal and organizational views, so do the questions in "legacy." Questions 17 and 18 test for personal satisfaction with the way the organization lives its values. Questions 19 and 20 test for whether legacy is present in decision making. Question 20 points to an important issue that is a good test for the importance of legacy: will we forego short-term results (filling slots with warm bodies, for example) for long-term benefit and consistency with our vision, mission, and values (filling slots only with the right people).

Approaches to Action

As a general principle, the results of this diagnostic should be shared and discussed with those who completed it, whether it is you and a couple of colleagues, a work team, a department, a discipline, or an organization. Obviously, the larger and more diverse the group, the more the sharing and discussion need to be orchestrated and may need to include, for example, skilled and trusted facilitators from the training and development department. This facilitation support is also useful to relieve you of the burden of both leading and participating freely in the discussion.

Be sure to allow sufficient time for the discussion. Participants need to be able to explore and absorb the implications of the findings and to reach a productive course of action. The resources about dialogue listed in endnote number 19 in chapter 4 may be useful in providing the tools to create a productive set of discussions.

Finally, you will need to model for others the disciplines of an ethical culture by being mindful, using your own voice to share your wisdom, listening with respect to the views of others (not necessarily agreeing with them, but taking them into account), being tenacious in seeking new thinking and moving the conversation beyond common complaints to positive action, and acting consistently with the legacy you and the group seek. This may require your courage in moving beyond the comfortable and the familiar. But as an act of personal integrity, it is an invaluable contribution to your co-workers and to your organization's integrity.

III

The Ethical Pathway of Leadership and Governance

6

Leadership, Governance, and Noble Purpose

This, therefore, is a faded dream of the time when I went down
into the dust and noise of the Eastern marketplace,
and with my brain and muscles, with sweat and constant thinking,
made others see my visions coming true.
Those who dream by night in the dusty recesses of their minds
wake in the day to find that all was vanity;
but the dreamers of the day are dangerous men,
for they may act their dream with open eyes,
and make it possible.

—T. E. Lawrence (Lawrence of Arabia)

THIS CHAPTER and chapters 7 through 10 focus on the ethical pathway of leadership and governance. The leadership focus is on senior leaders—CEOs and their executive team—as well as on the defining role these executives have in setting the ethical tone and standards of behavior throughout the organization, and the need for their absolute adherence to ethical pathways in producing results. That said, the principles and diagnostics presented for leadership can apply to leaders at any level in an organization, including frontline supervisors. The governance focus is on the board of trustees or directors and its critical role in setting and sustaining the ethical tone and standards for an organization.

The Disciplines of Leadership and Governance: An Overview

Figure 6-1 shows an overview of the ethical disciplines of leadership and governance. Noble purpose, an ethical discipline shared by organizational leadership and the board of trustees, is discussed in this chapter. The three other ethical disciplines of leadership—ceaseless ambition, candor, and passion—are discussed in chapter 7. A leadership diagnostic tool is presented in chapter 8. The three other ethical disciplines of governance—independent engagement, ethical culture, and ethical succession—are discussed in chapter 9. A governance diagnostic tool is presented in chapter 10.

Figure 6-1. The Disciplines of Leadership and Governance

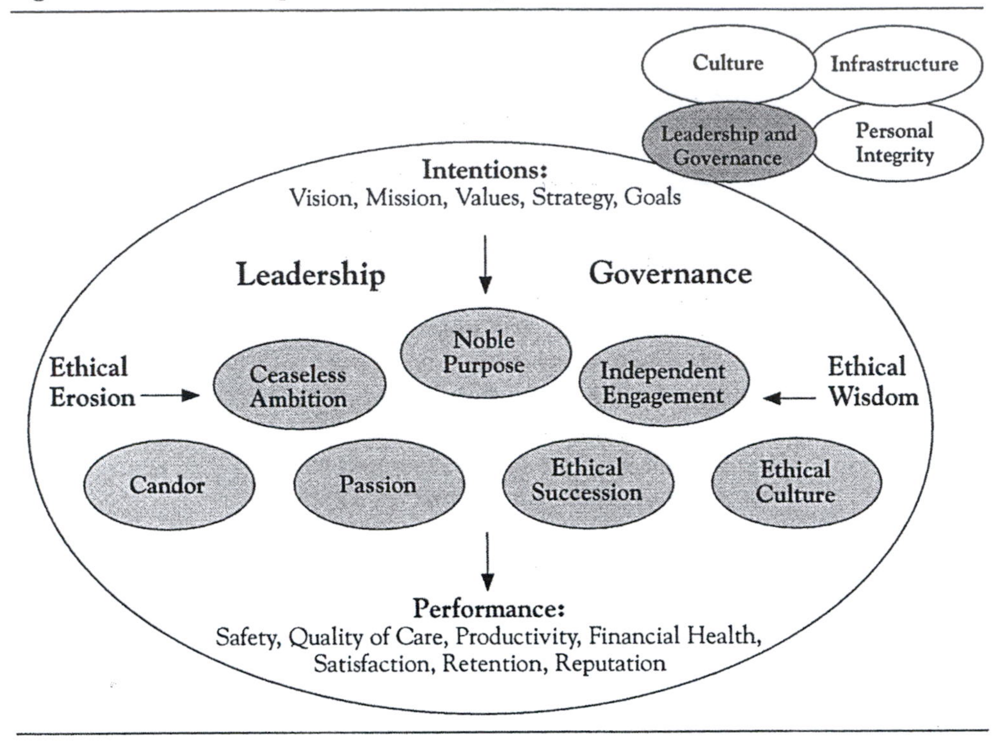

The Shared Discipline of Noble Purpose

Organizational consultant Barry Heermann calls noble purpose "a signature way of being of service in the world."[1] That "signature way" for those who work in health care is profound—they care for the health and welfare of individuals, families, communities, and society. Medicine is one of only three established professions in Western history; the other two are law and academia. Society entrusts a profession with the authority to establish and maintain the profession's standards and, in return, expects that the profession will act to promote the welfare of society. One definition of a profession is:

> A calling requiring specialized knowledge and often long and intensive preparation including instruction in skills and methods as well as the scientific, historical, or scholarly principles underlying such skills and methods, maintaining by force of organization or concerted opinion such high standards of achievement and conduct, and committing its members to continued study and to a kind of work which has for its prime purpose the rendering of a public service.[2]

Drawing from that definition, with an emphasis on purpose and behavior, the definition of *noble purpose* is:

> A calling . . . maintained by high standards of achievement and conduct . . . a kind of work, which has for its prime purpose the rendering of a public service.

Figure 6-2. The Shared Leadership and Governance Discipline of Noble Purpose

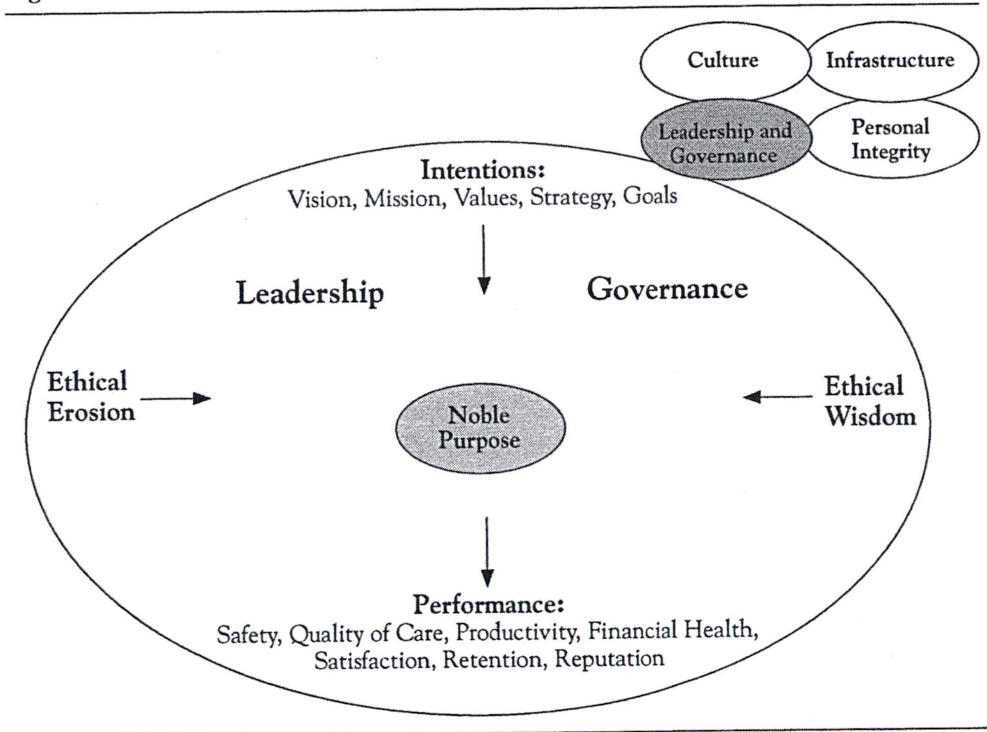

Dr. Robert Pearl is passionate about this calling. He wants health care professionals "to remember why they chose medicine, nursing, their chosen contribution, in the first place . . . to remember the first time they took care of a patient . . . to remind themselves of the privilege of caring for a patient."[3]

What applies to the practice of care also applies to hospitals as well as other health care organizations. The vast majority of American hospitals were created in response to community forces calling for the development of local medical services. The majority remain not-for-profit, tax-exempt organizations, and in return for that status, they have accepted special responsibilities to the communities they serve.[4] For-profit hospitals cannot turn away from this calling or do not wish to. For example, the Hospital Corporation of America's mission and values statement begins: "Above all else, we are committed to the care and improvement of human life."[5]

Noble Purpose and Financial Responsibility

We have already seen that great companies with celebrated leaders like Johnson & Johnson, Kyocera, and Southwest Airlines, while recognized for their financial success, are driven by something beyond it—their noble purpose. For Johnson & Johnson, it is the welfare of the people they serve through their products and services. For Kyocera, it comes from respecting the Divine and loving people. For Southwest, it is freedom to compete and to choose. Heroes of medicine, like Florence Nightingale and Mother Theresa, for example, although they may be the equal of any business executive in creating movements and organizations from nothing, are not celebrated for their financial accomplishments but for their contributions to the calling of medicine and the welfare of others—to their noble purpose.

Financial success is essential to organizational sustainability, and there are times in the life of an organization when financial challenges can be preoccupying. But when the persistent and overwhelming focus of a health care organization's leadership and board is on financial results, reimbursement optimization, physician business relationships, other financial partnerships, the search for capital, and so on, a strong focus on the noble purpose of the organization, as expressed in its vision, mission, and values, can become lost through lack of priority and measurement.

When 76 percent of hospital CEOs cite financial challenges as one of their top three issues, and 20 percent cite patient safety in their top three issues, it is both understandable and profoundly disturbing.[6] It is understandable because an executive spends a good deal of time on issues of productivity, expenses, budgets, revenue optimization, and the like. It is disturbing because patients are dying and being harmed by medical error while in the care of hospitals and other health care organizations. This prioritization may reflect the fact that measurement of nonfinancial performance is less routine and can be more complex than measurement of financial performance. In considering the low percentage of CEOs who place patient safety as the highest priority, Richard Breon noted: "Other issues eclipse patient safety as a concern because CEOs typically are more experienced in financial models, terminology, and operations than in clinical systems."[7] The increased focus on financial performance as a dominant measure of success has not gone unnoticed, as challenges to the not-for-profit status of hospitals have increased.[8]

This imbalance in prioritization and measurement is a prevalent condition throughout business. A global survey of priorities and focuses of boards of directors concluded that there is a "critical fault line between rhetoric and reality in the boardrooms of the world's leading companies. Nonfinancial factors are widely regarded as extremely important drivers of success for a company, yet they receive considerably less attention than financial data from the board and senior managers."[9] In fact, 86 percent of companies surveyed said their company was excellent or good at tracking financial indicators, but only 36 percent said they were excellent or good at measuring and tracking nonfinancial factors.

The admonition of Kyocera's founder, Kazuo Inamori, is worth repeating: "We have to carry out the right decision, which you as a human being can be proud of, surpassing shallow ideas about profit and loss to the corporation—or to any one individual. This is the most fundamental standard of conduct for all employees, including myself."[10] The primacy of noble purpose demands more of leaders than anyone else to decide what is important to focus on based on the aspirations of the organization, not on what is most commonly or easily measured. The issue of measurement and assessment is discussed more fully in part IV, "The Ethical Pathway of Infrastructure."

Noble Purpose and Employee Commitment

Putting noble purpose front and center in the operation of the organization provides employees with an emotional connection to the organization and evokes commitment. In the words of Kazuo Inamori: "Noble motives are a source of energy."[11]

A survey by the Corporate Executive Board[12] found that when employees have an emotional commitment (defined as the extent to which employees value, enjoy, and believe in their organization), they are more engaged and more committed to their organization's success. What is more, when that emotional commitment is combined with a rational commitment (defined as the degree to which employees believe the organization acts in their financial, developmental, and professional interest), a markedly stronger positive impact is made on their performance and on retention. In short, when employees believe in what they are doing and they feel taken care of, they will work harder happily and want to stay. A 2004 survey found that organizations that communicate and support their vision and values produce a dramatically improved impact on morale, commitment, and retention over those that do not.[13] For example, in organizations that communicate and support the vision and values, 16 percent of employees are thinking seriously of leaving, compared with 40 percent in nonsupportive organizations. In addition, 7 percent in supportive organizations are dissatisfied with the organization, compared with 39 percent in nonsupportive organizations, and only 6 percent in supportive organizations do not feel a strong sense of commitment, compared with 32 percent in nonsupportive organizations.

These findings underscore the importance of noble purpose. Employees in different health care organizations may be asked to do more with less, but those who work in organizations they believe in and feel supported by will voluntarily go above and beyond, will sustain that effort, and will stay when they believe their value of working in service of a noble purpose is shared by their leaders. This dynamic applies to challenges beyond increasing productivity, which is demonstrated by the 100,000 Lives Campaign.

Noble Purpose in Action: The 100,000 Lives Campaign

When the power and passion of those committed to health care align behind a noble purpose, they rise above parochial interests to focus on producing benefits that can be awe-inspiring, as in the response to the needs of the Asian tsunami victims, for example. The 100,000 Lives Campaign is a wonderful example of what happens when people come together to do the right thing. Initiated in December 2004 by the Institute for Healthcare Improvement (IHI), the 100,000 Lives Campaign is a national initiative with the goal of saving patients from unnecessary death in hospitals through improvements in the safety and effectiveness of health care. During the past several years, there have been many efforts driven by hospitals with similar goals in helping to create a general reduction in risk-adjusted mortality. One thing that distinguishes this campaign is its boldness, which is discussed more fully later in this chapter. The campaign set (and met) an unheard of goal of saving 100,000 lives in an 18-month pilot program. In addition, the campaign has had the effect of unifying and galvanizing the health care community around its noble purpose. Every hospital was invited to join the campaign, and about half representing 75 percent of hospital beds did so.[14]

Action-backed support for the campaign has come from across the health care community. Joseph McCannon, campaign manager for IHI, looking back on the 18-month pilot, wrote: "From the launch of the Campaign a very courageous group of partners, including the Joint Commission, the Centers for Disease Control and Prevention, the Centers for Medicare & Medicaid Services, the American Medical Association, the American Nurses Association, Leapfrog, and the National Patient Safety Foundation, have made the Campaign possible. The vibrant infrastructure is not going away—in fact we fully intend to build upon it in order to transform the health care system."[15] Why this unbridled enthusiasm? Because this improbable goal of saving lives has been easily exceeded in the 18 months since the campaign's inception, during which an estimated 122,300 patients have been saved from unnecessary death.[16]

One lesson of the campaign is that noble purpose in action evokes commitment, innovation, collaboration, and ethical wisdom in unexpected and potent ways. Rapid response teams, one of the approaches used by the campaign and already discussed in chapter 4, depend on tapping ethical wisdom for their success.

Another lesson is recognition of the extraordinary power of the health care community when it comes together in the service of its calling—its noble purpose. In Joseph McCannon's words, the impact of the campaign has "proven that it's possible for the health care community to come together voluntarily to rapidly make significant changes in patient care. I have never before witnessed such widespread collaboration and commitment on the part of health care leaders and front-line staff to move the system giant steps forward."[17]

In Short

Noble purpose is at the heart of the practice of care and the reason for being of health care organizations—most commonly expressed through their vision, mission, and values. The pressures of everyday work and the short-term challenges leaders and the board face may draw attention away from noble purpose, but it is critical that it is sustained as a focal point for leadership and board behavior, priorities, and decision making. Sustaining this focus is critical to support ethical pathways, heighten the meaning of work for leaders and others who work in the organization or come in contact with it, and evoke levels of employee commitment that enable an organization to perform at high levels of organizational and personal integrity.

Noble purpose is also a powerful unifying force. A focus on it brings together different parts of the health care community that otherwise may be in conflict, diminishes their differences, and mobilizes powerful collaborations for change.

References

1. Heermann, B. 2006. www.noblepurpose.com.
2. [No author cited.] 1961. *Webster's Third New International Dictionary*. Springfield, MA: Merriam-Webster.
3. Pearl, R. [CEO, The Permanente Medical Group, Kaiser Permanente] 2006. Interview with author, Oakland, CA, July 12.
4. Russell, J., and Greenspan, B. 2005. Correcting and preventing management mistakes, in P.B. Hofmann and F. Perry, eds., *Management Mistakes in Healthcare*. Cambridge, MA: Cambridge University Press.
5. www.hcahealthcare.com [Hospital Corporation of America Web site]. 2006.
6. Breon, R. 2006. Patient safety: a growing concern of CEOs. *CEO*, Spring.
7. Breon, Patient safety: a growing concern of CEOs, p. 1.
8. Sandrick, K. 2006. Defining and measuring community benefit. *Trustee*, October, p. 1.
9. [No author cited.] 2004. In the dark: what boards and executives don't know about the health of their businesses. Deloitte and Economist Intelligence Unit, p. 23.
10. Inamori, K. 2000. *Respect the Divine and Love People*. San Diego: Joan Kroc Center for Peace and Justice, p. 77.
11. Inamori, *Respect the Divine and Love People*, p. 52.
12. [No author cited.] 2004. *The Effort Dividend: Driving Employee Performance and Retention Through Engagement*. Washington: Corporate Executive Board.
13. [No author cited.] 2004. *Engaging the Workforce, Focusing on Critical Leverage Points to Drive Employee Engagement*. Washington: Corporate Executive Board, p. 98.
14. Institute for Healthcare Improvement. 2006. IHI announces that hospitals participating in 100,00 Lives Campaign have saved an estimated 122,300 lives. Press release, June 14.
15. Institute for Healthcare Improvement. 2006. Press release, June 14.
16. Institute for Healthcare Improvement. 2006. Press release, June 14.
17. Institute for Healthcare Improvement. 2006. Press release, June 14.

7

The Four Disciplines of Ethical Leadership

Never given in, never give in, never, never, never, never—
in nothing great or small—never give in
except to convictions of honor and good sense.
—Winston Churchill

LEADERSHIP HAS a profound influence on whether and how the vision, mission, and values of an organization shape its everyday life. We have observed leadership that ranges from the criminal (for example, Enron) to the saintly (for example, Gandhi) and everywhere in between. This chapter focuses on the leadership disciplines that foster and strengthen organizational integrity. It also focuses on the personal characteristics of an ethical leader. These disciplines are presented using examples of senior leaders, although they apply to all levels of leadership, from the top to front-line supervision. Without consistency of ethical leadership from top to bottom, employees will receive mixed messages, will become doubtful of the organization's commitment to its vision, mission, and values, and may or may not choose ethical behaviors or make ethical decisions. The four disciplines of ethical leadership are noble purpose, ceaseless ambition, candor, and passion (figure 7-1).

Noble purpose: Already discussed more fully in chapter 6, noble purpose is the calling of health care expressed in the vision, mission, and values of an organization and those who work in it, including its leaders.

Ceaseless ambition: The organization's noble purpose is an essential guiding light, but it will remain a commitment in name only unless it is matched by organizational action. Goals need to be bold if significant progress is to be made in closing the gap between where organizational performance is today and where it aspires to be. A high and consistent level of ambition is critical to stop ethical erosion and evoke and leverage ethical wisdom.

Candor: If the bold intentions of the organization are to be realized, all leaders need to be truthful in all their dealings and uncompromising in their demand for the use of ethical pathways to produce results. This discipline requires consistent self-awareness.

Passion: It is possible to have ceaseless ambition and candor in a cold-mannered approach to leadership, even if it is in service of noble purpose. But great ethical leaders drive change not only from rational arguments, but also from their infectious passion for the calling of health care and the vision, mission, and values of the organizations they lead.

Figure 7-1. The Four Disciplines of Ethical Leadership

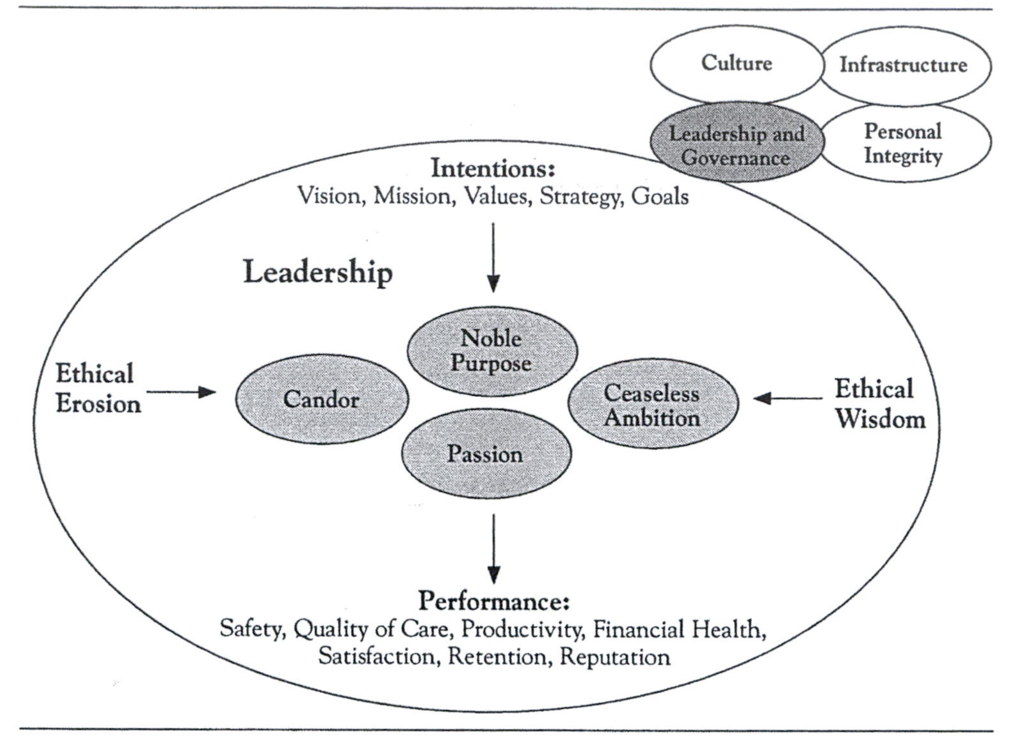

The Discipline of Noble Purpose

To recap from chapter 6, noble purpose is at the heart of the practice of care and must be sustained as a focal point for leadership and board behavior, priorities, and decision making. Sustaining this focus is critical to support ethical pathways, heighten the meaning of work for leaders and others who work in the organization or come in contact with it, and evoke high levels of employee commitment that enable an organization to perform with organizational and personal integrity.

As presented in chapter 6, noble purpose is also a powerful unifying force. A focus on it brings the health care community together and mobilizes powerful collaborations for change.

The Discipline of Ceaseless Ambition

It may seem wrong to suggest that the more greed for performance an organization has, the more likely the ethical pathways to performance will be healthy. How an organization can work harder and at the same time strengthen its vision, mission, and values is in part enabled by two ways of approaching performance: by taking on adaptive challenges, and by organizing and leading consistent with living system principles.

Taking on Adaptive Challenges

Ron Heifetz, co-founder of the Center for Public Leadership at Harvard University's John F. Kennedy School of Government, coined a valuable distinction in considering the challenges an organization faces or can undertake. He proposed two kinds of challenges: technical and adaptive.[1] A technical challenge may be very hard, but when it comes down to it, the current way of leading, current skills, usual behaviors, and established ways of operating are good enough to get the results you seek. You know you are faced with a technical challenge when you can fully plan the journey to success at the outset, even though the journey may be difficult to negotiate. An adaptive challenge is even harder to achieve because the results you are seeking are so bold, so unprecedented, so ambitious, that current ways of leading, current skills, usual behaviors, and established ways of operating are inadequate to get the results you seek. You simply cannot get from here to there without doing things very differently. Although you may have a strong sense of the journey, the road map for success is made by traveling it.

Simply put, technical challenges call for doing better what an organization already knows how to do. Adaptive challenges call for making things happen in the organization that cannot get done without significantly changing how the organization currently operates.[2] For example, saving 100,000 lives in 18 months when the infrastructure to accomplish the goal was not in place, and nothing like it had been done before, was an adaptive challenge—one that demanded creation of a broad coalition, new levels of collaboration, innovative approaches, and a high order of organizational integrity. Similarly, moving from the 18th percentile to the 75th percentile in patient satisfaction in 9 months (the initial goal at Baptist Health Care in Pensacola, Florida, discussed previously in chapter 4) was an adaptive challenge—one that demanded new ways of leading, new levels of teamwork, innovation in patient care, and again, a high order of organizational integrity. Such challenges are exciting, damaging to common practices, demanding of new skills and mindsets, energizing, and scary because success is uncertain.

Organizations as Living Systems

Living systems work based on four principles,[3] which taken together support the achievement of an adaptive challenge. Each of these principles is illustrated by using the examples of the 100,000 Lives Campaign and the Baptist Health Care transformation. These four principles are:

1. *Equilibrium is a precursor to death.* When a living system ceases to be responsive to changes in its environment, it has lost the ability to adapt, and its survival is placed at maximal risk. Organizations that fail to sense and respond to changes in their environment become victims of the way they operate, even if it has been successful in the past.

2. *In the face of a threat or when galvanized by a compelling opportunity, living things move toward the edge of chaos.* This does not mean that everybody runs around with arms flailing in a fit of mayhem and confusion. That *would* be chaos, not the edge of it. The critical point here is that when living systems move to the edge of chaos, this condition interrupts the status quo and evokes higher levels of change and experimentation through which fresh solutions are likely to be found.
3. *When the stimulation to meet a threat or a compelling opportunity takes place, living systems self-organize and new forms and sets of action emerge from the turmoil.* When an organization takes on an adaptive challenge, new forms of leadership, new skills, new behavior, and new ways of operating and producing results are needed. These shifts cannot be prescribed but will emerge by tapping the latent wisdom in the organization, ethical and otherwise, and the ability of people to self-organize and to adapt to meet new challenges or opportunities.
4. *Living systems cannot be directed along a linear path.* Unforeseen consequences on the adaptive challenge journey are inevitable because it is a road made by traveling it. The leadership challenge is to disturb the organization in a way that makes it impossible to not change, that provides a consistent focus on the challenge, and that provides an objective view of progress toward results. Leaders in this environment cannot instruct people on what to do in detail, or expect most problems to come to them for resolution. No leader knows enough to give perfect instructions, and employees close to the action are far better positioned to make decisions and adjust when they need to, consistent with the intentions of the challenge and ethical pathways.

Living System Principles and the 100,000 Lives Campaign

The following shows how the 100,000 Lives Campaign demonstrated each of the four living system principles:

1. *Equilibrium is a precursor to death.* Resignation about the number of unnecessary patient deaths and tweaking of old ways of looking at the problem reinforced a status quo that seemed incapable of making a telling, broad-based impact on the problem.
2. *A compelling opportunity moves a living system toward the edge of chaos.* By creating the 100,000 Lives Campaign, IHI provided a compelling opportunity—an adaptive challenge—for which new forms of action and organization were required for success.
3. *Living systems self-organize and new forms and sets of action emerge.* Each of the more than 3,000 hospitals that accepted IHI's invitation to join the campaign had the discretion to implement its principles and techniques in its own design, which involved many constituencies in the hospital, including patients and their families. This pro-

vided a hotbed for experimentation, which allowed best practices to emerge.

4. *Living systems cannot be directed along a linear path.* The IHI has not saved a single life. The organization had no authority to impose on campaign participants, nor did the organization have the ability to control the campaign's progress. What IHI did as a leader was to engage and focus the stakeholders and participants on the aims of the campaign, its operating principles, and its measures of success. And that made all the difference.

Living System Principles and the Baptist Health Care Transformation

The following shows how Baptist Health Care demonstrated each of the four living system principles in its transformation:

1. *Equilibrium is a precursor to death.* Baptist had become mired in poor performance in many aspects of its operation, including patient satisfaction, employee satisfaction, and financial health, and was on its way to extinction.
2. *A compelling opportunity moves a living system toward the edge of chaos.* By putting itself on the line for a transformational shift in performance, Baptist's leadership galvanized itself and the rest of the organization into many kinds of innovative action.
3. *Living systems self-organize and new forms and sets of action emerge.* At Baptist, part of what Al Stubblefield and his leadership discovered "when we stopped long enough to listen, was that our employees had remarkable ideas for improving our organization."[4]
4. *Living systems cannot be directed along a linear path.* At Baptist, leaders began to lead in an entirely different way, realizing that it was their employees who "must be the ones to discover and define the new culture,"[5] thus tapping their ethical wisdom.

Ceaseless Ambition, Ethical Erosion, and Ethical Wisdom

When an organization takes on an adaptive challenge and makes strict adherence to the vision, mission, and values an integral part of that challenge, the inevitable result is that ethical erosion is slowed or stopped, and ethical wisdom is tapped and leveraged.

Ethical erosion thrives in organizations that limit themselves to old ways of leading, rigid behaviors, and habitual ways of operating. Common practice rules the day, whether ethical or not, whether productive or not. Mindfulness is dulled. Faint signals of ethical lapses pass unaddressed, even unnoticed. Erosion continues unabated. But in an organization that is consistently breaking new ground through adaptive challenges, and that is committed to use ethical pathways to reach results, mindfulness is rewarded, faint signals are more quickly recognized, and the organization becomes practiced at intervening when it senses ethical erosion or barriers of any kind in performance. In this environment, in which people throughout the organization are empowered to act and have more voice, ethical wisdom is more readily accessed and leveraged.

That is why high performing organizations that have successfully met an adaptive challenge create new ones and, with them, create an environment of ceaseless ambition. Those organizations understand that there is no standing pat—that even the best organizations are vulnerable to drifting into habit, mindlessness, and erosion. New challenges, while testing, are invigorating to leaders and employees alike when in service of noble purpose. Having inspired a breakthrough in reducing unnecessary deaths, the IHI could have rested on its laurels. Instead, it created an even bigger challenge: the transformation of health care. In December of 2006, the IHI launched the "5 Million Lives Campaign," with an even wider array of partners, including America's Blue Cross and Blue Shield health plans, the American College of Healthcare Executives, and the American Hospital Association. The intention of this campaign is to reduce dramatically the estimated 15 million incidents of medical harm occurring in U.S. hospitals each year by 5 million in a 24-month time frame through the adoption of 12 improvements in care (the 6 original improvements in the 100,000 Lives Campaign and 6 others).[6]

In 1995 Baptist Health Care set a turnaround vision. After having accomplished and exceeding that goal, Baptist could have slowed the pace of change. But it did not. Baptist set a new vision and with it the new adaptive challenge "to be the best health care system in America."[7] By continuing to seek new challenges, Baptist and other organizations continue to innovate, and their people continue to create ways to achieve new levels of performance while testing and strengthening ethical pathways to produce results. The pace of change may vary depending on the organization's capacity to absorb it and on unforeseen obstacles to progress, but ceaseless ambition remains unabated.

The Discipline of Candor

Candor is the leadership demand to expose and face the facts of the current situation, whether good, bad, or indifferent. When demonstrated by leadership, candor provides a compelling model for truth telling throughout the organization at every level. Jim Collins observed: "There is nothing wrong with pursuing a vision of greatness. After all, the good-to-great companies all set out to create greatness. But unlike [the companies that did not make the leap and remained good] . . . the good-to-great companies continually refined the *path* to greatness with the brutal facts of reality."[8]

Jack Welch, ex-CEO of General Electric, went so far as to call lack of candor "the biggest dirty little secret in business," one that "blocks smart ideas, fast action, and good people contributing all the stuff they've got."[9] This includes their ethical wisdom. The cultural disciplines of an ethical culture (mindfulness, voice, respect, tenacity, and legacy) are all supported and encouraged by the leadership discipline of candor.

Candor as a Leadership Ethic

Larry Bossidy, a highly respected business leader, puts the leadership requirement for candor powerfully:

> A solid, long-term leader has an ethical frame of reference that gives her the power and energy to carry out even the most difficult assignment. She never wavers from what she thinks is right. This characteristic is beyond honesty or integrity, beyond treating people with dignity. It's a business leadership ethic.[10]

Bossidy lists four core qualities that sum up the view of an ethical leader who models the discipline of candor: authenticity, self-awareness, self-mastery, and humility.

1. *Authenticity* means that you are being the same as what you say and do. "Whatever leadership ethics you may preach, people will watch what you do. If you are cutting corners, the best will lose faith in you."
2. *Self-awareness* means knowing yourself, "then you are comfortable with your strengths and not crippled by your shortcomings."
3. *Self-mastery* means mastering your own actions. "You can keep your ego in check, take responsibility for your behavior, adapt to change, embrace new ideas, and adhere to standards of integrity and honesty under all conditions."
4. *Humility* means listening and admitting you don't know all the answers. "You exhibit the attitude that you can learn from anyone at any time. Your pride doesn't get in the way of gathering information you need to achieve best results."[11]

Each of the following examples demonstrates these four qualities in different ways. The leaders mentioned in these examples do not claim to be perfect, but they strive daily to "walk their own talk."

Chris Van Gorder and the Stoplight

Ask Chris Van Gorder, president and CEO of Scripps Health in San Diego, about his leadership, and he will tell you a story of his own growth in awareness about the essence of leadership.[12] In a previous career he was a police officer and was by his own admission driven to produce results—to get to the scene first and to get the bad guys. One night something happened that changed his life. He was alone in his squad car, rushing to answer a call, when he went through a stoplight and nearly caused a terrible accident before his car spun out of control. In that moment he realized that wanting to be first to the scene—to get the results without regard to the means—was putting others as well as himself in danger. He decided that the means to the result is equal in importance to the result itself. Today, listening to others and collaboration are critical values in his leadership.

When asked to look at the core of what gives him power as a leader, he responded: "All I have is my word."[13] Through these insights he models the behaviors he wants and his organization's values. In contrast, the village honest man (previously mentioned in part I, chapter 2) who follows conventional standards of conduct, shifting his own behavior as expectations and common practices shift, cannot lead but only follow, even if he has the appearance or the rank of a leader, at whatever level of the organization. True leadership means being out front on ethical issues, driven by an unwavering commitment to authenticity and candor, and not by the temporary demands of circumstance or expediency.

Doug Cropper and Joint Commission Accreditation

Doug Cropper was the relatively new CEO of Inova Fairfax Hospital in Virginia when the Joint Commission conducted an accreditation review.[14] Included in a long list of data requests was one for the temperature logs for refrigerators on the units containing patient food. One log was missing daily readings for three days. Food services did not have the records. The individual responsible for providing the data made a decision to write in measurements that were consistent with the valid log records in the days around the gap, and these data were given to the Joint Commission. This seems to be a small matter, but it is not. The penalties for submitting falsified data to the Joint Commission are harsh and are the same whether the falsification concerns clinical data, administrative data, or the temperature of a refrigerator. Yet in the larger picture, this seems to be a minor transgression involving a noncritical piece of data. Those involved only wanted themselves and the hospital to do well in the accreditation process. They were not covering up unfavorable data, just filling in a few blanks. But when you understand the nature of ethical erosion, the position of the Joint Commission, and the CEO's own values, the actions of Doug Cropper make sense.

On finding out about the falsification, the first thing Doug Cropper did was "blow the whistle" on himself and the hospital by informing the Joint Commission of what had occurred. Without this alert, it is possible, even probable, that the Joint Commission would never have noticed the irregularity. Asked how long it took for him to decide to advise the Joint Commission, Doug Cropper said: "A nano-second."[15] The second thing he did was order an inquiry into what occurred. As a result of his early intervention and decisive actions, the hospital was not sanctioned by the Joint Commission; although as a result of his internal inquiry, two employees lost their jobs. For many in the organization, this response was out of proportion to the incident, especially as long-standing employees who had not done any harm to patients or other such acts were punished so harshly. But for Doug Cropper and Knox Singleton, president and CEO of Inova Health System, truth telling is nonnegotiable. In a communication to all staff, Knox Singleton wrote about the significance of the incident and provided an unequivocal example of leadership commitment to ethical pathways and to the avoidance of ethical erosion:

> The [incident] . . . was very distressing to me. It was distressing because it spoke to a breach of our commitment to our patients and to each other for total integrity in everything we do. Someone decided it was a "minor thing"

> to fill in some missing data. Let me be clear about two things. First, it is never acceptable to be less than totally honest about errors or omissions in our work. Second, please know that there are no "minor things" in the daily work we do. As we have observed before, excellence comes not from doing great things nearly so often as it comes from doing our normal daily work with great consistency and careful thoroughness.[16]

Howard Putnam and the Ethics of Bankruptcy

Howard Putnam grew up on an Iowa farm and wanted to be a pilot.[17,18] By the age of 16 he was flying solo. But his career as a pilot was cut short when he discovered he was color-blind. Still, he loved aviation, even if he could not be an aviator. At 17 he went to Chicago and began work as a baggage handler on the late shift for Capital Airlines. During his first night on the job, he witnessed a supervisor take a hammer to the locks on customer baggage and rifle through their contents for items of value to steal. He went home that night upset, more at himself than the supervisor, for doing nothing to stop this theft. He saw clearly that he could not live this way. He made himself a promise that whenever he saw unethical conduct, he would confront it and not stand idly by—that he would be true to himself and do the right thing. He went to work the next night fully prepared to confront the supervisor and bear the consequences. As it happened, the supervisor was fired that very night for other inappropriate behavior.

After a career of increasing responsibility with United Airlines, Putnam became president and CEO of the fast-growing Southwest Airlines in 1978. Tremendous success occurred on his watch and, in 1981, he was offered the position of CEO of the much larger, and struggling, Braniff Airlines. Always loving a challenge, he accepted the job offer only to find after starting work at Braniff that he had been lied to about the financial condition of the airline, which was in fact dire. After keeping the airline alive for seven months, Howard Putnam and his board had no choice but to declare bankruptcy, and Putnam met the challenge head on. He has the distinction of being the first CEO to take a major carrier successfully into, through, and out of Chapter 11. He then went on to other business ventures. Braniff flew for a few more years under new ownership, but it failed again several years later.

The clarity that Howard Putnam had about his own values as a leader guided his actions through the extremely difficult bankruptcy process. His integrity in handling the event was so impeccable that Harvard University wrote a case study on his experiences at Braniff, "The Ethics of Bankruptcy,"[19] as a model of how to handle shareholders in crisis. This case study demonstrated how a leader's clarity and candor, forged by self-awareness, can be used as a beacon for action in even the most difficult of circumstances. In his book, *The Winds of Turbulence*, Howard Putnam writes: "Dedication to the truth and an ethical standard ensures respect for employees, customers, the environment—everybody and everything touched by the company."[20]

These examples reflect the actions of ethical leaders. Jack Welch, talking about the actions of such leaders, wrote: "People with integrity tell the truth, and they keep their word. They take responsibility for past actions, admit mistakes, and fix them. They know the laws . . . and abide by them. They play to win the right way, by the rules."[21]

The Discipline of Passion

Health care organizations are full of people who have a passion for health care and their self-expression as healers. They can be found everywhere in the organization: in the executive ranks, in physicians and nursing staff, in ancillary staff, in support staff, everywhere. There may be people with whom we work who are not our "cup of tea," or who seem to have gotten into health care by mistake, but they are not the norm. It is the job of leaders to ignite and sustain this passion, which is a key to asking for the very best that employees have to offer, including their ethical wisdom. A leader cannot do this with rational arguments and "smarts" alone. A leader can best ignite the passion of others by demonstrating his or her own passion and commitment to the noble purpose of the organization.

Jack Welch wrote: "By passion, I mean a heartfelt, deep, and authentic excitement about work. People with passion care—really care in their bones—about colleagues, employees, and friends winning. They love to learn and grow, and they get a huge kick when the people around them do the same. . . . [T]hey have juice for life in their veins."[22] If you speak to any of the leaders mentioned in this book, or others you know to be strong, ethical leaders, you will experience their passion for their work, for their fellow employees, for their patients and their families, for their community, and for doing things the right way. In the words of Dr. Robert Pearl: "When a leader does what is consistent with the beauty and values of medicine there may be fear, reluctance and legitimate concern, but ultimately doing the right thing creates so much personal and professional satisfaction that nearly all embrace the new direction."[23] And you will see and hear leaders' passion, not only through their words but through their eyes, their mannerisms, and their posture. For example, Chris Van Gorder of Scripps Health, reflecting on his day at work in a speech at an evening presentation, mentioned that he had been present that morning at the bedside of an employee's relative at the time of the relative's death. Gorder paused and said: "I am *passionate* about what we do; to be part of patient care from the beginning to the end of life."[24] It may be a "you had to be there" moment, but when he said the word *passionate*, it was as if it came from deep inside his being. This is the passion of a leader that resonates with and ignites the passion in others.

Al Stubblefield of Baptist Health Care is unapologetically passionate about the vision of the organization. He understands that a leader's passion is vital to unleashing the organization's passion and energy: "Our job as leaders is to recognize the passion that brings people into our profession and to empower them to live out those dreams."[25] Employees talk about the atmosphere at Baptist enthusiastically. Kenny Pressley, who works in the reimbursement department at Baptist Hospital, has worked at the hospital for six years and is excited about his work: "We want to be the number one hospital. I'm happy. I love working here. I'm here to help other people and I love it. It's fun to see the outcome when everybody works together."[26]

In Short

Ceaseless ambition, candor, and passion together with noble purpose comprise the essence of what drives ethical leadership. Through these disciplines, leaders model and promote an environment in which the other ethical pathways—culture, infrastructure, and personal integrity—can flourish, and the organization's noble purpose and organizational and personal integrity can become the everyday focus and means to performance. Leaders do not have to reach a perfect state to accomplish this. By doing their best to "walk their own talk" regarding ethical behavior and ethical decision making every day, and by freely acknowledging successes and failures, they provide a compelling model for the rest of the organization.

Chapter 8 provides a diagnostic through which you can measure the vital signs of the health of the ethical pathway of leadership.

References

1. Heifetz, R. 1994. *Leadership Without Easy Answers*. Cambridge, MA: Harvard University Press.
2. Gilbert, J. 2005. Co-creation: creating a new center of gravity to meet adaptive challenges. Unpublished paper, New Page Consulting Inc., Del Mar, CA.
3. Pascale, R., Milleman, M., and Gioja, L. 2000. *Surfing the Edge of Chaos*. New York: Crown Business.
4. Stubblefield, A. 2005. *The Baptist Health Care Journey to Excellence*. Hoboken, NJ: John Wiley & Sons, p. 44.
5. Stubblefield, *Baptist Health Care Journey to Excellence*, p. 41.
6. Institute of Healthcare Improvement. 2006. IHI launches national campaign to reduce medical harm in U.S. hospitals, building on its landmark 100,000 Lives Campaign. Press release, December 12.
7. Stubblefield, *Baptist Health Care Journey to Excellence*, p. 25.
8. Collins, J. 2001. *Good to Great*. New York: HarperCollins, p. 71.
9. Welch, J. 2005. *Winning*. New York: HarperCollins, p. 25.
10. Bossidy, L., and Charan, R. 2002. *Execution: The Discipline of Getting Things Done*. New York: Crown Business, p. 80.
11. Bossidy and Charan, *Execution*, pp. 81–82.
12. Van Gorder, C. [President and CEO, Scripps Health] 2006. Interview with author, San Diego, January 28.
13. Van Gorder, interview with author.
14. Cropper, D. [Executive Vice President, Inova Health System, and Administrator, Inova Fairfax Hospital, Inova Fairfax Hospital for Children, and Inova Heart and Vascular Institute] 2006. Interview with author, Reston, VA, September 20.
15. Cropper, interview with author.

16. Singleton, K. [President and CEO, Inova Health System] 2005. Memorandum to Inova staff, June 1.
17. About Howard Putnam. 2006. www.howardputnam.com.
18. Putnam, H. [President, Howard Putnam Enterprises] 2005. Interview with author, Reno, NV, June 13.
19. Goodpaster, K., and Whiteside, D. 1984. *Braniff International: The Ethics of Bankruptcy*. Cambridge, MA: Harvard Business School.
20. Putnam, H. 1991. *The Winds of Turbulence*. New York: HarperCollins, p. 135.
21. Welch, *Winning*, p. 83.
22. Welch, *Winning*, p. 87.
23. Pearl, R. [CEO, The Permanente Medical Group, Kaiser Permanente] 2006. Interview with author, Oakland, CA, July 12.
24. Van Gorder, C. [President and CEO, Scripps Health] 2006. Presentation to Society of Healthcare Leaders, San Diego, October 9.
25. Stubblefield, *Baptist Health Care Journey to Excellence*, p. 40.
26. Pressley, K. 2006. [Reimbursement Department, Baptist Hospital] 2006. Interview with author, Pensacola, FL, July 15.

8

A Diagnostic for the Ethical Pathway of Leadership

[Of the best leaders,] when their
task is accomplished, their work done,
The people all remark, "We have done it ourselves."

—Lao-Tzu

THIS CHAPTER provides a "vital signs" diagnostic to help you assess at a high level the health of the ethical pathway of leadership for your organization. After you have scored the diagnostic, you can use the results to choose a discipline for your focus of action. Read more on this choice in the section on "Interpreting the Diagnostic." The following are some broad guidelines for conducting the diagnostic:

1. Be sure to introduce the use of the questionnaire by sharing why you think completing and discussing the results will be a valuable use of time. Also share its purpose, which is about gaining understanding and making improvements, and is not about blame.
2. Assure those taking the diagnostic that it is safe to respond. Be sure the diagnostic will not be used to place blame on any one leader, but will be used to expose opportunities for improvement.
3. Because responses will be directed to an individual leader, consider using a trusted facilitator to administer, tally, and present the findings. As mentioned later in this chapter, that facilitator could also be used to manage discussions, coach a leader, and help build action plans.
4. Use the diagnostic and what you learn from it with caution. You would not make a diagnosis from a patient's vital signs, but you would use them as one input. This diagnostic and others in this book are best used in the same way, provoking questions, not answers, and opening up discussion and thinking, not closing them off.

Appendix 1 presents a comprehensive diagnostic survey to assess the health of all four ethical pathways. This is a better tool to gather a complete picture of ethical health. Instructions on how to complete an on-line version of the questionnaire can be found in appendix 1.

The "From-To's" of Ethical Leadership

The disciplines of ethical leadership exist to some degree in all organizations. They are not completely present or completely absent. Their condition can be thought to occur across a continuum. Figure 8-1 shows some of the "from-to's" of the ethical leadership disciplines and gives a sense of the "leadership mood" we want to minimize and the one we want to instill. The leadership from-to's reflect both leaders' view of themselves and how others view them.

The Ethical Leadership Diagnostic

This leadership diagnostic is designed to create an "outside-in" view of leadership, meaning that it is a nonleader's view of leaders, not the view of leaders of themselves.

For a leader looking for an ethics self-assessment tool, we recommend the American College of Healthcare Executives (ACHE) Ethics Self-Assessment, which can be taken on-line at www.ache.org. Like the diagnostics in this book, that self-assessment is designed to be thought-provoking and to help you identify those areas where you are on strong ethical ground, and where there are opportunities for reflection and improvement. The ACHE tool is intended for personal use and is not a tool for evaluating others' ethical behavior.

The questions in the following diagnostic are connected to a specific discipline. A short description of the discipline precedes the questions to remind you what discipline is being considered in the questions. The questions are written to assess an individual leader but can be rewritten to assess a leadership team. Figure 8-2 is a score sheet to use in producing a score for each discipline and a total score. There are three options for responding to each question:

- *Strongly Agree*—The behavior or point of view is pervasive, common practice. **Score a 5.**
- *Sometimes Agree*—You see the behavior or point of view, but it is inconsistent, and you cannot count on its happening routinely. **Score a 3.**
- *Strongly Disagree*—The likelihood of the behavior or point of view occurring is much more unusual than usual. **Score a 1.**

Circle the number that applies for each question. Score the diagnostic as you go along.

Noble purpose is the calling of health care expressed in the vision, mission, and values of an organization and those who work in it, including its leaders.

1. Our leader strongly believes in the vision, mission, and values of our organization.
2. Our leader reminds us that we are here to increase the health and welfare of the communities we serve.
3. Our leader focuses us on the vision, mission, and values of our organization.
4. Our leader will do the right thing for our patients and their families, even if it hurts the organization financially.

Figure 8-1. The "From-To's" of the Disciplines of Ethical Leadership

Discipline	From	To
Noble Purpose	It all comes down to operating performance: "No profit, no mission."	Our noble purpose is at the heart of our leadership: "No mission, no profit."
	Vision, mission, and values are all important, but realistically we cannot do our job as leaders and be bound by them.	Vision, mission, and values are our moral compass. Whenever we stray from them, our job as leaders is to refocus on them quickly.
	Mostly our leaders talk about tightening our belts.	Mostly our leaders talk about the difference we are making for our patients and their families.
	Our leaders do not care as much as regular employees do about our patients.	Our leaders set an example of what it takes to do the right thing for our patients.
Ceaseless Ambition	My job as a leader is to fight fires and keep the ship on an even keel.	My job as a leader is to accelerate our progress toward our vision and mission while living our values.
	My job as a leader is not about innovation; it is about making sure things are running smoothly with a minimum of disturbance.	As a leader, I will do whatever it takes to make this organization and our employees as great as they can be.
	Our leaders always seem to be in a crisis mode; all we seem to do is fight fires.	Our leaders really push us, but in a way that focuses us on our mission, vision, and values.
	Bold new ideas tend to be met by our leaders with a "we do not do it that way" response.	Our leaders get excited when they know we are trying out better ways of doing things.
Candor	Basically, my job as a leader is to protect employees from bad news.	I take every opportunity to tell employees how we are doing, good or bad. I expect them to do the same.
	I'm pretty much set in my ways as a leader; I know what I know and it works for me.	I love to learn about new ways of doing things and about how I can be a better leader.
	We have no clue what is going on; this place operates on a need-to-know basis.	I feel respected by my leaders because they treat me like a partner in resolving organizational issues.
	We never know what leaders have up their sleeves or what they are really thinking.	I trust our leaders to tell us what they can about what they are thinking.
Passion	I have a huge responsibility and do not have time to be frivolous or chatty with employees.	I love being around our employees; I enjoy and appreciate them.
	I have way too much to do to be out and about.	I love to get close to the action of patient care; it is inspiring to me.
	We never see our leaders unless they want to see us.	Our leaders are always available and asking what we need.
	It's never good news when our leaders do show up; you can bet that something is wrong.	I love being around our leaders; they are so enthusiastic and interested in what we are doing.

Figure 8-2. Ethical Leadership Diagnostic Score Sheet

	Strongly Agree	Sometimes Agree	Strongly Disagree	Discipline Total	÷ Number of Questions	= Average Score
Noble Purpose						
Question 1	5	3	1			
Question 2	5	3	1			
Question 3	5	3	1			
Question 4	5	3	1			
Score					4	
Ceaseless Ambition						
Question 5	5	3	1			
Question 6	5	3	1			
Question 7	5	3	1			
Question 8	5	3	1			
Score					4	
Candor						
Question 9	5	3	1			
Question 10	5	3	1			
Question 11	5	3	1			
Question 12	5	3	1			
Score					4	
Passion						
Question 13	5	3	1			
Question 14	5	3	1			
Question 15	5	3	1			
Question 16	5	3	1			
Score					4	
		Total Score			16	

Ceaseless ambition is a leader's high and consistent level of ambition for performance, critical to stop ethical erosion and evoke and leverage ethical wisdom.

5. Stretching us to take big positive steps in the way we do things is a major priority of our leader.
6. Our leader insists that we be innovative in our work.
7. Our leader trusts us to do the right thing when we try to improve how we do our work.
8. Our leader does not micro-manage us.

Candor is a leader's authenticity, self-awareness, humility, and self-mastery in all his or her dealings and the uncompromising demand for the use of ethical pathways to produce results.

9. When our leader tells us how we are doing, good or bad, we can trust what he or she tells us.
10. Our leader's values are clear to us.
11. Our leader is trying to improve the way he or she leads.
12. Our leader is rock solid in acting consistently with our values.

Passion is a leader's infectious enthusiasm and commitment for the calling of health care and the vision, mission, and values of the organizations he or she leads.

13. Our leader shows enthusiasm for the work we do.
14. We get fired up by our leader's enthusiasm for what we do.
15. Our leader visits our work area.
16. When we suffer, our leader suffers.

Scoring the Diagnostic

The following are steps to score the diagnostic to produce an average score for the questions for each discipline and an average score for all 16 questions. Figure 8-3 shows an example of a completed score sheet.

1. Go down the columns vertically and add the scores for each set of questions for a discipline.
2. Add the scores for each discipline across to produce a discipline total.
3. Divide the discipline total for each discipline by 4 (the number of questions) to find the average score for each discipline.
4. Add all the discipline totals vertically to produce the total score.
5. Divide the total score by 16 (the total number of questions) to find the average score for all of the disciplines combined.

Figure 8-3. Example of a Completed Ethical Leadership Diagnostic Score Sheet

	Strongly Agree	Sometimes Agree	Strongly Disagree	Discipline Total	÷ Number of Questions	= Average Score
Noble Purpose						
Question 1	(5)	3	1			
Question 2	5	(3)	1			
Question 3	5	(3)	1			
Question 4	(5)	3	1			
Score	10	6		16	4	4.00
Ceaseless Ambition						
Question 5	5	(3)	1			
Question 6	5	(3)	1			
Question 7	5	(3)	1			
Question 8	5	(3)	1			
Score		12		12	4	3.00
Candor						
Question 9	5	3	(1)			
Question 10	5	(3)	1			
Question 11	5	(3)	1			
Question 12	5	3	(1)			
Score		6	2	8	4	2.00
Passion						
Question 13	(5)	3	1			
Question 14	(5)	3	1			
Question 15	5	(3)	1			
Question 16	5	(3)	1			
Score	10	6		16	4	4.00
		Total Score		52	16	3.25

Interpreting the Diagnostic

You can decide your own approach in interpreting the survey, but consider the following questions and approaches in your interpretation.

Questions and Approaches to Interpretation

1. What is the total score average?
   Obviously, if the average score for an individual discipline is 3 or below, it is a red flag. "Sometimes" may be an acceptable average for some surveys, but leaders set the day-to-day tone of the organization through their actions. Their strong adherence to these ethical disciplines is important. You may well see scores of 5 for individual questions; however, an average score of 5 is an opportunity to acknowledge success and also to explore whether this perfect ethical leadership holds up under scrutiny.
2. On what one discipline would you focus for discussion and change?
   You can select a discipline on which to focus in at least three ways:
   - It can be the discipline with the lowest average score.
   - It can be the discipline with the most 1 scores.
   - It can be the discipline that you decide will produce the best opportunity for change (this may or may not be the lowest scoring discipline).

   Whatever discipline you choose to focus on, do not be surprised if discussion about it leads to discussion about one or more other disciplines. This is because the disciplines are related to each other.
3. To enrich a conversation about these results, you can choose the discipline with the best score and compare it to a selected, weaker performing discipline. This comparison provides an opportunity to not only ask what is not working about a weaker performing discipline, but also to ask what we can learn from what we are doing right with a high performing discipline.
4. Remember that this is a high-level diagnostic and, as such, should not be used to provide answers but to provoke focused questions and open discussion.

Thoughts for Each Discipline

Each discipline has its own characteristics. Ways to explore the implications of responses to the questions within each of the disciplines follow.

Noble Purpose

The underlying question being probed is whether employees believe that a leader strongly supports the calling of health care and always seeks to act consistent with the vision, mission, and values of the organization. If leadership cannot, with candor, say their behaviors and decision making are always shaped by these factors, then some of the following questions may prove useful: What is the cost of not acting consistently with the vision, mission, and values of the organization? Is an inconsistency of prioritization among leaders tolerated and, if so, why? What actions and decisions inconsistent with the vision, mission, and values have we tolerated in ourselves, in individual leaders, and in the leadership team?

If leadership, after sincere introspection, experiences a deep belief in the noble purpose of the organization when not seen by others to do so, the issue may be one of communication rather than values. Do leaders take the time in formal and informal settings to talk about their deep commitment to their own calling and the calling of others to serve patients and their families? Do they supplement these conversations with information that demonstrates the impact of noble purpose on decision making? Do we discuss how leaders are perceived and how employees and their leaders can alter negative perceptions?

Ceaseless Ambition

The focus of these questions is on the extent to which leadership has an appetite for adaptive challenges and the degree to which leadership lets go of control and taps the wisdom of the organization to do the right thing, consistent with the vision, mission, and values. Do employees feel stretched in a positive way, and does leadership trust them?

Low scores can be explored with the following questions: Are leaders challenging themselves to make changes in all aspects of performance, even those beyond financial performance? To what extent are leaders creating challenges for their organization? Are leaders challenging their employees to make changes in all aspects of performance, even those beyond financial performance? Do leaders trust in the wisdom and commitment of their employees to find better ways to do the right thing once those employees understand well the organization's situation and challenges?

Candor

The questions probe whether leaders are seen in the organization at one extreme as people whose motives are unclear, even suspected by employees, and who are perceived as not sharing (even hiding) facts about performance, compared with leaders at the other extreme, who are perceived as open and honest about their motives, concerns, and the facts of performance.

Low scores can be explored by asking the following questions: What do leaders do or not do to feed the perception that they are not trustworthy? What stories or events do employees use to support this perception, and are they organizational myths or current reality? Do leaders believe that candor has more of a downside than an upside? Do leaders share their values freely with others, or do they hold them as private beliefs, and if so why? What do leaders do or not do to feed the perception that they do not act consistent with the organization's values? What stories or events do employees use to support this perception, and are they organizational myths or current reality?

Passion

The questions for this discipline probe the emotional and personal connection leaders inspire in others. At one extreme, a leader may be perceived as remote emotionally and withdrawn physically, perhaps even unrecognizable to many employees. At the other extreme, a leader may be perceived as willing to share experiences, emotions, and concerns in both formal and informal encounters with employees that the leader seeks as a recognizable figure in all work areas of the organization.

Low scores can be explored by asking the following questions: Is it true that a leader does not spend much time outside of the administrative suite or his or her office? Why would employees perceive a leader as either remote or available? Does the leader believe that sharing experiences and emotions with employees matters, and if not, why not? What holds a leader back from seeking formal and informal encounters with employees?

Approaches to Action

As a general principle, the results of this diagnostic should be shared and discussed with those who completed it. As with diagnostics of this kind, if a leader is not willing to share the results and outcomes of the diagnostic and sincerely seek ways to strengthen his or her ethical leadership, it is better not to conduct it. Obviously, the larger and more diverse the group, the more the sharing and discussion need to be orchestrated and may need to include, for example, skilled facilitators from the training and development department. This facilitation support is also useful to relieve the leader of the burden of both leading and participating freely in the discussion.

Be sure to allow sufficient time for reflection and discussion. Leaders need to be able to absorb the implications of the findings and to reach a productive course of action. The resources about dialogue listed at the end of chapter 4 may be useful in providing the tools to create a productive set of discussions. Finally, action for areas of growth in ethical leadership that need immediate intervention should be approached with urgency.

9

The Four Disciplines of Ethical Governance

Directors should direct.
—Justice Hugo Black

ACCORDING TO Charles Ewell of the Governance Institute: "Health care is changing so much. The days when board membership was a feather in your community cap are gone. Now it's hard work. There are outside pressures from insurers and government; you have to bear down and take your responsibility more seriously."[1] Indeed, even though new laws and regulations are designed to support ethical oversight and behavior in public companies and have almost no direct impact on not-for-profit health care organizations, they are still likely to form the foundation for expectations and standards of behavior.

The four disciplines of ethical governance, which maximize the effectiveness of the board in leading, modeling, and overseeing organizational and personal integrity, are noble purpose, independent engagement, ethical culture, and ethical succession (figure 9-1).

Noble purpose: Already discussed more fully in chapter 6, noble purpose is the calling of health care expressed in the vision, mission, and values of an organization and those who work in it, including its leaders.

Independent engagement: Boards cannot discharge their duties, including their stewardship of the ethical pathways that transform intentions into performance, without having an effective partnership with the CEO. But when a board is dependent on the CEO, there is no partnership. The board becomes little more than a rubber stamp for the priorities, agenda, and recommendations of the CEO, and it cannot effectively fulfill its duties, both legal and ethical.

Ethical culture: Although the board is not involved in the day-to-day operations of the organization, it is a microcosm of it. As such, the board needs to attend to its own ethical health and to model the ethical culture it expects throughout the organization. The board cannot be an effective steward of the ethical health of the organization by holding itself to a lower standard of behavior than the organization it leads.

Ethical succession: The criteria for retaining or choosing new executives, including the CEO, and the criteria for the removal or addition of board members must include those criteria that reflect the need for executives and board members who exhibit the highest level of personal integrity that will make them effective stewards of the organization.

Figure 9-1. The Four Disciplines of Ethical Governance

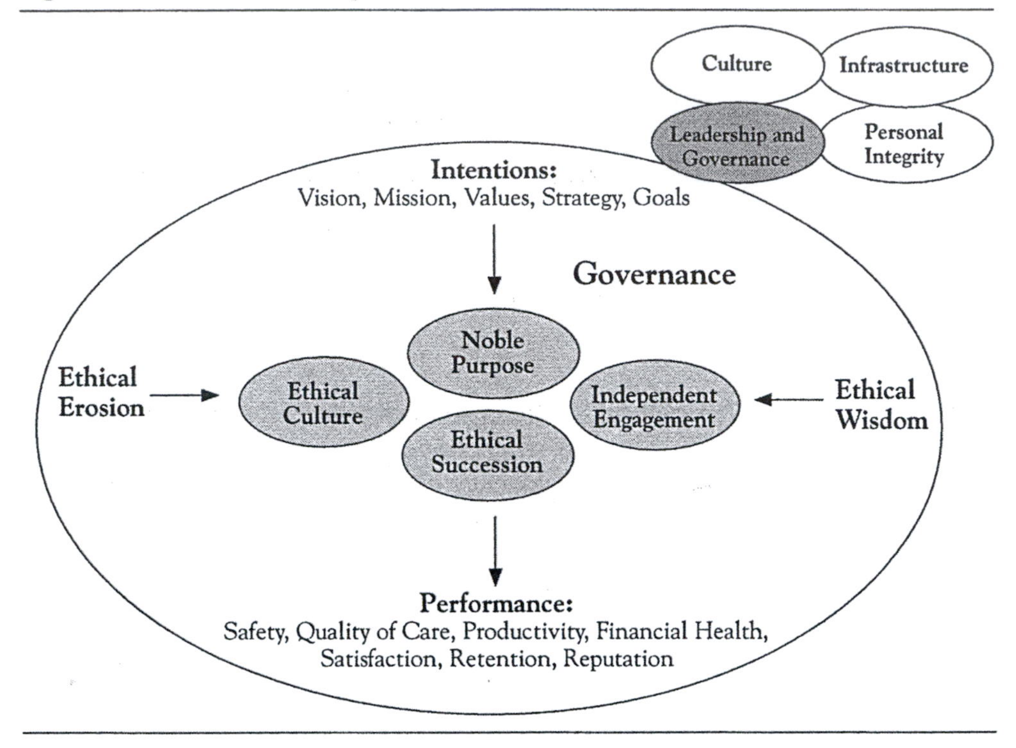

A Lasting Change in Board Scrutiny

Life has certainly changed for board members, and that is due to one reason: failure of the board members of some prominent public companies to prevent illegal and unethical lapses in the organizations they led, resulting in damage to the value and retirement prospects of millions of Americans. As a result, there is unprecedented scrutiny of the performance of public company boards, with serious consequences for lack of effective oversight. Board members used to sitting quietly in the background, enjoying the limited demands and sometimes handsome "perks" of board appointments, now find themselves in the hot seat.

Some board members who were identified as being asleep at the switch while their management cooked the books have been personally punished. For example, a shareholder suit against the board of Enron resulted in many directors' paying a total of more than $13 million out of their own pockets to settle the suit.[2] A similar suit against the board of WorldCom resulted in a payment of $18 million out of 10 directors' own pockets.[3] In each case the accusation was that the board ignored facts, or had not performed sufficient due diligence to expose facts, and that the company's leadership was engaged in unethical and illegal business practices, even though there were enough red flags to alert the board to the situation.

In a speech at Harvard University, Commissioner Roel Campos of the Securities and Exchange Commission (SEC) quoted U.S. Supreme Court

Justice Hugo Black as saying: "The law has no place for dummy directors."[4] The best advice for both for-profit and not-for-profit hospitals is for health care boards to get ahead of the curve and rigorously examine and improve their activities,[5] and take charge of the board's own focus, agenda, and information flow.[6]

This was the hard lesson learned by the board at Granada Hills Community Hospital in Granada Hills, California.[7] Plunged into Chapter 11 bankruptcy, the board hired a turnaround crisis management firm to handle day-to-day operations while the board attempted to reorganize. During the next seven months, the turnaround company's assigned hospital CEO and CFO painted a positive picture of financial progress. But it was false. The turnaround company's contract was terminated for cause after the board found out that payroll taxes were unpaid. The hospital closed a short time later after filing for Chapter 7 insolvency.

This was not the end of the story for this beleaguered volunteer board of a not-for-profit community hospital. Three years later the board members were charged in district court with breaching their duty to the hospital and were threatened with substantial personal liability damages, although eventually the board was found to have acted appropriately and in keeping with its duties. Many of those involved in board governance consider this a warning to not-for-profit boards that they had better act in keeping with their fiduciary responsibilities or face serious consequences.

The Discipline of Noble Purpose

To recap from chapter 6, noble purpose is at the heart of the practice of care and the reason for being of health care organizations—most commonly expressed through their vision, mission, and values. The pressures of everyday work and the short-term challenges leaders and the board face may draw attention away from noble purpose, but it is critical that it is sustained as a focal point for leadership and board behavior, priorities, and decision making. Sustaining this focus is critical in supporting ethical pathways, heightening the meaning of work for leaders and others who work in the organization or come in contact with it, and evoking levels of employee commitment that enable an organization to perform at high levels and with organizational and personal integrity.

Noble purpose is also a powerful unifying force. Its focus brings together different parts of the health care community that otherwise may be in conflict, diminishes their differences, and mobilizes powerful collaborations for change.

The Discipline of Independent Engagement

When the CEO is the board's sole conduit to information that is used to support board discussions and decision making, it is difficult for the board to exercise the independent judgment that is part of its duty. It is hard for such a board to be anything but a rubber stamp. The vast majority of members of not-for-profit health care boards are unpaid, and many have found their way onto boards because they are known in the community and have shown an interest in serving. With limited time to spend on board work, the members depend on management and perhaps the chairman and a few other board members to do the "heavy lifting" of analyzing issues and making recommendations, often coming into discussions late in the process, even at the point of decision.

This reactive way of operating will no longer suffice. The biggest ethical vulnerability of well-meaning people in well-meaning organizations is the unmanaged erosion of ethical standards. At Enron, for example, some of the greatest excesses began on a small scale and escalated over time. In fact, the board became complicit by waiving a portion of the code of ethics to allow what was to become a centerpiece of major fraud at the company.[8] Waiting until standards of integrity have deteriorated so far that they have precipitated harm to patients or employees, a loss of financial integrity, damage to public reputation or other breaches is a failure in the duty of the board to attend to the ethical health of the organization. Boards need to be proactive, independent, and engaged. Alex Pollock, a resident fellow at the American Enterprise Institute who serves on several boards, has written:

> The most diligent directors cannot possibly match the detailed and specific knowledge of an enterprise . . . that a competent management must have. . . . However, directors should bring a general knowledge relevant to the business in question, sufficient stature to confront and address problematic situations, and sufficient experience to be meaningful counselors in matters of importance. It depends on a combination of relevant knowledge and independence of the right kind.[9]

The antidote to a reactive board dependent on the CEO for education, guidance, and even instruction is a board that practices independent engagement by (1) setting and managing the board agenda and placing a priority on ethical oversight, (2) becoming educated about current and prospective ethical issues impacting health care organizations, (3) demanding performance measures sufficient to manage not only the financial condition of the organization but also important nonfinancial measures, including the health of ethical pathways, and (4) the engagement of the hearts, minds, and energies of board members themselves.

Board Responsibilities, Priorities, and Ethical Pathways

A fundamental responsibility for a board is to prioritize its focus. Of six board priorities identified in a survey of corporate boards,[10] three related directly to ethical standards and ethical pathways:

- Ensuring that management not only performs, but performs with integrity [not only during hiring decisions but continuously]
- Setting expectations about the tone and culture of the company [to ensure that management is promoting an appropriate ethical culture]

- Ensuring that the corporate culture, agreed strategy, management incentive compensation, and the company's approach to audit and accounting, internal controls, and disclosure are consistent and fully aligned [true and fair being the goal of all of these issues]

Making the ethical health of the organization a formal part of the board agenda is a critical step. A Hastings Center Report on ethics in trusteeship in health care noted that "in the past, trustee ethics have been largely tacit. But these tacit understandings are being unraveled by the current health care marketplace and cannot be taken for granted. . . . It is necessary to reestablish and revivify a sense of ethical mission and obligation for hospital trustees on an explicit footing."[11]

Independent Education

If the board is to be independent in its thinking, it must go beyond the CEO for its knowledge. This is not a criticism of the CEO, nor is it meant to discount the importance of a strong partnership between the board and CEO. But for a partnership to exist, it requires that both parties bring substantial assets to the table. A confident CEO will welcome new perspectives as an enrichment of his or her own effectiveness.

There are two major ways to infuse independent education: third-party education and board composition. Through third-party education (for example, presentations to the board by appropriate subject matter experts, attendance at conferences or meetings on board and health care best practices, discussions of important trends in health care, and best practice visits), the board will develop a shared understanding that supports its independent thinking. The second way to infuse independent education is through board member selection, that is, identifying the competencies needed for more effective board deliberations and importing those competencies through the choice of new board members. This is discussed more fully in the section in this chapter on the discipline of ethical succession.

Frank Sardone, president and CEO of Bronson Healthcare Group in Kalamazoo, Michigan, in partnership with his board, instituted a governance educational program that, in his words, has resulted in "a more engaged board." One hour is set aside at monthly board meetings for education and discussion. The board attends an annual national educational conference focused on governance issues and also a board education retreat. Education is linked to board priorities. One specific benefit of the program is that it has prepared board members for policy decisions they will need to make before issues become a crisis.[12]

Baptist Health Care in Pensacola, Florida, supports board education in part by a regularly published newsletter, titled "Board Briefs," available on its Web site.[13]

Independent Measurement and Assessment

Asking a CEO or members of the executive team how they are performing—and receiving replies based on their feelings, impressions, and anecdotes—is a risky business. A board certainly would not be satisfied by such responses about financial status. Difficult to supply or not, it is essential that the board receive information through which it can assess the ethical health of the organization on a regular basis. The ethical health survey diagnostic from this book or other surveys that report on the health of ethical pathways are critical to accomplishing this task.

The Role of Ethics Officer

Many health care organizations have introduced the management position of ethics officer. It is an important role and, in the best cases, is a powerful conduit for information between the organization, the executive team, and the board—a truly independent voice. In the worst cases, it is merely "window dressing"—the officer's voice is muted and managed by the CEO. To be able to do the job effectively, the ethics officer requires the absolute support of a highly ethical management and board, which creates the paradox that ethics officers may be most needed in organizations where what they have to say is least welcome.

One potential pitfall for the ethics officer is a narrow definition of the role when it is limited to issues of legal and regulatory compliance. These are important considerations; however, an overwhelming focus on legal or regulatory exposure can lead to an absence of focus on broader issues of organizational integrity, ethical erosion, and ethical pathways. The spying and pre-texting scandal involving the board at Hewlett-Packard was facilitated by the now disgraced senior counsel and compliance officer who gave the board a narrow legal opinion, not an ethical one.[14] The opportunity for the board is to be sure that the role of ethics officer spans compliance, risk assessment, organizational integrity, and ethical pathways in equal measure.

Another potential pitfall and opportunity lie in the relationship of the rest of the organization to the role of the ethics officer. Simply put, management and even the board might let themselves off the hook for being aware and proactive in seeking out and addressing ethical issues by placing those responsibilities on the shoulders of the ethics officer. Or they may ask the ethics officer for permission to take actions that are close to the line between what is ethical and what is not. But such an approach is irresponsible and dangerous. It is exactly the approach of the Hewlett-Packard board in the pre-texting example just mentioned, and it led to the resignation of the company's board chair. Board members cannot delegate their accountability for the integrity of the organization. The opportunity is to use the ethics officer as an expert resource who can analyze and recommend, but who is not expected to assume responsibility for, ethical decisions properly made by senior management or the board.

Engaged and Ethical Board Members

The board can adopt many practices to enhance independent engagement; but at the end of the day, it is the responsibility of each board member to establish and address board focus and priorities. Being a steward of the noble purpose of the organization, making decisions that have a profound influence on the future of the organization and those it serves, being proactive in assessing financial and nonfinancial performance (including ethical health), having independent knowledge of issues, participating actively and responsibly in discussions, and building board relationships in and beyond meetings, call for a level of engagement that can only be met by an appropriate devotion of time, energy, and commitment to board work. The serious challenges facing every health care organization demand it. Those who work full time in health care deserve it. Patients, their families, and the community expect it.

For these reasons, expectations of board members need to be clear. The expectations include their time commitment, their role in decision making and other board matters, the style of their participation, regularity of attendance, their full and responsible participation at board meetings, and their integrity. The ideal profile of board members is that of smart, independent-minded, inquisitive people who can disagree without being disagreeable and who have the ability to engage, inquire, and debate. Unpaid board members on not-for-profit boards can be willing but not able to meet these requirements. Board membership can no longer be seen as a "perk" with limited demands on the board member. The stakes are too high. It is a matter of the integrity of the board.

What is more, regulators are awake to issues of board performance. For example, the Joint Commission has developed a section on governance in its accreditation process. The expectations include that board members will have term and age limits.[15]

Integrity of Reporting and Conflict of Interest

The Sarbanes-Oxley Act of 2002 (SOX) demanded more accountability by public companies, especially in financial reporting, CEO accountability, and avoidance of conflicts of interest. Most of the measures required by the act were a direct response to the illegal acts that came to light as some public companies "cooked the books." Many private and nonprofit companies have since voluntarily adopted SOX requirements, which have emerged as best practices in corporate governance standards.[16] These standards include the following:

- An independent audit committee (with no inside directors) that is responsible for directly appointing and overseeing the audit firm (with the firm reporting directly to the audit committee)
- Prohibition of auditors from providing consulting services to the organization
- Rotation of audit partners every five years
- CEO and CFO certification of financial statements
- Board compensation committee review of executive compensation and incentive pay, with attention to marketplace arrangements

- Prohibition of loans to officers and directors
- Avoidance of conflicts of interest for officers and directors

The persistent expectation of heightened board accountability from regulators, legislators, and the public requires more professional health care boards, even if still unpaid, that have a strong, consistent focus on the organization's ethical health.

The Discipline of Ethical Board Culture

Discussing what constituted an effective board member, SEC commissioner Roel Campos said, "We at the SEC are committed to a strong 'tone at the top' culture throughout Corporate America. . . . You—as directors—should commit yourself to encouraging and implementing a proactive and responsible board culture. You are at the front line—therefore, we will look to you to set and implement the proper tone and compliance environment at your respective companies."[17]

But what is the culture to which commissioner Campos is referring? Just as every organization has a culture, so does every board. The board is subject to the same ethical erosion as any other part of the organization and needs to exercise ethical wisdom to stop its own ethical erosion. To do this, the board needs to be strong in the five disciplines of an ethical culture, which were discussed more fully in part II: mindfulness, voice, respect, tenacity, and legacy.

Mindfulness at the Board Level

When mindfulness is present, each board member is sensitive to his or her own reactions and discomforts between and during board discussions. For this to occur, board members must be personally attuned to the noble purpose of the organization and be independently engaged. The two questions that will help in prompting mindfulness are: (1) Is the tone and content of the discussion we are having or decision we are making consistent with our vision, mission, and values? (2) What issues and trends should we be addressing as a board that we are not presently addressing? The board can employ simple practices to encourage this personal questioning, including posting the questions or a version of them at every meeting, positioning them prominently in the board packet, or posing the questions as a standing agenda item. After enough repetition the board will come to a point when the question no longer needs to be asked because it is consistently being considered without the need for encouragement. When there is a concern, an awareness of something being "off" with a discussion or an agenda, it needs to be shared.

There are also board practices that suppress mindfulness of ethical wisdom. They are the same practices that limit the independent engagement of board members, such as decision making controlled by the CEO or board chair without proper time for reflection or substantive discussion, which by design or as an unintended consequence suppresses mindfulness.

Voice at the Board Level

If mindfulness is welcomed, then board encounters need to be organized to provide members with the opportunity to express questions or concerns even when they have not mustered a strong body of facts to support what they have to say. Sometimes a board will have members who are vocal and seem only to want to sound off on their favorite grievance, no matter what the topic is at hand, even to the extent that they have not taken the time to understand the topic before expressing their own views. These members need to be managed or removed. But their behavior is not a reason to suppress voice in others who are responsible and engaged contributors. In fact, limiting airtime for more vocal board members, responsible or not, and allowing time for quieter voices to be heard, will strengthen the voice of the board as a whole.

Board members are subject to the same pressures as employees when it comes to speaking up. They may be concerned about their not being perceived as team players; they may not want to slow down a meeting that already has a full agenda; they may not want to appear uninformed or unintelligent by seeking more understanding of the topic under discussion; or they may think "if the CEO who works on this stuff all the time thinks this is a good idea, who am I who shows up every now and then to raise doubts." In a board culture where voice is discouraged, the board becomes, at best, a junior partner and, at worst, a rubber stamp for decisions. In either case it is exposed to failing in its duties as a board.

Respect at the Board Level

A board healthy in respect spends time acknowledging and strengthening the process by which it holds discussions and makes decisions—the board's own rules of engagement. It is unreasonable to expect a group that only comes together periodically to work through very busy agendas to behave as a high-performing team unless it carves out time to do so. A board, like any strong team, takes time to assess the effectiveness of its own collaboration, discussions, and decision making, and to build relationships between members at and beyond meetings, often in more relaxed social settings, such as lunch or dinner. This will only happen when development as a team is elevated to the importance of a significant board focus.

Tenacity at the Board Level

The board must be tenacious in fulfilling its fiduciary responsibilities. It is a constant challenge for board members to be satisfied that they and the leadership and employees of the organization are acting with integrity. Tenacity means being willing to ask the hard questions and to stick with them until they are resolved. Selection of motivated board members and clarity of expectations of their role are critical elements. The understanding of issues through independent engagement is also critical to tenacity. It's hard to be tenacious when board members do not believe they are on solid ground in their position on an issue. This importance in understanding issues underscores the value of board education.

Legacy at the Board Level

Now we come full circle back to the organization's noble purpose and the board's stewardship. Similar to the challenge for leaders and employees, the challenge for the board is to avoid being so preoccupied with short-term pressures and expediency that it loses sight of larger intentions and goals. Every board decision needs to reflect line of sight—a clear connection from the vision, mission, values, strategies, and goals of the organization to the board's decisions. An understanding of vision, mission, and values should imbue all board education.[18] In addition, measures of performance asked for by the board need to extend beyond financial measures to nonfinancial measures, including those that measure the ethical health of the organization and its leadership. Again, difficulty in measuring those elements of the operation do not make their effective measurement less important but more so.

The Discipline of Ethical Succession

There are two kinds of succession important to organizational integrity that the board has a direct influence in shaping: CEO succession and board member succession. Each has its own challenges and influence on the future of the organization.

CEO Succession

CEO turnover in hospitals has ranged from 14 to 18 percent; the average tenure of a hospital CEO is 5.6 years.[19] CEO succession is a crucial and predictable board accountability. There are conflicting views about what boards value in a health care CEO, from which it is fair to conclude that board expectations of the CEO are inconsistent.

According to a hospital CEO leadership survey,[20] the three most important CEO characteristics to hospital boards are: (1) experience and results—a proven track record, including a history of building and sustaining successful leadership teams, (2) operational strength and compatible strategic focus on key success factors, and (3) exceptional ability to articulate the vision and service as the mission keeper and moral compass of the organization. The last point speaks strongly to most of the ethical disciplines of leadership: noble purpose, ceaseless ambition, candor, and passion.

A less encouraging white paper published by the American College of Health Care Executives included the characteristics of internal CEO candidates who had impressed board chairs as likely CEO successors.[21] Basically, these nine attributes boiled down to being a good problem solver (able to handle difficult assignments, able to imaginatively develop ideas to resolve hospital/physician conflicts, able to think broadly, and able to be entrepreneurial and solid at crunching numbers) and working well with others (a winning personality, a "joiner" active in clubs and community groups, a good speaker at public presentations, and a person able to work well with the culture of the community). For the most part, current CEOs reflected the same characteristics as the board chairs but added five more, many in the same tone (a sharp focus on benchmarking and performance improvement, a shrewd negotiator with managed care organizations, a leader visible to medical staff, knowledgeable about quality and safety issues, and skilled at navigating the state's political arena). Every one of these attributes is important. However, the terms *passion, integrity, ethical, moral compass, vision, mission, values, health and welfare of communities served, candor,* or *passion* are either nonexistent or at best tacit in this list of valued CEO characteristics.

Leadership integrity cannot be assumed. Even after making integrity and ethical leadership disciplines part of the selection criteria, due diligence is still needed. Laxity can have adverse consequences. Take the case of Radio Shack. When CEO Leonard Roberts moved into the chairman's role, he promoted his COO, David Edmondson, to the position of CEO. Edmondson had been with Radio Shack for 11 years. A news article revealed that Edmondson had lied on his résumé, stating that he held two degrees when he, in fact, did not hold even one.[22] The breakdown in the basic process of due diligence by the board and the CEO—the newspaper was able to discover that Edmondson had distorted his résumé simply by checking with the colleges from which he claimed to have graduated—led to his immediate resignation and to embarrassment and disruption at Radio Shack at a difficult time in the company's history.

Due diligence regarding a candidate's integrity and track record in promoting organizational integrity goes beyond merely establishing an absence of lying. Evidence of ethical compatibility can be demonstrated by how he or she has previously exhibited the disciplines of ethical leadership and how effectively he or she has promoted ethical pathways.[23] These criteria need to be part of the selection process. A personable nature is not evidence of integrity. Judy Thompson is an executive recruiter who places a premium on performing due diligence on the backgrounds of candidates she offers to clients. During a search for a CFO, it came to light at a late stage of the selection process that the leading candidate had ethical irregularities in his previous work. This information had not been provided by the candidate. In spite of this information, the board members involved in the selection still chose the candidate primarily because they liked him. Any board member with an appreciation for identifying ethical erosion would have red-flagged the candidate. He had a prior record of unethical acts, compounded by the fact that he had hidden that record. How could he be entrusted with this critical financial position?

Because CEO turnover can be anticipated, boards need to be proactive in determining their role and the process of successor selection, and in making it as seamless as possible. A research study published by the National Association of Corporate Directors in collaboration with Mercer Delta Consulting yielded 10 best practices in board handling of CEO succession:[24]

1. Plan three to five years out before a CEO transition is expected.
2. Ensure full board involvement. The process should not be relegated to a committee.
3. Establish an open and ongoing dialogue and an annual review. The board and CEO should collaborate on succession planning and devote substantial time to discussing the topic.
4. Develop and agree on selection criteria. Criteria for the new CEO should be developed with the organization's future strategic needs in mind.
5. Use formal assessment processes. They provide information that helps boards assess candidates objectively and identify development needs.
6. Interact with internal candidates. Board members should give ongoing opportunities to interact with internal candidates in various settings, such as off-site meetings and social environments.
7. Stage the succession to avoid horse races. Place potential successors in progressively challenging roles, but never announce they are being considered for CEO.
8. Develop internal candidates rather than recruit externally. Internal candidates know the company's culture, employees, and directors.
9. Have the outgoing CEO leave or stay on for a limited time. The outgoing CEO should either leave the board immediately or stay on for a maximum transitional period of 6 to 18 months.
10. Prepare a comprehensive emergency succession plan. Emergency succession planning should be dealt with as soon as a CEO takes the helm, and the board should review the plan annually.

Assessment of candidates through the lens of the disciplines of ethical leadership—noble purpose, ceaseless ambition, candor, and passion—needs to be interwoven into this process to ensure the candidate with the best necessary capabilities is selected, including the capability of ethical leadership and the capacity to work in partnership with the board.

Board Succession

It's not unusual for not-for-profit health care boards to select new board members based on someone's idea that they would make good board members and have a willingness to serve. In addition, it's not unusual for the member replacement process to take place under pressure: "It's September. We need two new board members by January 1. We need to get on it. Ideas, anyone?" However, many organizations are being much more thoughtful and proactive in their approach to board succession. They realize that board make-up influences effectiveness. The emerging best practices are expressed succinctly by James Orlikoff:

> The best boards stave off potential shortages by cultivating individuals with "boardsmanship" in an ongoing fashion. Board members assess the present board composition against the competencies they need and identify gaps. They rely on an explicit selection process after developing a list of competencies the board needs, including areas of expertise, skill sets, perspectives they would bring from their own professions and personal attributes, such as integrity and commitment to community.[25]

Focusing on the disciplines of ethical governance needs to form part of the selection process, just as focusing on the disciplines of ethical leadership forms part of the CEO selection process. A voluntary board may not be able to find a perfect candidate for the competencies it needs, but being aware of what is needed takes the selection far beyond getting willing bodies in the chairs. If the board cannot find a candidate who is committed to the noble purpose of the organization, is willing to learn and to exercise independent engagement, compatible with the ethical culture of the board, and is willing to adopt a rigorous approach to CEO and board succession, then it may well be better to leave the chair unfilled.

In Short

Ethical governance is critical to building and sustaining the ethical pathways that transform intention into performance. An ethical board and its individual members understand their special position of stewardship and their duties to strengthen and sustain organizational and personal integrity throughout the organization and, not least, in their own actions. An ethical board always has its focus on the noble purpose of the organization. It works in partnership with the CEO in a spirit of independent engagement. It understands that its own culture is a microcosm of the organization's culture, and as such, the board needs to model the disciplines of an ethical culture. Succession, the CEO's and the board's, is handled proactively and with a rigorous process that includes integrity as an important selection criterion.

The following chapter provides a diagnostic through which you can measure the vital signs of the health of the ethical pathway of governance.

References

1. Larson, L. 2003. What every board should know. In K. Gardner, ed., *The Excellent Board*. Chicago: Health Forum, p. 94.
2. [No author cited.] 2005. UC reaches $168 million settlement with Enron directors in securities fraud case. Press release, University of California, January 7.
3. Masters, B., and Day, K. 2005. 10 ex-WorldCom directors agree to settlement. www.washingtonpost.com, January 6.
4. Campos, R. 2006. How to be an effective board member. Speech at HACR Program on Corporate Responsibility, Boston, August 5, p. 1.
5. Orlikoff, J., and Totten, M. 2003. The governance audit: assessing and improving the board. In K. Gardner, ed., *The Excellent Board*. Chicago: Health Forum.

6. Millstein, I., Gregory, H., and Grapsas, R. 2006. Six board priorities for boards in 2006. *Directors Monthly*, April, p. 1.
7. Sandrick, K. 2006. Judging fiduciary duty. *Trustee*, April, p. 6.
8. Eichenwald, K. 2005. *Conspiracy of Fools*. New York: Broadway Books.
9. Pollock, A. 2006. Achieving balance in corporate governance. *Directors Monthly*, April, p. 5.
10. Millstein, Gregory, and Grapsas, Six board priorities for boards in 2006. *Directors Monthly*, April, p. 1.
11. Jennings, B., and others. 2002. *Ethics and Trusteeship in Health Care* [Special Supplement]. Garrison, NY: The Hastings Center, July-August, p. S6.
12. Sardone. F. [President and CEO, Bronson Healthcare Group] 2006. Interview with author, Kalamazoo, MI, July 21.
13. Stubblefield, A. 2005. *The Baptist Health Care Journey to Excellence*. Hoboken, NJ: John Wiley & Sons, p. 55.
14. Darlin, D. 2006. Advisor urges H.P. to focus on ethics over legalities. www.nytimes.com, October 4.
15. Wegmiller, D. 2006. Beyond Sarbanes-Oxley: accountability and CEO behavior. CEO, Summer, p. 1.
16. Broude, P. 2006. The impact of Sarbanes-Oxley on private and nonprofit companies. National Directors Institute, March 9.
17. Campos, How to be an effective board member, p. 12.
18. Larson, What every board should know, p. 94.
19. Khaliq, A., and Thompson, D. 2006. *The Impact of Hospital CEO Turnover in U.S. Hospitals*. Chicago: American College of Healthcare Executives.
20. White, T. 2006. The long-tenured CEO. *CEO*, Fall, p. 1.
21. [No author cited.] 2006. The paradox of CEO succession planning [CEO Circle White Paper]. Chicago: American College of Healthcare Executives, January.
22. [No author cited.] 2006. Radio Shack CEO resigns amid résumé questions. *USA Today*, February 20.
23. Hofmann, P. 2006. Evaluating ethical fitness. *Healthcare Executive*, May/June, p. 34.
24. [No author cited.] 2006. The role of the board in CEO succession. *Directors Monthly*, September, p. 1.
25. Glabman, M. 2006. The future of voluntary governance. *Trustee*, June, p. 12.

10

A Diagnostic for the Ethical Pathway of Governance

Leaders have a significant role in creating the state of mind that is society. They can serve as symbols of the moral unity of the society. They can express the values that hold the society together. Most important, they can conceive and articulate goals that lift people out of their petty preoccupations, carry them above the conflicts that tear society apart, and unite them in pursuit of objectives worthy of their best efforts.

—John W. Gardner

THIS CHAPTER provides a "vital signs" diagnostic to help your board assess at a high level the health of the ethical pathway of governance for your organization. After you have scored the diagnostic, the board can use the results to choose a discipline for its focus of action. Read more on this choice in "Interpreting the Diagnostic" below. The following are some broad guidelines for conducting the diagnostic.

1. Be sure to introduce the use of the questionnaire by sharing why you think completing and discussing the results will be a valuable use of time. Also share its purpose, which is about gaining understanding and making improvements, and is not about blame.
2. Assure those taking the diagnostic that it is safe to respond. Generally, the board is a small group, in which case it will be more difficult to maintain anonymity and more important that those taking the diagnostic trust your good intent.
3. You may still consider using a trusted facilitator to administer, tally, and present the findings. As mentioned later in this chapter, that facilitator could also be used to manage the discussions, coach the board, and help build action plans.
4. Use the diagnostic and what you learn from it with caution. You would not make a diagnosis from a patient's vital signs, but you would use them as one input. This diagnostic and others in this book are best used in the same way, provoking questions, not answers, and opening up discussion and thinking, not closing them off.

Appendix 1 presents a comprehensive diagnostic survey to assess the health of all four ethical pathways. This is a better tool to gather a complete

picture of ethical health. Instructions on how to complete an on-line version of the questionnaire can also be found in appendix 1.

The "From-To's" of Ethical Governance

The disciplines of ethical governance exist to some degree in all organizations. They are not completely present or completely absent. Their condition can be thought to occur somewhere on a continuum. Figure 10-1 shows some of the "from-to's" of the disciplines of ethical governance and gives a sense of the "board mood" we want to minimize and the one we want to instill. The governance "from-to's" reflect the board's view of itself. The diagnostic score sheet should also be completed by executive staff who are familiar with how the board functions.

The Ethical Governance Diagnostic

Similar to other diagnostics in this book, the questions in the following diagnostic are connected to a discipline. A short description of the discipline precedes the questions to remind you what discipline is being considered in the questions. Figure 10-2 is a score sheet to use in producing a score for each discipline and a total score. There are three options for responding to each question:

- *Strongly Agree*—The behavior or point of view is pervasive, common practice. **Score a 5.**
- *Sometimes Agree*—You see the behavior or point of view, but it is inconsistent, and you cannot count on its happening routinely. **Score a 3.**
- *Strongly Disagree*—The likelihood of the behavior or point of view occurring is much more unusual than usual. **Score a 1.**

Circle the number that applies for each question. Score the diagnostic as you go along.

Noble purpose is the calling of health care expressed in the vision, mission, and values of an organization and those who work in it, including its leaders.

1. The vision, mission, and values of the organization are always at the forefront of our thinking when the board makes decisions.
2. When stakeholders in the community ask me as a board member what are the organization's priorities, I tell them it is realizing our vision, mission, and values.
3. The board takes time to reflect on how its work contributes to the vision, mission, and values of the organization.
4. We actively seek means and forums to speak about the noble purpose of our organization with our stakeholders in the community.

Figure 10-1. The "From-To's" of the Disciplines of Ethical Governance

Discipline	From	To
Noble Purpose	The board's duty comes down to oversight of operating performance: "No profit, no mission."	Noble purpose is at the heart of our work as a board: "No mission, no profit."
	Vision, mission, and values are all important; but realistically, the board cannot do its job and always be bound by them.	Vision, mission, and values are the board's compass; whenever we stray from them, the board needs to refocus on them quickly.
	Board agendas stress the current condition of the organization and its immediate issues.	Board discussions always seek to assess the organization's progress toward realizing our vision, mission, and values.
Independent Engagement	The board agenda and focus are provided by the CEO.	The board agenda and focus are the result of a partnership reflecting the priorities of the board and the CEO.
	The board follows the CEO's recommendations with little if any debate.	The board makes sure it understands any issues for which the CEO is recommending action, and makes informed decisions.
	The board assumes that the CEO and the board would not be in their positions if they were not ethical.	The board conducts an annual evaluation that includes a close look at the ethics demonstrated by the CEO and the board.
	The board counts on the CEO to keep board members up to date with what they need to know.	The board directs a structured educational program to keep it abreast of current and future issues and trends in health care.

(Continued on next page)

Figure 10-1. (Continued)

Discipline	From	To
Ethical Culture (Mindfulness)	Board agendas are so crowded that I don't have time to reflect on what I am feeling.	As a board member, part of my duty is to be sensitive to when I feel something might be "off" ethically with a decision.
(Voice)	We go along with decisions even if there might be concerns; that is what it means to be a team.	Board meetings are designed so someone who has concerns can be heard, even if they do not have a lot of facts.
(Respect)	The board values members who think along the same lines.	The board cultivates and encourages needed diversity of views and experience.
(Tenacity)	The board is what it is. We are lucky to get people to serve.	The board wants to excel at its duty; we are always looking for ways to improve our own effectiveness and the organization's ethics.
(Legacy)	The board is mostly focused on putting out fires and making whatever decisions are needed to get through immediate problems.	All board decisions, even those made to solve immediate, pressing issues, are made with the impact of any decision on the organization's noble purpose clearly in mind.
Ethical Succession	The board expects the CEO to give fair notice if he or she plans to leave, hopefully with a recommendation for a successor.	The board has an emergency executive succession plan in place, along with continuously updated successor selection criteria.
	As long as nothing comes to its attention, the board assumes the CEO is acting with integrity.	The board has a regular and objective CEO and executive evaluation process that probes the integrity of our leaders.
	The board starts looking for decent people willing to serve on the board a few months before they are needed.	The board has a member succession plan that maps the competencies needed to identify suitable candidates; planning for board replacements is at least a year out.

Figure 10-2. Ethical Governance Diagnostic Score Sheet

	Strongly Agree	Sometimes Agree	Strongly Disagree	Discipline Total	÷ Number of Questions	= Average Score
Noble Purpose						
Question 1	5	3	1			
Question 2	5	3	1			
Question 3	5	3	1			
Question 4	5	3	1			
Score					4	
Independent Engagement						
Question 5	5	3	1			
Question 6	5	3	1			
Question 7	5	3	1			
Question 8	5	3	1			
Score					4	
Ethical Culture						
Question 9	5	3	1			
Question 10	5	3	1			
Question 11	5	3	1			
Question 12	5	3	1			
Score					4	
Ethical Succession						
Question 13	5	3	1			
Question 14	5	3	1			
Question 15	5	3	1			
Question 16	5	3	1			
Score					4	
		Total Score			16	

Independent engagement is the board setting its own priorities and agenda, becoming informed on the issues before it, and partnering with the CEO with its own point of view.

5. The board, not the CEO, sets board priorities.
6. We have regular educational sessions that help us understand current issues and trends impacting our organization, including ethical issues.
7. The board's exchanges with the CEO are conversations between equal partners in decision making.
8. The board has a firm grip on the ethical health of the organization.

Ethical culture is modeling by the board of the disciplines of an ethical culture.

9. I am sensitive to personal discomfort with a decision signaling something may be "off" ethically.
10. I can speak freely and directly about any concerns I have about our integrity as a board and as an organization.
11. The board encourages and respects different points of view on issues and decisions we face.
12. The board deals effectively with conflicts and disagreements among board members or with the CEO.

Ethical succession is the consistent inclusion of criteria for integrity in CEO and board succession planning.

13. The board's review of CEO and executive performance regarding ethical leadership is regular and rigorous.
14. A validated incident of unethical behavior results in the removal of a board or executive candidate from succession consideration.
15. The board uses a rigorous process to screen prospective executive candidates, which includes a thorough assessment of their track record as persons of integrity.
16. The board uses a rigorous process to screen prospective board members that includes a thorough assessment of their track record as persons of integrity.

Scoring the Diagnostic

The following are steps to score the diagnostic to produce an average score for the questions for each discipline, and an average score for all 16 questions. Figure 10-3 shows an example of a completed score sheet.

1. Go down the columns vertically and add the scores for each set of questions for a discipline.
2. Add the scores for each discipline across to produce a discipline total.

Figure 10-3. Example of a Completed Ethical Governance Diagnostic Score Sheet

	Strongly Agree	Sometimes Agree	Strongly Disagree	Discipline Total	÷ Number of Questions	= Average Score
Noble Purpose						
Question 1	⑤	3	1			
Question 2	5	③	1			
Question 3	5	③	1			
Question 4	⑤	3	1			
Score	*10*	*6*		*16*	4	*4.00*
Independent Engagement						
Question 5	5	③	1			
Question 6	5	③	1			
Question 7	5	③	1			
Question 8	5	③	1			
Score		*12*		*12*	4	*3.00*
Ethical Culture						
Question 9	5	3	①			
Question 10	5	③	1			
Question 11	5	③	1			
Question 12	5	3	①			
Score		*6*	*2*	*8*	4	*2.00*
Ethical Succession						
Question 13	⑤	3	1			
Question 14	⑤	3	1			
Question 15	5	③	1			
Question 16	5	③	1			
Score	*10*	*6*		*16*	4	*4.00*
		Total Score		*52*	16	*3.25*

3. Divide the discipline total for each discipline by 4 (the number of questions) to find the average score for each discipline.
4. Total all the discipline totals vertically to produce the total score.
5. Divide the total score by 16 (the total number of questions) to find the average score for all of the disciplines combined.

Interpreting the Diagnostic

You can decide your own approach in interpreting the survey results, but consider the following questions and approaches in your interpretation.

Questions and Approaches to Interpretation

1. What is the total score average?
   Obviously, if the average score is 3 or below, it is a red flag. "Sometimes" may be an acceptable average for some surveys, but in the case of organizational and personal integrity, lack of consistency in living the organization's values is an invitation to ethical erosion. You may well see scores of 5 for individual questions; however, an average score of 5 is both an opportunity to acknowledge success and also to explore whether this perfect ethical culture holds up under scrutiny.
2. On what one discipline would you focus for discussion and change?
   You can select a discipline on which to focus in at least three ways:
   - It can be the discipline with the lowest average score.
   - It can be the discipline with the most 1 scores.
   - It can be the discipline that you decide will produce the best opportunity for change (this may or may not be the lowest scoring discipline).

   Whatever discipline you choose to focus on, do not be surprised if discussion about it leads to discussion about one or more other disciplines. This is because the disciplines are related to each other.
3. To enrich a conversation about these results, you can choose the discipline with the best score and compare it to a weak-performing discipline. This comparison provides an opportunity to not only ask what is not working about a weak-performing discipline, but also to ask what we can learn from what we are doing right with a high-performing discipline.
4. Remember that this is a high-level diagnostic and, as such, should not be used to provide answers but to provoke focused questions and open discussion.

Thoughts for Each Discipline

Each discipline has its own characteristics. Ways to explore the implications of responses to the questions within each of the disciplines follow.

Noble Purpose

The underlying questions being probed are (1) whether the board sees itself as the steward for the calling of health care as expressed by the vision, mission, and vision of the organization, and (2) whether the board always acts consistent with the organization's noble purpose. If the board cannot say with conviction that its behaviors and decision making are always shaped by these factors, then some of the following questions may prove useful: Can we assume that our vision, mission, and values drive our decisions even if we do not talk about them? To what extent do we talk about our noble purpose when discussing and making strategic and policy decisions, and is it sufficient to be guided by it? Would we describe ourselves as vigilant in making sure the board, our leadership, and the organization are acting with integrity?

Independent Engagement

To the degree the board educates itself on the issues of the organization and the health care environment, it is able to bring its ethical wisdom to bear in deciding board priorities and in decision making. Otherwise it is likely to be dependent on the CEO as the sole provider of board focus, intelligence, and decisions. The following questions may be useful when results of the diagnostic show low scores: To the degree we rely on our CEO for board priorities, understanding of issues, and decision recommendations, in what ways may we be compromising our duty as stewards of the vision, mission, and values of the organization? If it is important that we educate ourselves better to fulfill our duty as a board, what prevents us from doing so? What price does the community we serve, including patients, their families, and employees, suffer when we are not a full partner with the CEO in decision making? What do we really know about the ethical health of the organization? How do we measure the organization's ethical health?

In addition, the following like-minded questions offered by Paul Hofmann and Wanda Jones can aid in a discussion with your CEO on the effectiveness with which key relationships are managed: "What are the ethical foundations of our relationships and behaviors? How do we know how well we are maintaining our standards? Are there areas where we are at ethical risk? Are we open with the public about issues the public considers important?" And further: "Do we scan for the ethical breaches of others as a signal to audit our own practices? Do we have a 'crisis management' policy that favors prompt disclosure and problem solving (e.g., billing abuses, misuse of patients, or an infectious outbreak)? How recently has an ethical audit been conducted?"[1]

Ethical Culture

The key issue being probed is whether the board appreciates that to be effective it needs to act as a high-performing team. The following questions may be useful: Do we view ourselves as a team or merely a group of people who come together for a short time to resolve questions about organizational performance? If we are a team, do we need to be a strong team to get our job done? If we view ourselves as a team, what specific plans and actions do we have in place to improve our individual and team effectiveness, including our ethical health? How do we measure team effectiveness, especially when it comes to our own ethical health? Do we avoid issues, including ethical issues, either because we do not handle conflict well or because we lack the time or will to work through those issues to resolution?

Ethical Succession

The key issues being probed are the primacy of ethical criteria and orderly succession planning. The following questions may be useful: Do our board and CEO evaluation processes stress ethical performance? If not, why not? Is it clear that the board has no tolerance for unethical behavior by a board member, the CEO, or any executive, and how is this made clear on an ongoing basis? Have we tolerated any unethical behavior or acts on the part of a board member or senior staff? If so, what has been our rationale and what has been the cost of our tolerance? Do we perform a rigorous screening to ensure that a prospective board member has a strong track record of ethical behavior and decision making? Do we perform the same screening for CEO succession candidates, even an in-house candidate? Do we assume that internal succession candidates are ethical because they are already employed and, if so, is this an adequate screening criterion for evaluating their ethical behavior and actions?

Approaches to Action

As a general principle, the results of this diagnostic should be shared and discussed with the entire board. Obviously, the discussion needs to be orchestrated and may need to include a skilled facilitator trusted by the board. This facilitation support is also useful to relieve the board chair or the CEO of the burden of both leading and participating freely in the discussion.

Be sure to allow sufficient time for the discussion. Participants need to be able to explore and absorb the implications of the findings and to reach a productive course of action. The resources about dialogue listed at the end of chapter 4 may be useful in providing the tools to create a productive set of discussions.

Finally, the board has the opportunity in this discussion to strengthen and model the disciplines of ethical governance, especially the discipline of ethical culture, by being mindful, allowing voice to the perceptions and ethical wisdom of all members, listening with respect to the views of others (not necessarily agreeing with them but taking them into account), being tenacious in seeking new thinking and moving the conversation beyond predictable outcomes to positive action, and acting consistent with the legacy members seek to leave beyond their tenure on the board. These actions may require courage in moving beyond the comfortable and familiar. But as an act of personal integrity, it is an invaluable contribution to fellow board members and to the community and other stakeholders the organization serves.

Reference

1. Hofmann, P., and Jones, W. 2003. Tough love: ten questions to ask your CEO. In K. Gardner, ed., *The Excellent Board*. Chicago: Health Forum, p. 157.

IV

The Ethical Pathway of Infrastructure

11

The Three Disciplines of Ethical Infrastructure

Just as good morals, if they are to be maintained, have need of the laws, so the laws, if they are to be observed, have need of good morals.
—Niccolo Machiavelli

ETHICAL INFRASTRUCTURE refers to management systems and processes that influence the sustainable strength of organizational and personal integrity. Many of these systems and processes fall under the broad heading of compliance, for example, risk assessment, internal and external auditing, investigatory services to identify offenses, policies and procedures, training, communication methods (such as ethics hotlines), newsletters and intranets, and disciplinary guidelines. These systems and processes are essential foundations for ethical infrastructure and other ethical pathways.

However, this part of the book is not intended as an extensive presentation of the many elements of infrastructure. The focus is not on broad-based compliance but on animation of some processes to strengthen organizational and personal integrity, to leverage ethical wisdom, and to stop ethical erosion.

The term *compliance* implies that something is imposed. The definitions of compliance reinforce this implication: the act of conforming, acquiescing, or yielding; a tendency to yield readily to others, especially in a weak or subservient way; conformity or accordance, cooperation, or obedience.[1] And compliance has not yielded the favorable impact on ethical performance it intended. As first noted in chapter 4, the findings of the 2005 report of the National Business Ethics Survey, a study of employees across for-profit, not-for-profit, and governmental sectors in the United States, found that while the frequency of formal compliance processes and programs have increased, they have not produced the positive outcomes expected, and there is little change in the extent to which employees have observed misconduct in the workplace since 1994.[2] The implication is that these programs do not inspire higher standards of ethical behavior but are related to "have-to-do" actions that yield completed activities but no real change; that is, the organization's relationship to the ethical pathway of infrastructure is more about compliance, not engagement, and is about procedure rather than heartfelt action.

The term *animate* means to give life to, to make alive, to make lively, vivacious, or vigorous, give zest or spirit to, to move to action.[3] The focus of another section in this part of the book is to look at key elements of ethical infrastructure, some more novel and some more common, and ways to animate them so they more vigorously support ethical pathways, strengthen ethical wisdom, and stop ethical erosion.

The Three Disciplines of Ethical Infrastructure: An Overview

The three disciplines of ethical infrastructure are engagement, accountability, and management by facts (figure 11-1). While it is useful to look at those disciplines individually, it will become evident that it is their intertwining that results in a strong ethical infrastructure. Engagement of the workforce is expressed in shared accountability for results. Employees are "incentivized" and rewarded based on meaningful measures that link individual, group, and organizationwide action to the intentions of the organization, including its vision, mission, values, and performance.

Ethical engagement is the commitment to ethical pathways through structures and processes that strengthen and sustain engagement of employees, which evoke the commitment of their hearts and minds.

Accountability builds on ethical engagement to create a shared accountability for organizational and personal integrity in common management processes, such as hiring, performance appraisal and incentive structures, policies and procedures, and ethical decision making. Accountability breathes life into those processes so that they are positive contributors to the ethical health of the organization.

Figure 11-1. The Three Disciplines of Ethical Infrastructure

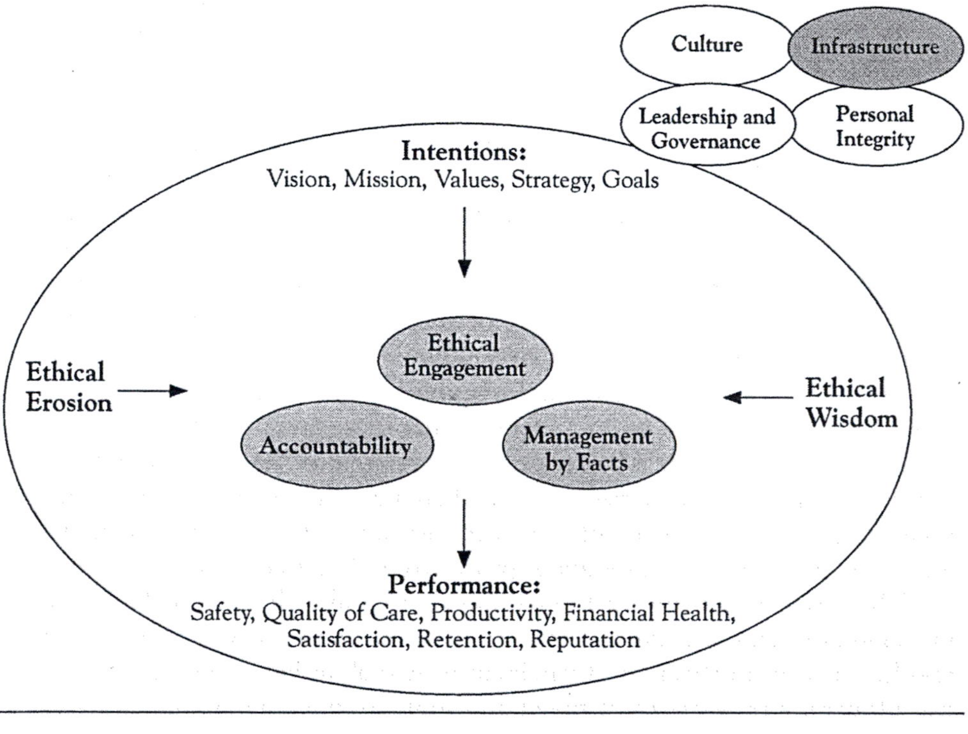

Management by facts consistently seeks to convert informal ideas of what constitutes ethical health into formal performance metrics, which are actively tracked and, whether good, bad, or indifferent, are freely shared with employees and other stakeholders to prompt recognition and performance interventions.

Two organizations used as examples in this part of the book are Baptist Health Care in Pensacola, Florida, and Bronson Healthcare Group in Kalamazoo, Michigan. Both are Malcolm Baldrige National Quality Award recipients and regulars on *Fortune* magazine's annual list of the nation's 100 Best Companies to Work for. Baptist and Bronson are by no means alone in these successes. What is noteworthy is that Baptist and Bronson have reached this level of recognition, especially in being awarded a Baldrige, by working very hard in building ethical infrastructure, and they continue to do so. The Baldrige award criteria stress ethics (it is mentioned 51 times in the criteria)[4] and also place a premium on measurement. Frank Sardone, president and CEO of Bronson, noted: "Following the Baldrige criteria really strengthened the discipline of measurement here."[5]

The Discipline of Ethical Engagement

Engagement of employees is critical to the health of ethical pathways. Engaged employees are more mindful of ethical erosion and more willing to share their ethical wisdom. Ethical engagement reflects the greater willingness of employees to give their discretionary effort to organizations that support and communicate the organization's vision and values.[6]

Although it is not necessary to engage all employees, it is necessary to engage a crucial number or "critical mass" of them, especially during the beginning stages of an adaptive change or transformation, and to expand that number until momentum is established to sustain and strengthen ethical pathways. There is always a critical mass at work regarding ethical behavior in an organization, and at times, it can sustain an unhealthy ethical environment. For example, figure 11-2 is a view of an organization that talks about ethics but does not show an authentic commitment to ethical pathways. For clarification, figures 11-2, 11-3, and 11-4 are not intended to show precise proportions but to illustrate the principles being discussed.

At one end of the curve shown in figure 11-2 are employees who could be called "hard-wired ethical"—self-motivated to do the right thing even in the absence of consistent leadership or organizational support. At the other end of the curve are employees who could be called "hired-wired unethical"—self-motivated to do whatever it takes to get results without having ethical behavior on their radar. In the middle of the curve are the majority of employees who are not hard-wired ethical or unethical, but are observant. Like the village honest man, they are on the lookout for what the leadership of the organization values regarding a wide range of behaviors, including ethical behavior. These employees will follow, but they will not lead. Good words from leadership mean nothing to this group, and rightly so. What matters is what the leadership of the organization tolerates and what it rewards.

Typically, in this kind of ambivalent organization, the commitment to ethical behavior is mixed. Some leaders may build strong ethical values in their part of the organization, and some may choose not to waste their

Figure 11-2. Ethical Engagement: Critical Mass in an Organization with a Mixed or Ambivalent Commitment to Ethical Pathways

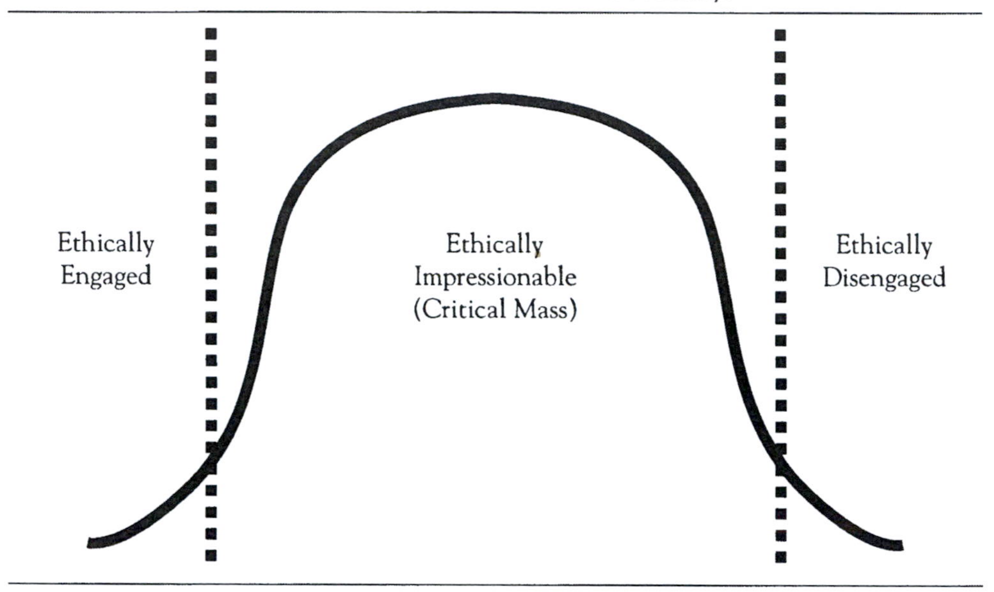

Figure 11-3. Critical Mass of Ethically Engaged Employees Committed to Ethical Pathways Led by a Committed Leadership

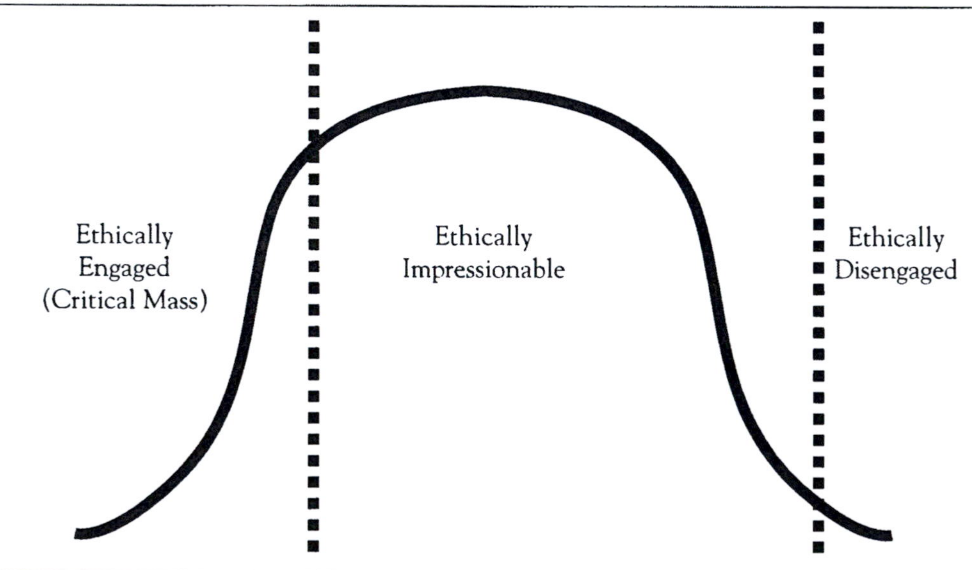

Figure 11-4. An Ethically Engaged Organization with Self-Sustaining Momentum

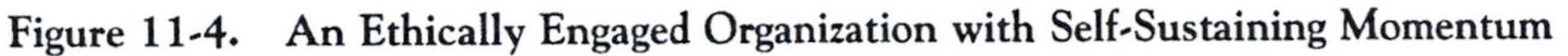

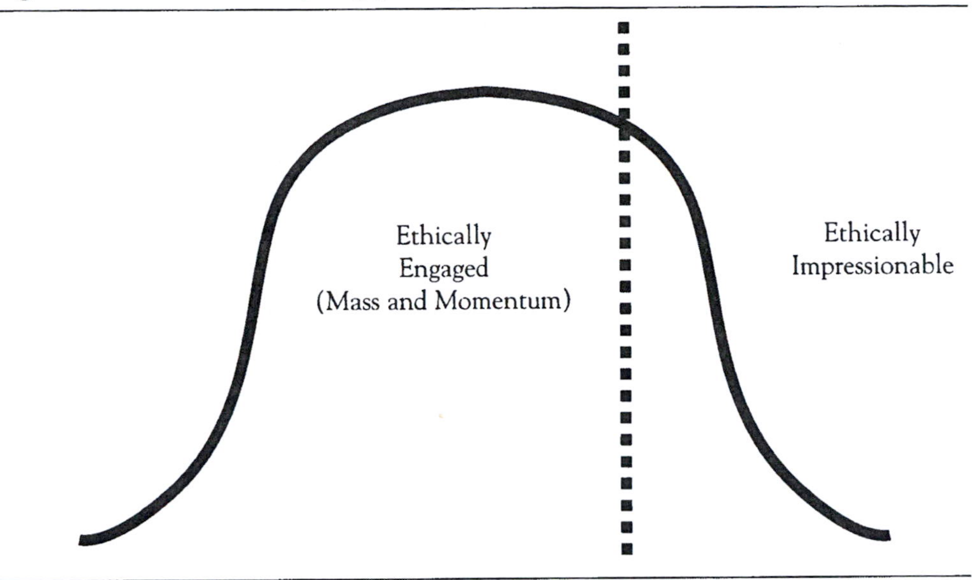

energy on what they see as a potential distraction from a full focus on financial results. Thus, there is no consistent leadership passion for high ethical standards or noble purpose. "Hard-wired ethical" people do not get more recognition or better increases than the "hard-wired unethical" people. In fact, because financial performance is the most readily available measure of success, hard-wired unethical people may be better recognized for the financial or budgetary results they produce, even if they do so in ways inconsistent with the stated values of the organization. Observing this pattern of recognition, ethical impressionable employees, seeking recognition themselves, will move toward unethical behavior, which will become more and more the norm. This shows another way of how ethical erosion works. When the critical mass is made up of the ethically impressionable, and leadership commitment to integrity is mixed, ethical erosion is more likely to prosper.

Figure 11-3 shows the initial shift when formal and informal leaders are engaged in leadership's uncompromising commitment to meet an adaptive challenge through ethical pathways. The challenge expands the number of key employees who become animated and ethically engaged, so those employees, not the ethically impressionable, become the critical mass. The key to success is not the size of the group. It is the group's unified commitment to change. In the transformation at Baptist Health Care, one of the first acts of CEO Al Stubblefield was to remove leaders who, given an opportunity to sign up for the transformation, chose to remain skeptical about its prospects for success.[7]

Figure 11-4 shows an organization that has achieved momentum in adhering to ethical pathways. The hard-wired unethical people can no longer find a place in the organization. For example, David Butts, when he was an executive for a traditional utility company moving from a rigid command and control structure to a culture of engagement of employees and their ethical wisdom, observed that, as the change took hold, managers who clung to dictatorial ways of leading were "illuminated" and obliged to change or to leave the organization.[8] Butts' company still had ethically impressionable employees, but they were outnumbered by the ethically engaged who have chosen to embrace whole-heartedly the change and ethical pathways to performance. Although continuing to operate as the village honest man, the ethically impressionable have one path to follow—the one modeled by the ethically engaged.

Even when momentum is achieved, an organization cannot relax thinking that its ethical pathways are secured. On the contrary, organizations in this stage of change understand that there is always work to do. They know that ethical pathways are always vulnerable to erosion and that continuing to develop the ethically engaged is critical to sustaining the ethical health of the organization. Organizations accomplish this sustained strengthening of ethical pathways not by encouragement alone, but by establishing and nurturing the processes and structures that keep the organization moving forward; in other words, they make ethical engagement an integral part of their infrastructure. They sustain ethical engagement (1) through leadership expansion, (2) by providing "line of sight" for every employee, (3) by enthusiastic recognition of the ethically engaged, and (4) through servant leadership. The following sections discuss each of these critical elements in more detail.

Leadership Expansion

Leaders of adaptive change maximize innovation and commitment to better ways of doing things; however, they do not do this by dictating action throughout the organization or even in their area of accountability. Knowing they rely on others for success, such leaders drive decision making downward and let go of control while providing a clear focus for responsible action. In this way they create an engaged and self-generating workforce committed to higher levels of performance and to ethical pathways.

A key element of letting go successfully is an expansion of the leadership base in the organization. Bronson's 230 leaders (defined as the CEO through all levels of management, including every front-line supervisor) meet offsite in an intensive leadership retreat for up to two days three times a year. This commitment of management time reflects the importance of employee engagement to the organization in meeting its intentions. At Baptist Health Care, a larger organization with more entities, a similar process includes 450 leaders (defined as anyone who fills out a performance appraisal for another employee or who runs, at the least, a one-person department). The distinction of leaders and managers is removed, and the expectation is for leadership at every level.

The size of the leadership group is not the challenge; pervasive excellence in leadership is the challenge. At Bronson the leadership retreats are part of a five-year initiative called "LEADERship" whose mission is "to fully develop excellence within each leader to move Bronson from good to great."[9] The leadership initiative at Bronson is designed to be challenging and recognizes that some leaders will not make the shift needed in leadership. In the words of Marilyn Potgiesser, director of human resources, "The process is not comfortable. Some will not be traveling with us on the journey and it is our job to help them leave with dignity."[10]

At Bronson, retreat outcomes and agendas are based on input from leaders themselves and are orchestrated by four committees composed of eight to ten leaders. These committees coordinate their efforts through a steering committee. So the development of each retreat is in itself a practice of expanded leadership. The four committee names give a sense of the content and tone of the retreats: the curriculum committee (to deliver a curriculum that educates, inspires, and develops superior leaders), the communications committee (to educate employees about leadership development and to act as a resource to communicate important messages throughout the organization), the performance management and leadership accountability committee (to develop methods to hardwire key learning, tools, tips, and best practices into the organization), and the social and logistics committee (to energize the retreats and make them fun, to provide opportunities for networking, and to handle all the physical arrangements).[11] The initiative is an animated process designed to consistently improve the leadership of the organization.

There are about 4,000 employees at Bronson. All 230 leaders (1 in 18 employees) are involved in this extensive leadership initiative, which they share with the CEO and the executive team—an initiative in which they have a voice. Employees who do not attend leadership retreats know their leaders are involved in the initiative, and they know that what they hear from their own leader about Bronson's challenges, performance, and prospects has not been filtered or distorted through multiple management levels. In this way the leadership initiative also builds trust throughout the organization, reinforces the ethically engaged, and positively influences the ethically impressionable.

Engagement and Line of Sight

Ethically engaged employees are committed to the intentions of the organization. But if they cannot make a connection from those intentions to their own everyday actions, their commitment will lack impact or satisfaction. Organizations that have engaged their employees sustain that engagement by creating and institutionalizing that connection—"line of sight"—between organizational intentions and everyday work for an individual employee. The beauty of line of sight is that it provides the opportunity for all employees at every level in every part of the organization to find their part and voice in supporting the organization's noble purpose and intentions, and encourages them to use their initiative and ethical wisdom to strengthen organizational and personal integrity.

A limited, clear, and consistent set of priorities facilitates engagement. At Bronson it is the corporate strategies or three "Cs": clinical excellence, customer and service excellence, and corporate effectiveness. At Baptist it includes the five pillars of operational excellence: people, service, quality, finances, and growth. Consistency is provided by adherence to those priorities, not by changing them on an annual cycle or with every shifting circumstance. If these priorities should change, there will be a compelling and well-communicated reason for that change. Ethical engagement is promoted by putting such priorities consistently in the forefront of organizational communications, conversations, and decisions.

Contrast the environment of consistent focus with a client situation this author faced. The client had 12 strategies for success. Nobody in the organization of 4,000 employees could remember them, let alone be engaged in them. Even the company president needed a written copy in front of him as a prompt to get beyond the four or five he could recite from memory. The strategies were not spoken about with any consistency. The one thing the organization could count on was that the strategies would change at the beginning of the next fiscal year, so nobody took any time to consider how the strategies connected to their own work—and rightly so. It would have been a wasted effort.

At Bronson, employees use a tool called a "Badge Buddy," a card worn by employees behind their ID badge on which they have written their personal goals for the year. Every employee has three personal goals, one for each strategy or "C." The cards with their goals provide a constant reminder to employees of how they contribute to the intentions of the organization, and are part of their performance appraisal.

At Baptist, "The Baptist Health Care Daily" (BHC Daily) is a prominent tool for animating line of sight. The BHC Daily is a document to use in the ongoing discussion of the importance and relevance of organizational values to the actions of every employee. The BHC Daily focuses on what the organization thinks it is timely to reinforce—for example, an item identified by a lower score on a performance measure.

Figure 11-5 is part of the BHC Daily cover sheet for one week. Other parts not shown relate to updates about what is new at Baptist, including process changes. The week, like any other, has a focus: "Ethical Behavior, Our Way of Life." Every day of the week has a "daily learning" connected to that focus.

Attached to the cover sheet are five sheets, one for each weekday. Every daily sheet presents a "learning" consistent with the weekly focus. Figure 11-6 is part of the BHC Daily for Tuesday of this week. Not shown, the daily sheet includes information relevant to the "pillar of the day," a quote of the day, and a healthy living tip for the day.

Here is how the BHC Daily works. Every work group is expected to meet for 10 minutes to review the BHC Daily for that day. This meeting occurs in different ways in different departments. For example, the laboratory

Figure 11-5. The BHC Daily Cover Sheet (Extract)

The BHC Daily

Week of August 14, 2006

Weekly Focus: Ethical Behavior, Our Way of Life

Day	Date	Daily Learning
Monday	August 14	Ethical Behavior = Integrity
Tuesday	August 15	Ethical Denial, Who, Me?
Wednesday	August 16	Morality Versus Ethics
Thursday	August 17	BHC's Code of Conduct
Friday	August 18	Ethical Challenges
Saturday and Sunday	August 19 and 20	Summary of Week

Figure 11-6. The BHC Daily for One Day (Extract)

The BHC Daily

Tuesday, August 15, 2006: Ethical Denial: Who, Me?

All of us at one time or another have been vulnerable to being in ethical denial, or dismissing, distorting, or discounting ethical questions. This can occur when we become overwhelmed by the responsibilities of work, or when outside factors beyond our control enter our daily lives. We can become guilty of attempts to rationalize unethical behavior, which can make even the most hurtful of behaviors appear ethical.

The following are some common rationalization statements: "It's not unethical as long as you are unaware of an ethical principle or standard that prohibits it." And another example is: if you can name five other colleagues off the top of your head doing the same thing, it's not unethical. Or, that something is considered ethical because no one has ever complained about it. And, finally, it is not unethical as long as your boss wants you to do it.

Even though some of these excuses may seem silly, at some time or another you have probably heard at least one of these.

Question for discussion:

Try entering your department as if it were the first time. What ethical first impressions are you creating?

has six daily meetings to attain the fullest coverage possible. Administrative departments working on a single shift are more likely to meet once at the beginning of each day. Some departments post the BHC Daily, but that is not as effective as a face-to-face discussion between colleagues. Accountability is expected and monitored (more on that in the section on "discipline of accountability"). Given the results produced through employee engagement at Baptist, the question is "not so much why do it as why possibly would you not do it?"[12] Although unmeasured, the impact may be significant, given that the total time spent on education through the BHC Daily (50 minutes a week) adds up to as many as 40 hours a year for every employee.

The overall impact of the BHC Daily is to support employee mindfulness, encourage employees' voice, and constantly invite employees to create their own line of sight between Baptist's intentions and their everyday life and actions at work.

Engagement, Recognition, and Reciprocity

For David Butts, "illumination" and effective resolution of negative management behaviors were critical in gaining momentum for change. It is true that negative influences need to be turned around or removed and in a compact time frame; otherwise they will remain a significant drain on the organization's capacity to meet adaptive challenges and to strengthen ethical pathways. Engaged employees will become discouraged by leadership's tolerance of cynics and chronic complainers. Negative employees will distract organizational energy, cast doubt on leadership's commitment to change, and attract impressionable employees to their point of view. In organizations such as Bronson and Baptist, and in others deep into their transformation, sufficient strides have been taken in establishing strengthened adherence to organizational values. Yet these organizations and others like them need to stay vigilant in dealing with those employees whose values and behaviors still do not match those of the organization. Otherwise ethical erosion will be encouraged. But focusing on the hard-wired unethical employees cannot remain the preoccupation of an organization committed to sustaining great change.

There is another, more positive kind of illumination: the celebration and recognition of those who exemplify the vision, mission, and values of the organization, both through the performance of their everyday tasks and by going above and beyond. This recognition creates a relationship of reciprocity. Employees commit themselves to support organizational intentions, and in turn, the contribution of those employees is recognized whole-heartedly in a continuous circle of mutual support. The examples outlined below are more than motivational devices. They are animated, whole-hearted expressions of mutual appreciation. Without that spirit, the ways of recognition are manipulative and seen as such by employees.

Fun and Celebration at Bronson

At Bronson, leaders work hard to create a culture of fun and celebration. It is an important part of their leadership—to catch people in the act of doing the right thing. Bronson has empowered its leaders to use "on-the-spot" reward and recognition by dipping into their personal "recognition tool box." The organization has created a recognition budget for each department and purchased file boxes so leaders can stock their "tool box" with low-cost items such as logo items, mugs, pens, notepads, candy, and small denomination gift certificates. Bronson also prints and distributes "Bronson Bucks"—$1 and $5 gift certificates redeemable at the cafeteria, coffee shop, concierge services, or "snack shack."

Leaders are also required to send thank-you cards regularly to employee homes. On one occasion a manager in human resources worked particularly hard on a project that kept her at work later than normal for several days. The director of human resources sent a thank-you card from "mommy's boss" to the manager's children at home to express what a hard worker their mother was and how much the director appreciated her. Included with the note was a gift certificate from a neighborhood ice cream parlor, so the children could take their mom out for ice cream as the director's thank-you to them all.

Bronson is an organization looking for reasons to celebrate and have fun. It celebrates department or team accomplishments with pizza parties, potlucks, or other celebrations, as well as organizationwide celebrations, such as when Bronson was recognized by *Fortune* magazine as one of the 100 Best Companies to Work for. At this event, every employee received a $10 gas gift card to thank them for their contributions in making Bronson a great place in which to work. In a spirit of fun, the leadership acknowledged that "gas costs a fortune." That year Bronson was ranked 36th on the *Fortune* list, so in the mailing with the gas cards, 36 randomly selected employees were invited to attend an all-employee celebration event in the hospital auditorium, where fun and food were provided and where each of the 36 spun the Bronson Wheel of Fortune to win "fabulous" prizes—a round of golf, movie tickets, restaurant gift certificates, or other kinds of gift cards or services—as their co-workers cheered them on.

When Bronson was named to *Working Mother* magazine's list of 100 Best Companies for Working Mothers for the fourth year, it held a family event where parents could drop off children between the ages of 4 and 12 for a Bronson-paid evening at a local Chuck E Cheese with pizza and complimentary arcade tokens. Children stayed under the supervision of Bronson leaders. Parents could then choose either to go shopping next door at an exclusive Bronson employee-only shopping night at Toys 'R' Us or to go out to dinner.

Implementation of a new dress code with new uniforms can be a touchy subject. Bronson kicked off this initiative by sponsoring an employee fashion show. It invited employees to model the new uniforms, calling the event the "Bronson Spring Collection." It was so popular Bronson held two seatings complete with sparkling nonalcoholic juice, appetizers, and music. The implementation went well.[13]

Recognition at Baptist

At Baptist Health Care there are many ways individuals, teams, and physicians are recognized. For example, individual forms of recognition include the following:

- Handwritten thank-you notes. These notes are sent to an employee's home to acknowledge progress, achievements, or outstanding service.
  Sending thank-you notes to the home is a similar practice to the one used at Bronson. Perhaps Baptist got the idea from Bronson or adapted the idea from another organization. Regardless, the lesson is one that Jack Welch imbued at General Electric. When he took over the company, there was a strong resistance to any practices that were "not invented here." Parts of a GE company were even reluctant to learn from other parts of their own company. Fewer wanted to learn from a non-GE company. Jack Welch's admonition to GE when it came to best practices inside or outside the company was to "steal" ideas shamelessly (but ethically, of course).[14] You do not have to reinvent the wheel to become a best practice organization. You can do so by learning from the successes and failures of others.
- "WOW" service certificates given by leaders or co-workers in acknowledgment of a fellow employee's excellent service. After an employee receives five, the cards are listed in the employee's personnel file and a certificate is awarded.
- New employee cards. After 90 days of employment, a card with a photo of the employee's co-workers and signed individually by them is presented as a "glad you are here and you are important to us" message.
- One-year appreciation awards. A certificate and a pin are awarded after a year of service.
- Multi-year service awards. The longer an employee serves, the higher the recognition and celebration he or she receives.
- Employee of the month. An employee chosen from a list of nominees is surprised and feted at a small reception. He or she receives a $50 gift certificate, a special pin, a special parking space for a month, and a photo posting.
- Employee of the year. At a yearly awards ceremony, the 12 employees of the month are celebrated, and one is chosen as the employee of the year.
- Champions. Employees whose performance has gone "above and beyond" in service of the vision, mission, and values of the organization are recognized quarterly. Two or three are introduced by their respective managers at the monthly board meeting, where they are applauded by the board.

- Legends. Ten to 12 employees are recognized annually from the list of champions and are celebrated in great style, with a limo ride for them and their guests to the annual two-day retreat for board members from all nine Baptist entities. At the retreat the "legends" dine with their administrator, are showcased in a special video presentation, receive a framed certificate and special pin, and are applauded by the 200 board members and administrators in attendance. The recognition does not stop there. Their "stories" are printed in a booklet made available at the retreat and back at work, and they are featured in a full-page newspaper advertisement so the local community will recognize their service.[15]

The cumulative effect of these examples of institutionalized, widespread recognition is to animate recognition every day. The leaders at Baptist and Bronson understand that recognition can become commonplace, but it never grows old. More than that, it can inspire by featuring stories of organizational and personal integrity as models for others, like the "legends" at Baptist.

Two Baptist Legends: Lynda Payne and Betty Smith

It was this author's honor to meet Lynda Payne and Betty Smith, who work in the laundry at Baptist Hospital. They are legends of Baptist Health Care. The following story describes why. A patient called down to the laundry asking if the laundry staff could put aside some undersheet pads for her because she liked using them. Some pads were saved for her but were never picked up before the patient's discharge. So Lynda and Betty tracked down the patient's address, called, and asked if they could bring the pads to her home. When they arrived at the home, what they found was shocking. The house was in terrible condition and the woman was in a sad, neglected state—bedridden, with no family to care for her. There and then Lynda and Betty took ownership of the situation. They asked if they could bathe her, and they cleaned her house. They connected the woman with social services and home health. Lynda and Betty involved their department manager in the process, and they made regular visits to deliver undersheet pads to the former patient. In the words in the booklet acknowledging them, "Lynda and Betty are Legends of Baptist Hospital because their compassion leads them to do great things for people in need."[16]

Lynda and Betty are the fullest expression of ethically engaged employees who are supported by their organization, and whose values and integrity, and those of the organization, are fully aligned. Lynda says her work in the laundry "is a profession—not just a job—connected to patient care," and states proudly: "I own Baptist!"[17]

Engagement and Servant Leadership

It takes a particular kind of leadership to establish successful and sustainable processes to engage employees or other stakeholders—a kind of leadership that opens its arms wide to the individual and collective ethical wisdom of the organization. The term that best captures this spirit is *servant leadership*, a natural expression of the leadership disciplines discussed in part III. This kind of leadership certainly includes an "open door" for two-way communication between leadership and employees. However, it goes beyond that. "Servant leadership," wrote McGee-Cooper and Loper, "is not about a personal quest for power, prestige, or material rewards. Instead the servant as leader begins with a true motivation for nurturing others."[18]

Greg Schaffer, president of Johns Hopkins Bayview Medical Center, reflects the spirit of a servant leader. As a teenager, Schaffer worked as an aide, and the experience continues to help him when responding to requests for assistance from leaders in clinical nursing areas. "I put a great deal of trust in their judgment and do my best to immediately respond to their needs . . . trusting their judgment is a wise thing to do."[19] This spirit is also exemplified by Garry Ridge, CEO of WD-40. His leadership focus is not on critiquing his people's performance but on helping them get an "A." The focus is on what the employees need to succeed, while putting the leaders' welfare second.[20]

The spirit of servant leadership takes the leader to the front lines of the organization—nursing units, treatment areas, ancillary areas, support areas, the cafeteria—to listen for and trust proactively and regularly the wisdom and requests of employees. The change at Baptist was dramatic and a strong and straightforward example of the kind of leadership that engages employees and other stakeholders. "We went from a culture of 'command and control' to one of 'ask, listen, and act.'"[21]

The leadership culture cannot be left only to the good intentions of leaders. It will be vulnerable to ethical erosion. Other priorities will pull at a leader and draw attention away. Servant leadership needs to become part of the infrastructure of the organization, as it has at Bronson and Baptist. As you read the examples that follow, bear in mind that it is possible for the organization's leadership to adopt all these processes and still not build an engaged workforce if these processes are used solely as motivational devices without an authentic desire to act as servant leaders.

Baptist has employed and continues to employ several processes to support its leadership and provide a platform for employees to become and to stay engaged. Those processes include the following: (1) employee involvement in the setting of department goals and action planning to meet the goals; (2) solicitation of suggestions through the "Bright Ideas" program; (3) leaders' getting out of their offices and eating lunch in the cafeteria whenever possible, making it a point to sit with employees they do not know; (4) a monthly lunch with the hospital administrator and 15 randomly selected employees; and (5) senior leaders' making themselves available to employees in daily rounds at employees' work locations to listen, address concerns, and model exemplary service.[22]

Leaders are busy people who work long hours. Knowing this you might think: "I might want to do these rounds, but frankly there is no way I can take on more work on a daily basis." But this was not the view of John Heer, past president of Baptist Hospital. He experienced such powerful results from "rounding" that, however busy, he "didn't have time not to round."[23] The importance of rounding and other engagement processes is made all the more so when appreciating the dangers of unnoticed ethical erosion and the power of accessing and leveraging ethical wisdom throughout the organization.

Servant leadership is not about satisfying every employee's request, need, or concern. Employees will accept their not having a request fulfilled if they are given a clear explanation of why not. Nor is the intention for leadership to collect a laundry list of "to-do's" from employees. Optimally, problem solving is a synergy of a leader's view and scope of authority and an employee's wisdom and innovation.

The Discipline of Accountability

The difficulty with common processes is that they often begin as animated, but over time they lose their vitality and move from value-based processes to compliance-based processes. They become "things to do"—necessary, but not welcome; done with proper attention, but not with enthusiasm. Those essential processes do not actively promote ethical health or evoke inventive accountability in employees—the kind of accountability that has employees engaged in ways to maximize the relevance and effectiveness of those processes to strengthen ethical pathways.

This discussion of the discipline of accountability focuses on ways to sustain and strengthen organizational and personal integrity through selected management processes and through the animation and use of broadened accountability. This discussion does not provide an exhaustive list, but it does provide key process elements that can significantly impact the health of all ethical pathways. Those processes are: (1) vision, mission, and values; (2) policies and procedures, including compliance programs and codes of conduct; (3) values-based decision making; (4) hiring practices; and (5) incentive and reward programs and performance appraisals.

Vision, Mission, and Values

There are two challenges in broadening accountability for the organization's vision, mission, and values. The first occurs in their creation. The second and harder challenge is in sustaining the organization's vision, mission, and values long after the initial excitement of their creation. The infusion of engagement and accountability in the creation of mission, vision, and values, and even more so in sustaining them, is critical to the health of ethical pathways. The processes for doing so need to be systemic and grounded in measurements that determine the degree to which the vision, mission, and values shape everyday ethical behavior.

Vision Creation: Illinova

When Illinova, a regulated electric and gas utility in downstate Illinois with a long-standing tradition of command and control leadership, decided to gear itself up for a more competitive marketplace in the mid-1990s, the executive team aligned behind a vision for the company that would guide it in the coming years. The executive team worked hard on owning this vision, as well as on articulating the engaged way of leading they decided was required for success. The next challenge facing the executive team was to enroll the entire organization in this new vision and in new ways of leading to achieve it. A major step in this process was the engagement of the top 500 people in this 4,000-person organization in a work session designed to generate their ownership of a new vision. Larry Haab, CEO of Illinova, stood in front of his leaders and told them that they were about to engage in work focused on the adoption of a new vision, and that one of three things would happen: they would decide to own the vision presented by the executive team, they would own it with recommended changes, or they would reject it out of hand, in which case he would tear it up and start over. Haab said that it was up to them.[24]

In those words Larry Haab demonstrated both his commitment to engagement for everyone present (a meeting of this size, let alone one that gave full voice to employees, was unheard of at Illinova until that time) and his recognition that top leadership's ownership alone would be insufficient for the vision and all it implied to guide action throughout the organization. Larry Haab liked the vision, but what mattered more to him was Illinova's winning in the new unregulated world by unleashing the latent wisdom and commitment of its employees. At the session the vision was embraced unchanged, and the company moved forward.

Values Creation: The Oklahoma Heart Hospital

In 2002 the Oklahoma Heart Hospital in Oklahoma City opened as a joint venture of the Sisters of Mercy Health System and more than 30 local cardiologists. Participants in the joint venture came from different backgrounds with different ways of working and potentially different values reflected in the behaviors they might encourage, tolerate, or reject. Before the hospital opened, the physicians and Sisters of Mercy leadership came together in two four-hour sessions to hammer out what values at the new hospital would be important to them, what behaviors they would expect from physicians and hospital staff alike, and what policies and structures they would put in place to ensure that those values and behaviors would be "hard-wired" into the new organization. They did this by working through 72 scenarios, including the two examples shown in figure 11-7.

Using a real-time scoring method, participants voted for their preferred response: a, b, or c. This method sometimes led to a quick consensus and sometimes to major differences of opinion and extended discussion. In every case where different views were expressed, the issues were "hashed out." From these many scenarios and their analyses, the values and behaviors expected at the new hospital emerged and were implemented. The 600-employee Oklahoma Heart Health Hospital is today financially successful and consistently scores in the highest percentiles in patient and employee satisfaction—due in no small measure to what emerged from those intense value-creation sessions.[25]

Figure 11-7. Examples of Scenarios Used for Values Creation

Selected Interview Scenarios for Leaders and Physicians

Scenario: Verbal abuse

A physician continually criticizes the nursing staff, referring to them derogatorily as incompetent and constantly pointing out what he believes to be inadequacies in the quality or timeliness of their care giving. On a number of occasions caregivers have been brought to tears by his rudeness, negativity, and fault finding.

How would you view and respond to his behavior? Give me an example when you encountered this, and how did you respond?

a. Unfortunate but understandable given the personality of this particular physician, and it probably will have to be tolerated unless it begins to negatively impact patient care or contributes to employee turnover.

b. Undesired but can be tolerated if it is exhibited occasionally, but the physician should be spoken to if it occurs regularly.

c. Intolerable and specific measures should be undertaken to prohibit this behavior if the physician wishes to continue to practice here.

Scenario: Greet each person appropriately using preferred names

A nurse walks down the hallway heading for a patient's room. "I'll be right back," she hollers to another nurse. "I'm going to check on the CABG in room 120." She walks into the patient's room. "Am I what you called a cabbage?" the elderly, distinguished looking patient asks with surprise and some indignation. The nurse laughs. "It's just how we refer to people around here." "I'd prefer to be called by my proper name," he replies. She glances up at his name above his bed. "Sorry about that George." The patient retorts, "You don't know me that well to call me by my first name. I prefer to be called 'Mr. Henson.'" "My, my," responds the nurse, "a little testy today, are we, honey?"

How would you view and respond to her behavior? Give me an example when you encountered this, and how did you respond?

Addressing people by their preferred names is:

a. Something we should do if that is what an individual asks.

b. A sign of respect; everyone should try to do that with all their patients.

c. The right thing to do; nurses and physicians are being disrespectful if they don't do this.

Sustaining Vision, Mission, and Values

Most employees, including leaders, do not have the opportunity to create their organization's vision, mission, and values; rather, they are presented with them. In the worst case, vision, mission, and values are little more than organizational decorations, fading into the walls on which they are displayed or filed out of sight. Forgotten is the fact that they began as living documents. However, it is always possible to recreate them as living documents, even for employees who never had a hand in creating them. We could gather the vision, mission, and values of any number of health care organizations and might conclude that they all sound like variations of each other, composed of the same set of clichés, such as "to be the best" or "to be the leader in . . . safety, service excellence, caring, and respect for the individual." But this is to miss the point. Those in an organization who are actively engaged in carrying out the vision, mission, and values have the opportunity to experience for themselves the enthusiasm and self-expression of the people who first created them. In short, they relate to the creation as their own. For example, every employee at Bronson has a copy of Bronson's Plan for Excellence and knows how he or she contributes individually to the organization's vision, mission, and values. In the words of Frank Sardone of Bronson: "This has resulted in a palpable feeling of pride and energy within the culture."[26]

Progressive organizations create a relationship between the organizational vision, mission, and values and the personal aspirations and values of employees and other stakeholders (such as physicians), so that organizational and personal integrity work in harmony. As we have seen and will see more in this discussion of the discipline of accountability, progressive organizations create new processes and leverage existing processes to animate the vision, mission, and values of the organization by linking them to the values of their employees, creating line of sight, enthusiasm, and inventive accountability.

The leadership of organizations that are led by a ceaseless ambition challenge themselves with a critical question: "Do our vision, mission, and values still animate the organization?" Those elements should not be subject to continuous change; otherwise they will not provide necessary focus. But they do need to inspire the organization. At Baptist Health Care the vision adopted at the outset of its transformation focused on "service excellence." After service excellence improved dramatically, that vision became, in a way, used up. A new vision was created that reflected a new ambition, "To be the best health system in America."[27]

Johnson & Johnson and the Credo Challenge

Much has been made, even in this book, of Johnson & Johnson's credo and how it guided ethical action during the Tylenol tampering incident of 1982. What is not as well known is that the credo could have been discarded six years earlier. This story is another example of a leader's feeling passionate about a vision and being willing to let it go rather than have others in the organization not own it.

Johnson & Johnson had blossomed ever since its inception in 1887. By 1976 it had plants in over 50 countries and was experiencing rapid growth in the number of employees. It had been more than 30 years since the inception of its credo. James Burke, who was soon to be chairman of the company, upset a lot of people when he questioned the credo's relevance. In Burke's words: "I began to suspect that the Credo wasn't as meaningful to everyone in the company. While many adopted it as our guideline for conducting business, this wasn't universally true."[28] Burke held a two-day meeting for 25 senior managers covering what was called the "Credo challenge." Burke goes on, "What we said, in effect, was this: If you do not believe in the Credo, and you aren't urging your employees to abide by it, then it is an act of pretension. In that case you should take it off the wall of your office and throw it away."[29] Thus began a rigorous and extensive process that resulted in recommitment by the company's leadership to the credo (with some updating of language), including the rededication to it by many who had no direct connection to the energy and enthusiasm of its original adoption and application.

Charley Corace manages Johnson & Johnson's annual Global Credo Survey of the company's 115,000 employees. This 78-question survey tests for the health of the credo and the engagement of employees. The rationale for the survey is simple: "We are proud and passionate about our Credo but we cannot assume that it is being followed in the thousands of decisions being made every day across the organization."[30] Many of the processes set in place by the company are focused on the question, "How can we make our leaders accountable champions of the Credo or have them leave if they cannot do so?"[31] The senior leadership recognizes it is the daily behaviors and decisions of leaders throughout the company that support employees in their own journey from awareness of the credo to belief in it, or conversely, to diminish the credo's relevance. The spirit of the credo is always at risk, always subject to erosion: "Our Credo has taken a lifetime to develop and we know it can be lost in a moment."[32] There is intentional pressure on leaders by means of 360-degree evaluations to determine if they are choosing to live the credo. If they are not, they will not stay with the company.[33]

Policies and Procedures, Codes of Conduct, and Compliance Programs

When first written, policies, codes, and compliance programs are a codification of ethical wisdom generated in response to a particular event or trend. They offer guidance to others who follow on the best course of action in similar circumstances. This guidance is the original intention, whether those policies are generated internally or by third parties with regulatory or oversight authority. But like the vision, mission, and values, these policies and programs are susceptible to erosion and loss of vitality. Again, the challenge is to recreate their value and their importance to the vision, mission, and values of the organization. The examples that follow remind us of how policies and procedures often stem from ethical wisdom and how they can be used to stop ethical erosion and to infuse values into compliance processes.

Policy as Ethical Wisdom

In the following example of a novel situation, there was a demand for a quick decision but no policy to guide it. A partner in a large consulting firm was leading the firm's bid to provide services to a state government. During the final vendor selection process, he received a call from a person he had never met who worked in the state governor's office. This person asked for the consulting firm to donate to a fund associated with the governor's office. A great deal depended on this substantial contract, both for the firm and for the partner's reputation in the firm. With no policy to guide the decision on whether to donate to the governor's fund, the partner immediately met with two other partners. Bringing the company's values and their own ethical wisdom to bear, they decided the company would not donate. There and then, they wrote a policy forbidding the company to donate in response to such requests. This policy served two purposes. The first was to allow the partner to decline the request and explain it was against company policy, thus taking it out of the realm of personal preference. The second was to codify the policy so others would be guided by it when facing similar circumstances. By the way, the consulting firm was awarded the contract.[34]

Many patient care policies and procedures were created in the same way—to avoid harm and to support high standards of patient care. For example, a patient was mistaken for another patient, and something harmful happened or could have happened. The wisdom of those involved was brought to bear, and policies were written with accompanying procedures to ensure the proper identification of patients. Today, policies and procedures for patient identification are long-standing, common practices along with many others intended to ensure patient safety. And yet, tens of thousands of deaths and many more incidents of harm occur every year from medical error. What happens? Over time many policies become routine; they lose their connection to the ethical wisdom that created them. Ethical erosion occurs, and pressures such as volume of work make strict adherence to policies a sometimes redundant formality driven by the need for compliance rather than an expression of a value. The critical issue is to animate policy, or alter it, in order to recreate its connection to the noble purpose of the organization and, by doing so, elevate its relevance and importance to employees.

Animating a Long-Standing Policy

Richard Esgate, president of Esgil Corporation, understands the danger of ethical erosion and the power of policy to forestall it. Esgil provides plan review and building safety services for local county governments. An absence of conflict of interest is a large part of its value proposition in a business fraught with potential conflicts of interest. Most of Esgil's 40 employees are building inspectors, and at times, applicants for permits, contractors, architects, engineers, or investors in a project may want to show their appreciation by offering gifts to inspectors employed by Esgil. The company does not have many policies, but it has one that has been in effect for more than 25 years, almost as long as the company has been in existence: the policy on acceptance of gifts. It prohibits any employee from accepting any gift, at any time, from anyone, for any reason, with a further requirement to document the offer and the employee's response and to make the documentation part of the employee's personnel file. The documentation is required in case any accusation of impropriety is made against Esgil at a later date. Breach of the policy is cause for termination.[35]

The policy is animated in three ways. The first is by regular discussion of it at staff meetings; the second is by reinforcement of the policy when novel situations arise; and the third is by "stories" that show the importance of the policy in conducting business. For example, in one of those stories, an Esgil building inspector was called to inspect a patio addition on the residence of an elderly lady. The contractor's work was poor and did not meet code requirements. The inspector forced the contractor to perform the necessary work, both to conform to code and to produce an overall better standard of work. The lady was very appreciative, and on the Esgil inspector's final sign-off visit, she proudly presented him with a batch of brownies she had baked especially for him. What did he do? He declined the brownies and documented the offer.[36] You could say that declining a harmless offer of appreciation from an elderly lady he likely would never meet again was excessive. But when you understand the nature of ethical erosion, this absolute intolerance for exceptions to the policy is critical in a business that is a potential minefield of conflicts of interest. The story roots employees, old and new, in the importance of the policy.

The contribution of stories to sustaining policy in everyday actions is crucial. Stories have life, and through their lessons, values embedded in policy become animated. For example, the often moving stories of the legends of Baptist Health Care serve to evoke values (and policies) of the organization within employees without overtly teaching them. Johnson & Johnson uses personal stories in its orientation program to create a connection to the credo among new hires. The company also uses its intranet to feature personal stories that demonstrate commitment to the credo.[37] This "line of sight" from a policy to the intentions of the organization illustrates the policy's importance.

Drawing a Hard Line with the Pharmaceutical Industry

The examples of the consulting firm and Esgil discussed above show how policy embodies ethical wisdom and how it can stop ethical erosion. This is the case in a shift occurring in the relationship between physicians and pharmaceutical companies.

Supplying physicians with drug-labeled pens, notepads, mugs, prescription pads, samples, and the like has been a long-standing and relatively low-key practice of pharmaceutical companies. However, more aggressive marketing of an increasing number of competing drugs culminated in the late 1990s in a new level of inducements to physicians to buy their time and ordering preference. These inducements include tickets to sporting events, golf outings, expensive dinners, and even cash. In an effort to rein in their own behavior and perhaps to avoid regulatory intervention, the major pharmaceutical companies have taken a number of inducements off the table.[38]

Led initially by Kaiser Permanente, whose Northern California medical group of 6,000 physicians adopted a stringent new policy in 2005,[39] an increasing number of health care organizations, including Stanford University Medical Center, Yale, and the University of Pennsylvania, have instituted new policies that draw a hard line on any gifts from pharmaceutical companies, including mugs, pads, pens, and drug samples.[40] The driving force behind these policy changes and what gives them power is a concern for patients and their pocketbooks. Pointing to the nature of ethical erosion, an article in the *Journal of the American Medical Association* noted: "The bias thus introduced [by inducements] . . . violates both the best interests of patients and the standards of scientific integrity."[41] And "because gifts of even minimal value carry influence and because disclosure is an inadequate safeguard . . . many current practices should be prohibited and others should be more strictly regulated to eliminate potential sources of unwarranted influence."[42] There are exceptions even in some of these stringent policies. For example, at Stanford the rules do not prohibit an industry representative from taking a doctor out to dinner in the doctor's off time, although the policy strongly cautions against it.[43] From what we know is predictable about ethical erosion, we can expect such exceptions to become the basis for chipping away at the policy. However, as long as the policy remains animated with the understanding of its higher purpose and is continually discussed and emphasized, with exceptions open to the light of day, it can be sustainable—as can any policy in the organization under the same scrutiny.

There is no doubt that an organization can make employees accountable for a policy, procedure, or compliance process by creating adverse consequences for a breach of policy. It is a relatively easy process to have employees read a code of conduct, answer questions on it, and sign that they have read and understood the code. But it does not mean that they will embrace it in everyday work. A code or policy that employees can connect to the vision, mission, and values of the organization and their own values will evoke employees' commitment and sense of accountability because they will see that the code or policy is in the service of the organization's noble purpose and not merely a "have-to" to tolerate and even bypass.

Values-Based Decision Making

Many disciplines discussed in this book are directed at ethical decision making that calls for immediate action or intervention without deliberation. Other ethical decisions are so significant in their impact that an orderly decision process is required for the best solution or that enough time is allowed for a well-considered process. Appreciation of the impact of organizational values on such decisions, and the impact of the decisions on organizational values, is needed for values-based decision making. Figure 11-8 shows the steps made in a values-based decision by Scripps Health in San Diego. The figure shows a framework designed to assist employees in making decisions that are aligned to Scripps' mission and values and that tap know-how and know-what.

Figure 11-8. Values-Based Decision Making Framework

Steps to Making a Values-Based Decision

Individual Steps (1 through 4)

1. State the issue in the form of a question. Determine when the decision has to be made.

   Is it appropriate to ____?
2. Ask yourself:
   - Are there Scripps policies and procedures that address this issue?
   - Are there applicable laws and regulations?
   - Who are the stakeholders? (internal and external)
3. Identify and analyze options that:
   - Comply with the law and Scripps' policies.
   - Are aligned with Scripps' values.
   - Provide greatest benefit to the largest number of stakeholders.
   - Provide the best precedent for guiding similar decisions in the future.
4. Implement and monitor the decision.

If the Decision Is Still Unclear:

Consider a more "consultative" decision-making process by seeking assistance from a situational advisor or advisory group.

5. Review and reconfirm the options.
   - Define the decision needed, identify the decision maker, and review options.
   - Formulate questions and identify information needed. Gather facts and data.
6. Discuss the related values.
   - Which values are relevant?
   - Identify values in conflict?
   - Which values are affirmed/not affirmed? How can we mitigate the values not affirmed?
7. Reflect.
   - Allow each person to reflect and express their opinion in light of personal and organizational beliefs.
8. Discuss the best option and agree on an action plan for the final decision.
   - Articulate consensus.
   - Communicate recommendation to the decision maker.
9. Implement and monitor the decision.

The framework shown in figure 11-8 contains all the disciplines of ethical culture: mindfulness, voice, and respect (in step 7), tenacity (in working through even difficult issues to completion), and legacy (in steps 3 and 6).

Every executive and manager in the Scripps system is trained in this framework. Vic Buzachero, senior vice president for human resources, has seen multiple benefits from use of the framework. It has provided a guide for employees about how to discern a path forward when there is a conflict of interest. It has heightened transparency of values-based decisions for employees as well as for other stakeholders in the community and the media. Such benefits are similar to those offered by Paul Hofmann in his article on critical questions to answer in responding to clinical mistakes. For example, the first critical question is: "How should the organization's vision, mission, and core values influence the disclosure of errors and the actions taken?"[44]

The values-based decision framework has also affirmed the importance of Scripps' values. In an incident before the framework was formalized, but while it was informally applied, the organization decided to offer financial relief to employees earning below an hourly rate threshold by asking them for a deductible for benefits provided by Scripps that was lower than the deductible for high wage earners in the system. This offer was in recognition that an equal deductible for all creates a greater hardship for low wage earners. Scripps' decision was driven by its value that "we demonstrate complete respect for the rights of every individual," and was made without regard to market practice. Not only were the low wage earners appreciative of the financial relief, but the leadership also received expressions of appreciation from higher wage earners who were adversely affected by having to carry a larger share of the organizationwide employee contribution. For those employees, living the organization's values meant a great deal.[45]

In another instance, the decision-making framework was used to evaluate closing a visible patient service during the financial turnaround of an underperforming hospital. The leadership team of the hospital assessed community needs and the stakeholders impacted, and was able to close the service and to redeploy the people and resources to other services that met greater community needs, all with full support of the stakeholders. The action was a major element in the success of the financial turnaround.

Hiring on and Letting Go

Organizations that place values front and center animate them by putting a strong emphasis on the "fit" of prospective employees with the organization's values during and after the hiring process. And these organizations do it in a way that broadens accountability for the hiring decision. There are many ways to do this, but the following five elements and processes prove effective: (1) moving away from just hiring warm bodies, even in times of shortage; (2) signaling to prospective employees the importance of fit with the organization's values; (3) probing for values in the interview and selection process, often through the use of peer interviewers; (4) inculcating the values and organizational priorities post-hire; and (5) letting go of those who cannot live by the values. Taken as a whole, those elements and processes animate the vision, mission, and values of the organization and broaden accountability for success in hiring decisions.

Moving Away from Warm Bodies

There is enormous pressure to deliver a high quality of care. That commonly translates into having more staff, some of whom may be in short supply. This is the rationale for lowering employment standards, but it does not work, especially when the organization has taken on a compelling adaptive challenge that requires the engagement of employees for its success. When employees who are a poor fit with the values of the organization continue to be hired, the effect is the same as retaining existing employees who do not exhibit the organization's values: ethically engaged employees become discouraged; ethically impressionable employees decide that ethical conduct is not a prime commitment of the organization and act accordingly; ethically unengaged employees become more justified in their cynicism; and needed change is defeated.

Bronson took a critical look at workforce development in the late 1990s and decided to become more discerning in the selection of new hires with the skills and values suited to the emerging culture of excellence. In 2001 Bronson's turnover was 19.4 percent. By 2006 it was below 8 percent. In 1998 turnover among registered nurses was 16 percent. By 2006 it was 5 percent.[46] Being more selective in hiring actually resulted in stronger staffing levels, although not in isolation, but along with overall strengthening of the organization's ethical pathways.

Signaling the Importance of Values to Prospective Employees

Organizations intent on finding employees whose values are consistent with those of the organization screen for values at every stage of the hiring process—before an interview, during the interview and selection process, and post-hire.

Before an Interview

Tom's of Maine makes natural personal care products. If you go to the employment section of their Web site, you can read how much they care about their beliefs, purpose, and mission. You can also read: "As a company, we strive to hire the whole individual, someone whose personal values align with our company values. So, we'd like to know more about you than the typical employer might ask. As part of the application process, we will ask that you complete the following Personal Interest and Skills Questions, in addition to submitting your resume."[47] Those questions are shown in figure 11-9. The primacy of those questions signals the organization's emphasis on the importance of values and their identification before the company decides to speak to an applicant.

At Baptist an applicant is asked to read and sign the code of conduct before an interview. A prospective employee cannot fully assess the importance of the code of conduct from this request, but he or she cannot mistake the message that the code is important to the organization.

Figure 11-9. Tom's of Maine Web Site Questions for Applicants' Written Response

Tom's of Maine Personal Interest and Personal Skills Questions

Personal Interest Questions:

- Think of a time in your life when you felt most alive. Describe the circumstances and what you were doing. Why is this particular time important to you?
- Are there certain elements of our beliefs, mission, and culture that you feel more connected to than others? Which of your personal qualities will be of the greatest benefit to the Tom's of Maine culture?
- Tell us about a time when you had to draw upon your personal values to solve a problem, either in a personal or professional setting.

Personal Skills Questions:

- Describe a time when you faced opposition to your ideas in a group in which you played a key role, and yet were able to achieve the results you wanted.
- Give us examples of ways in which you have improved efficiency and effectiveness in an area of importance in your professional life.
- Describe a time when you had to communicate honestly with another person or group of people about a difficult situation. How did you establish common ground with others who may have had different viewpoints?

We suggest that you take some time to reflect on these questions before answering.

Used with permission.

During the Interview and Selection Process

At hospitals in the St. Louis–based Sisters of Mercy Health System, prospective employees are graded on how well their personal characteristics are aligned with those of Mercy. Figure 11-10 is an extract from one of the tools used in the interview process for this purpose. Each item is scored on the following scale: a score of 2 means the candidate is desirable in regard to a specific characteristic (a natural fit); a score of 1 is acceptable (the candidate has the basics and the possibility of further development); and a score of 0 is unacceptable (the candidate is not a fit for Mercy). In aggregate, these scores tell the story of the applicant's suitability for the organization. In addition to providing clarity about the potential for the candidate's success as an employee, the use of this and other documentation demonstrates a sound and transparent hiring decision process in case of challenge.[48]

Figure 11-10. Characteristics for Applicants to Sisters of Mercy Health System (Extract)

Score	Characteristics More Aligned with Mercy	Characteristics Less Aligned with Mercy
	Sense of personal mission and clarity of purpose	Unclear what is personal mission and core values
	Integrity—"Walk the talk" and for the right thing when no one is looking	Concerned with appearances and meeting others' expectations
	Forthright—raise issues when disconnected from mission and values	Unable or unwilling to challenge the status quo
	Willing to take risk; do whatever is needed to accomplish the good	Plays safely and by the rules; concerned with personal failure
	Willing to make tough decisions	Cautious and slow to decide or act
	Accountable	Shares fault and blame with others
	Comfortable with moral ambiguity	Uncomfortable without absolutes
	Blend of compassionate care and good business	Over-emphasis on business or compassionate care to the detriment of the other
	Special concern for the poor	Little interest in or judgmental about the poor
	Open and candid	Hard to get to know
	Present to others	Concerned with self or with senior person in interview
	Friendly, joyful, good sense of humor	Un-engaging and overly serious

2 (Desirable) — 1 (Acceptable) — 0 (Unacceptable)

Peer Interviews

Peer interviewing is a feature of the hiring process at Baptist, Bronson, and Mercy. If you are interviewing for a nursing position at Baptist, you will be interviewed by some of your future peers, and you will be scored by them as to your fit into the culture. Your responses will be scored as poor, good, or very good over several criteria: attitude, teamwork, integrity, initiative, communication, values, and service. For example, possible questions concerning integrity include: "What are your personal values?" "Give us an example of a time when you found it necessary to make an exception of the rules in order to uphold your values." And "How would your co-workers describe you to us?"[49]

The process above is the same if you are interviewing for *any* position in a Baptist hospital. If you are an internal candidate looking for a transfer, you will go through the same screen. If you are a prospective leader (even if you are an internal candidate), you will be interviewed by peers and by selected future subordinates. Peers and subordinates do not have the final decision, although their recommendations carry weight. The final decision remains with their respective leaders.

The peer review process has many benefits. Peers and subordinates have a high stake in the hiring of someone with whom they will work, and on whom they will depend every day; so they will bring all their wisdom to bear in evaluating a candidate. Because their knowledge and expectations of the position are second to none, they are less likely to be "snowed" by the candidate in the interview. The possibility of hiring ethically engaged employees is heightened, and accountability for the hire is expanded. Employees experience themselves as partners in the hiring process, not merely observers hoping for the best from their leader's decision.

Inculcating the Values Post-Hire

New employees at Bronson have preceptors who are responsible for teaching and training them in technical matters. In addition, Bronson provides a "friend at work" who acts as the social and cultural contact in the department for a new employee. The friend's job is to make sure that the new employee feels welcomed, is smoothly integrated into the work team and the hospital community, is inculcated with Bronson's values and culture, and is brought into the social environment. Like peer interviewing, this approach is an expansion of staff accountability for ensuring that every new employee fits in at Bronson.[50]

If you did not think the code of conduct was important when you were asked to sign it before being interviewed at Baptist, you would certainly get the message at the two-day new employee orientation. A full 8 hours of the 16-hour orientation are devoted to culture orientation activities, including a 2-hour presentation by the hospital administrator.[51] New employees leave the orientation with two questions for their own manager: "Where do we do The Daily?" and "At what time?"[52] This orientation strengthens accountability on the part of the employee and the manager and supports a further focus on values.

The post-hire processes at Bronson and Baptist are meaningful symbolically and in substance. They give a clear message to new employees that the organization is committed to their success and to ethical pathways to performance.

Letting Go of Those Who Cannot Live by the Values

Most people who work in health care have a great deal of compassion and caring, having chosen to work in an environment committed to the welfare of others. It is not unusual for this caring to extend to co-workers, even those who do not perform well or may have personalities inconsistent with the values of the organization. We may not give up on these co-workers easily, especially if we have worked with them for some time and have accommodated their limitations. This tolerance might apply to a senior leader, a physician, a nurse, or anyone anywhere in the organization. It may have worked in the past; but given the many challenges faced by health care organizations, including patient safety, quality of care, financial integrity, patient satisfaction, and employee satisfaction and retention, it is no longer tenable. Again, keeping such individuals, whether long-standing employees or new hires, saps ethical engagement and damages performance.

The pain of letting go old friends who no longer fit the organization's values or needs is hard. A consulting colleague recounted the time he was sitting with a CEO who was about to let go hundreds of people in the organization, including close colleagues. The CEO was distraught. He was about to lay off people whose weddings he had celebrated, whose children's birthdays he had attended, and with whom he had shared joyful experiences and difficult times. But the reasons for the layoff were compelling and necessary to preserve the jobs of other employees. The CEO held to his course of action and his duty in spite of personal grief.[53]

Bronson has high aspirations and continues to undergo a demanding transformation. Employees at Bronson say things like, "It is harder to do the wrong thing around here; there will be peer pressure and consequences," "We can't afford to carry the burden (of unproductive employees)," and "We assist all people to be as successful as they can be, but still this may not be the right place for them."[54] There is a similar mindset at Baptist: "We hire the best who align with our values; others leave," and "We weed out the people who don't share the same drive."[55] To let such people go may seem harsh, but actions guided by the vision, mission, and values of the organization, especially for what is best for patients, their families, and the community, will exhibit the greatest integrity—hard sometimes, but always true.

Incentives, Performance Appraisals, and Reward Programs

In 1975 Dr. Steven Kerr, currently chief learning officer and a managing director with the Goldman Sachs Group, wrote a classic article on management with a title that says all you need to know about the content: "On the Folly of Rewarding A, While Hoping for B."[56] Its message is as instructive today as it was then. Health care organizations that tell employees that organizational and personal integrity are of paramount importance, then do not place an emphasis on ethical behaviors and decision making in performance appraisals, for example, will not and should not be taken seriously. In addition, when an organization does measure organizational and personal integrity in employees, but then rewards ethically engaged, ethically impressionable, and even unethical employees with equal wage increases, that leadership is again trapped in the folly of rewarding "A" and hoping for "B." However, there are other models that create a strong connection between the vision, mission, and values of the organization and employee incentives, rewards, and performance appraisals—models that reward "A" and expect "A."

Gain Sharing at Bronson Healthcare Group

Gain sharing has a long history in many industries, although it is not prevalent in health care organizations. The concept is based on the work of Joseph Scanlon and is sometimes labeled the Scanlon Plan. In the difficult economic times of the 1930s, Scanlon, a cost accountant in a small and struggling steel mill, developed his concept of management and labor cooperation to ensure productivity and profitability. Successful plans vary in their scope and approach, but they rest on four critical principles, which echo previous discussions in this book: (1) meaningfully informing employees of the organization's circumstances, objectives, and priorities to build their ownership for change; (2) a structured and guaranteed opportunity and responsibility for employees to influence decision making in their area; (3) the opportunity for all employees to realize financial benefit from their increased accountability and commitment to reach critical performance measures; and (4) the need for management to provide the means and competencies necessary to be successful. Thinking of gain sharing as no more than an incentive plan discounts its broader impact as a vehicle for organizational development consistent with those four principles.[57,58]

Bronson Healthcare Group's gain-sharing program is driven by the organization's plan for excellence and, in particular, the three Cs: clinical excellence, customer and service excellence, and corporate effectiveness. The gain-sharing program policy has three objectives: (1) to provide an orderly and consistent means for the distribution of gain-share dollars to eligible employees; (2) to set goals and targets that consistently challenge each organizational component to improve quality, service, satisfaction, and organizational performance; and (3) to provide a method for communicating to employees the strategic importance of achieving organizationwide targets related to the three Cs. Those objectives show clearly that the Bronson program is not an incentive program but an organizational development program in which nonmanagement and management employees in all of Bronson's entities participate. Part-time and on-call employees also can participate, depending on the number of hours they work in a quarter. Any employee who is the subject of a serious disciplinary action in a quarter cannot participate.

Goals for nonmanagement personnel differ slightly (there are higher obligations for management personnel), but the program's principles are the same for all. Here is how it works for a full-time nonmanagement employee who is eligible to participate:

1. Payouts are made quarterly.
2. The maximum total quarterly payout is $300.
3. If Bronson does not meet or exceed its bottom line for profitability, there is no payout for the quarter because the organization will not pay out gain-share dollars it has not earned through financial performance. If the profitability target is met, then steps 4 to 6 take place.

4. If your department makes its target for clinical excellence, you receive the maximum quarterly payout of $100 for meeting the clinical target. Every department has a clinical excellence target, even those that do not provide clinical care. For example, human resources' clinical care target is focused on the speed with which open positions are filled by qualified candidates, which assumes fuller staffing means better clinical care.
5. If your department makes its target for customer and service excellence, you receive the maximum quarterly payout of $100. The customer and service payout is dependent on the department's patient satisfaction score as measured by The Gallup Organization or on internal survey data for those departments not measured by Gallup.
6. The third $100 payout for corporate effectiveness is made if a department meets its target. Corporate effectiveness focuses on reduction of cycle times, wait times, or other efficiencies.[59]
7. Whether there are payouts or not, all employees receive a card from their leader that tells them their payout for the quarter (figure 11-11).

Through this program Bronson strengthens its values and performance, increases the accountability of its employees and managers, and evokes their engagement and commitment to promoting the vision, mission, and values of the organization every day.

Figure 11-11. Example of Employee Gain-Sharing Program Quarterly Report Card

Congratulations!

Thanks to your focus on Bronson's Plan for Excellence
last quarter, we met these targets for gainshare:

____Clinical Excellence
____Customer & Service Excellence
____Corporate Effectiveness

You will receive a payout of $___________.*

Thank you for your dedication to Bronson and our
vision to be a national leader in healthcare quality.

Frank J. Sardone

*minus statutory taxes

Performance Appraisals at Sisters of Mercy Health System

Performance appraisals at Sisters of Mercy Health System hospitals and other Mercy locations provide another example of rewarding "A" and expecting "A." Employee appraisals at Mercy contain nine behavioral service standards that assess an employee's performance (figure 11-12).

To receive a passing grade on any behavior, an employee needs to be scored as demonstrating the behavior all the time or at least consistently.

Figure 11-12. The Nine Mercy Service Standards

Sisters of Mercy Health System Service Standards

I. **Treat everyone as a valued individual.**
Give your complete attention and appropriate time to the individual you are serving.

II. **Seek out and address customer needs.**
Make it a priority to be out among your customers and co-workers on a regular basis.

III. **Make eye contact, greet and welcome everyone.**
Appropriately smile and look at everyone with sensitivity to situations and cultures.

IV. **Display a positive presence.**
Use positive body language and tone of voice while avoiding negativity and whining.

V. **Keep customers and co-workers informed.**
Do what you say you'll do in a timely manner, and be cooperative and willing to help team members.

VI. **Work as a team.**
Be pleasant, polite, and kind.

VII. **Maintain privacy and confidentiality.**
Ensure that whatever is intimate to a person is not disclosed or revealed.

VIII. **Keep a clean environment.**
Ensure all work areas (halls, parking lots, restrooms, entry ways, lobbies, etc.) are clean by picking up trash and addressing other cleanliness issues. Maintain your own personal appearance and hygiene.

IX. **Live the Mercy Spirit.**
- Respect our Christian heritage and traditions.
- Show compassion and care.
- Embrace the spirit of joy.

There are both positive and negative consequences for an employee from this assessment. An employee's aggregate score for these standards can have an impact on his or her potential annual increase in compensation. If an employee scores unacceptably in five of the nine behavioral standards, then he or she will be placed on a job performance improvement plan with the understanding that the employee may be asked to leave the organization if the job performance does not improve. This improvement process supports engagement by helping to ensure good organizational fit by specifying behaviors that reflect the organization's values. It also acknowledges and rewards ethically engaged and accountable employees and imposes adverse financial and disciplinary consequences on those who are not.

Leadership Accountability and Assessment at Bronson

Every one of the 230 leaders in Bronson Healthcare Group signs a leadership commitment statement. It is a statement of accountability and commitment to the demonstration of leadership, with criteria against which leaders' performance will be assessed. The beginning of the statement sets the tone for those expectations (figure 11-13).

The rest of the statement focuses on how leadership's commitment will be shown in the following 11 areas:

1. Self-confidence, including a commitment to model visibly positive behaviors and to seek feedback on their own behavior
2. Organizational commitment, including promoting Bronson's plan for excellence and aligning their behavior to the needs, priorities, and goals of the organization

Figure 11-13. Beginning of Bronson's 2007 Leadership Commitment Statement

As a leader at Bronson, I commit to accepting accountability. Therefore, I can be counted on to:

BEHAVE in a manner that is consistent with the mission, values, and vision of Bronson and is in keeping with the highest standards of integrity and ethical behavior.

ACT in a manner that is consistent with my job duties, responsibilities, and working requirements.

PERFORM in a manner that is consistent and supports the strategic objectives of the corporation: Clinical Excellence, Customer and Service Excellence, and Corporate Effectiveness.

3. Flexibility, including understanding and appreciating different and opposing perspectives on issues
4. Innovative thinking, including challenging and involving their staff and encouraging constructive conflict and debate
5. Achievement motivation, including developing their own leadership skills, being present and participating at LEADERship retreats, and providing honest feedback on the retreats
6. Customer service, including making a positive difference for patients, families, physicians, and each other
7. Organizational awareness, including supporting the clear connection between Bronson's goals and values through the alignment of strategies and actions
8. Teamwork and cooperation, including providing open and honest feedback to employees, physicians, fellow leaders, patients, and other customers in a timely manner
9. Development of others, including regular coaching and mentoring of their reports
10. Team leadership, including supporting and holding the leader's employees and colleagues accountable for achieving success
11. Judgment and decision making, including using existing information to make the best of a difficult situation and to make intelligent and sound decisions while under pressure.[60]

One of the principles of gain sharing is the need for management to provide the means and competencies necessary to be successful. Organizations committed to leader and employee engagement and accountability make training an expectation for all those who work in the organization and provide the best training opportunities. At Bronson, every leader is expected to attend 60 hours of training annually. They can choose what courses they attend from a LEADERship Development Toolbox series. Other employees are expected to attend 40 hours of training annually.[61]

The complement to the leadership commitment statement is performance appraisal criteria that measure those commitments in action. Leaders who sign the statement are evaluated in part using the leadership accountability minimum requirements form (figure 11-14). Commitments are made and performance is evaluated based on the expectation that those commitments will be met.

A theme of this discussion on accountability is that the emphasis on performance—when it is linked strongly to the vision, mission, and values of the organization—animates those intentions. When animated, the organization's vision, mission, and values evoke commitment and accountability through positive consequences for ethically engaged performance, and negative consequences for ethically disengaged performance. Those positive consequences encourage ethically engaged employees. The sustainable health of organizational and personal integrity is strengthened by inculcating this commitment and accountability into the fabric of common management processes.

Figure 11-14. Bronson's 2007 Leadership Accountability Minimum Requirements

To meet Bronson leadership requirements, all new leaders must complete requirements on an ongoing basis and document them annually. If working requirements are not met, corrective disciplinary action may occur.

Demonstrates commitment to Bronson's Plan for Excellence as evidenced by:

___ Completion of 2007 annual goals

___ Completion of 90-day work plans and one-up review

___ Attendance at all LEADERship Sessions (3 times per year)

___ Completion of assigned homework and accountability grids

___ Compliance with, and readiness for, regulatory and accrediting agencies

___ Completion of the Leadership Development Summary and creation of a Personalized Leadership Development Plan

___ Signing the 2007 Leadership Commitment Statement

Demonstrates commitment to Bronson's Customer Service Standards as evidenced by:

___ Recognizes and rewards employees

Completion of a minimum of 12 Rounds per quarter
___ # rounds completed

Completion of a minimum of 12 Thank You notes per quarter
___ # Thank You's sent

___ On-time completion of employee performance evaluations

___ Develop action plan for areas below industry norm on Employee Satisfaction

Demonstrates commitment to Bronson's Plan for Corporate Effectiveness as evidenced by:

___ Attends or obtains information from Monthly Management Update (MMU) meetings (must attend a minimum of 75% of meetings)

___ Completion of required reports, documentation, or mandated educational sessions

Assist at Bronson sponsored and community events (minimum of 6 points)
___ # of points obtained

The Discipline of Management by Facts

The discipline of management by facts seeks to convert informal ideas of what constitutes ethical health into formal performance metrics that are actively tracked and, good, bad, or indifferent, are freely shared with employees and other stakeholders to prompt recognition and performance interventions.

The Malcolm Baldrige National Quality Award criteria for performance excellence are built on 11 core values and concepts.[62] One of those core values/concepts is management by facts:

> A major consideration in performance improvement and change management involves the selection and use of performance measures or indicators. The measures or indicators you select should best represent the factors that lead to improved health care outcomes; improved customer, operational, financial, and ethical performance; and healthier communities. A comprehensive set of measures or indicators tied to patient/customer and organizational performance requirements represents a clear basis for aligning all processes with your organization's goals.[63]

This concept is consistent with research on companies that have moved from good to great. As already noted, one of the characteristics those companies share is the willingness to confront and openly share the "brutal facts of reality" of their business.[64]

Management by Avoidance of Facts: The Tragic Story of Arthur Andersen

Arthur Andersen was long considered the gold standard of accounting firms. In 2002 Arthur Andersen was indicted for its involvement in fraud at Enron, where it served as auditor. Ensuing events led to the closure of Arthur Andersen later that year (almost 90 years after it was founded), with great job loss and irreparable damage to the pensions of its retirees.[65]

It may seem like the company's demise was a result of its corrupt relationship with Enron, but that does not tell the whole story. It was due to a profound avoidance of the facts of the firm's ethics. Within a four-year span from 1998 to 2002, Andersen was indicted (and sometimes settled cases at significant financial cost to the company) or had been criticized as the auditor for many companies forced to restate earnings, as well as some that had gone bankrupt because their financial statements hid a "house of cards."

These legal actions started with Waste Management, followed by The Baptist Foundation of Arizona, Qwest Communications, Sunbeam, Boston Chicken, McKesson-HBOC, WorldCom, Global Crossing, and Enron—the last three representing the three largest bankruptcies in American history. At no time was a senior partner disciplined or let go until the dismissal of David Duncan, the partner in charge of the Enron account, although his dismissal was more an act of desperation than of principle. Despite internal warnings of pervasive ethical problems, the leadership of Andersen continued on a fatal path, taking many legal actions and warnings as isolated events.[66]

Andersen's fall is an example of not facing the brutal facts of the business, a case study in avoidance of louder and louder signals of ethical erosion, and a demonstration of stifling the voice of ethical wisdom within the company as the leadership ignored warnings of danger. It is also evidence of the maxim: "You manage what you measure." There is no question that the leadership of Arthur Andersen had its eye on results, almost exclusively on financial results, and by that measure their performance was spectacular. Had the leaders of Arthur Andersen as aggressively measured adherence to their own traditionally high ethical standards, they would have seen the signs of erosion long before compromising those standards became common practice—and much grief may have been avoided.

Health care organizations are vulnerable to the same measurement dynamic; and willingness to face the facts of performance by means of regular measurement of a range of ethical performance indicators is critical to strengthening ethical health, leveraging ethical wisdom, and stopping ethical erosion.

Management by Facts in Health Care

Driven by increasing consumer awareness as well as pressure from regulatory and governmental agencies, there is an increasing focus on health care outcomes. For example, not-for-profit hospitals are under increased scrutiny to justify that the community benefit they provide is sufficient to retain their current tax status. And it is the lack of consistency and transparency in measurement and reporting of community benefit that may be the problem rather than a lack of benefit being provided.[67] This situation is at the heart of management by facts. It is not enough to have anecdotes or a list of activities that demonstrate there is a process in place to provide community benefit. The key question is: what benefit has been gained by the community, as measured by the outcomes of any process designed to provide benefit?

In the case of deaths from medical error, it was not anecdotal evidence that brought a strong focus to the issue. It was the Institute of Medicine's research-based assertion that between 44,000 and 98,000 people die from medical errors every year[68] that galvanized the current focus and activity on patient safety.

The need for credible measures of results was an important consideration in the design of the 100,000 Lives Campaign. To have saved more than 120,000 lives in 18 months demands attention. If the results had been anecdotal, the campaign would not have captured our attention and our imagination as strongly. The measurements used in this case were straightforward and met the following standard: "The measurements need not be of research quality, but they must be honest."[69] The campaign calculated lives saved by tracking mortality rates. It compared the mortality rates for each month of the campaign with the mortality rates of the months in the year preceding the campaign. In addition, a national case-mix adjustment was applied to account for the overall change in acuity between the campaign pilot period and the prior period. The campaign also provided tools to participating hospitals to track progress on specific interventions.[70]

Indicators of Organizational Ethical Health

A lagging indicator is a measure that only changes after a shift has happened. Such measures are valuable, but we are left reacting to the shift they report rather than anticipating that shift. It is like finding out that the condition of the electrical wiring in your house was below par by walking through your house's charred remains, too late to take action to stop the fire. Indictments, successful whistleblower actions, discovery of incidents that cause harm to patients and to reputation, billing irregularities that result in public criticism or legal actions, and financial loss through negligence are all lagging indicators—the result of insufficient health of ethical pathways.

A leading indicator is a measure of a shift before it has occurred. In the electrical wiring example, an appraisal of the condition of the wiring would have anticipated the probability of a breakdown causing a fire, which gave time to avoid the fire. Proactively measuring, assessing, and identifying ways to strengthen the health of ethical pathways forestalls ethical breaches by using leading indicators. For example, if an organization has a strong ethical pathway of culture in which employees are consistently mindful ethically, have voice for their ethical concerns, can consistently work in a spirit of collaboration across the organization to resolve ethical issues, have the tenacity to see difficult problems through, and make decisions in keeping with the long-term benefit of the organization and its stakeholders, then the exposure to unethical acts will be reduced. The same is true of the health of the ethical pathways of leadership and governance, infrastructure, and personal integrity.

The diagnostic approach in this book is one example of an ethical health survey focused on leading indicators. Other common leading indicators of ethical health include employee satisfaction data and retention rates. The assumptions are that satisfied employees stay with the organization (evidenced by high retention) and that their satisfaction both reflects and supports the values of the organization, which yields stronger ethical behavior and decision making.

Leveraging the Value of Indicators of Ethical Health

Organizations that manage by facts seek to leverage both lagging and leading indicators of ethical health. They do this by employing at least four methods: (1) they focus on common measures that infer ethical health; (2) they leverage knowledge of comparative performance by participating in national reporting data bases focused on those performance indicators; (3) they reduce the time between results reporting and response so that even though an indicator may be lagging, it can be acted on quickly; and (4) they share the facts of performance freely and regularly with their employees and other stakeholders.

Common Measurements That Infer Ethical Health

The common measures that infer ethical health include patient satisfaction, employee satisfaction, staff retention, safety performance, quality of care, and financial integrity. As we have already discussed, some of those measures are lagging, and some are leading. Bronson's gain-sharing program is an example of linking the facts of performance in clinical excellence, customer and service excellence, and corporate effectiveness to the system of financial rewards. The underlying assumption is that higher performance in core values will strengthen organizational and personal integrity, allowing for even higher performance through ethical pathways.

Leveraging Facts to Understand Comparative Performance

Organizations with ceaseless ambition care about how they stack up against others as well as about their internal performance trends. Such organizations compare themselves to other organizations by using many of the performance criteria mentioned above. In every case they identify gaps between themselves and best practice organizations, and they use those facts to strive to become better or to sustain themselves as a best practice if they are already one. For example, at Bronson HealthCare Group the human resources department publishes a HOT (Human Resources Organizational Trends) report twice a year. Performance criteria include "top box" patient satisfaction (measured every three months), employee satisfaction, job mobility (percentage of positions filled internally), results of the employee referral program, time to fill positions, employee turnover, RN turnover, the vacancy rate for unfilled positions, the RN vacancy rate, and the number of employees. Trends are tracked from 4 to 12 years depending on available data. Each chart tracks three sets of facts: actual performance, national average performance, and best practice. The Bronson target is always to be at best-practice levels of performance. Figure 11-15 shows results for RN turnover at Bronson Methodist Hospital, the flagship

Figure 11-15. 2006 Mid-Year RN Turnover Report, Bronson Methodist Hospital

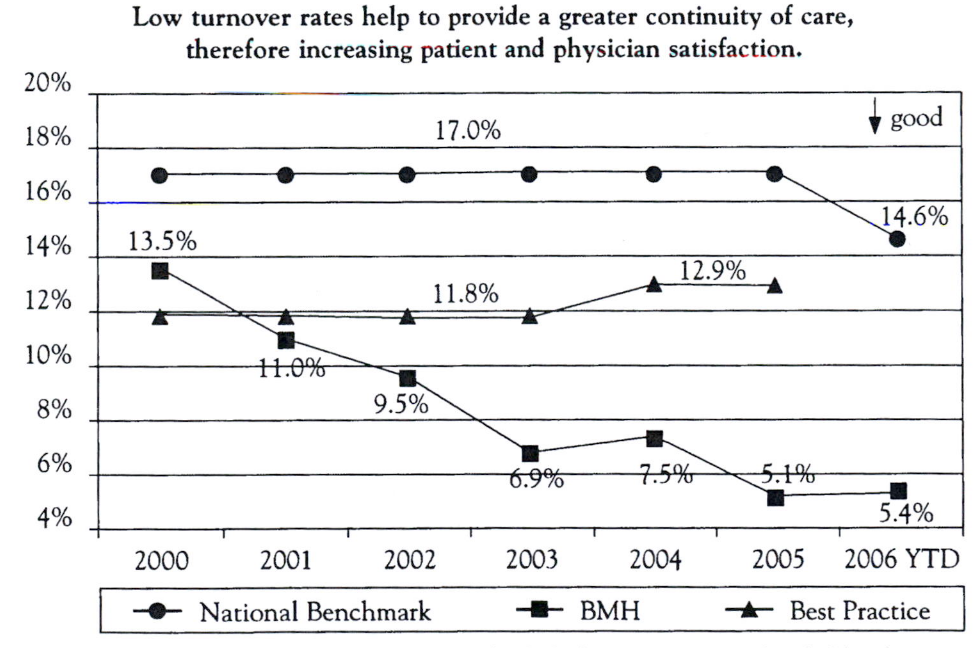

RN turnover is the number of staff nurses who left the organization divided by the average total number of staff nurses.

Source for National Benchmark: NACHR-JWT. Source for Best Practice: ANCC.

hospital in the Bronson system. The trend is positive. Bear in mind that Bronson started its drive for excellence in the late 1990s. In 2000 turnover was 13.5 percent, which was below the national average (17 percent) but not as good as the best practice (11.8 percent). By the end of 2005, turnover had dropped to 5.1 percent, which was below the national average (17 percent) and was a best practice (that level was set at 12.9 percent). These facts encourage further improvement in the case of positive performance, or they call for action in the case of worsening performance or performance that is below best-practice targets.

Management by Facts on Short Timelines for Fast Action

It is feasible to have a gain-sharing plan that pays out annually. However, by providing a quarterly opportunity for a payout, Bronson is shortening the time from actual performance to reporting of that performance. In this way Bronson is providing faster feedback on key performance criteria. Employees have at least four opportunities a year to assess what their performance has been and what they need to do to meet the next set of targets. Similarly, at Baptist, employees have 90-day plans, so there too, performance is known and is managed on a short-term basis.

Baptist has shaped the concept of short-term reporting to a fine art with the facts of patient satisfaction. In 1995, before its transformation, Baptist received quarterly patient satisfaction reports from Press Ganey about 45 days after the quarter had ended. By the time the reports were circulated, it was hard to make the connection between the results and the conditions that may have impacted them, as much as nearly five months before. It was not the major reason that Baptist was in the 18th percentile of hospitals in patient satisfaction, but it did not help matters.

Fast forward to today, when Baptist commonly places in the 99th percentile of hospitals for patient satisfaction and has done so for many years. Baptist achieved best-practice levels, but it still strives to improve. The system for reporting patient satisfaction data has evolved to the current weekly process. The following explanation shows how it works. Every Thursday at 3 p.m., Baptist hospitals receive an e-mail tabulation of the week's patient satisfaction scores. The results are quickly circulated throughout the organization. The report shows weekly patient satisfaction results by unit and by survey question, as well as the results required, also by unit and survey question, to achieve a 99th percentile score and to support the organization as a whole in meeting its 99th percentile goal. If there is a problem, it can be addressed quickly, and everyone involved knows within a week the impact of his or her intervention. If low scores persist in a particular unit or for a particular survey question, then the appropriate leaders create a 90-day action plan to turn the situation around. The department with the most favorable weekly results gets bragging rights for the week.[71] Al Stubblefield sums up the impact: "We have found that the closer to real-time our results are communicated, the more our performance improves. Real-time measurement eliminates many excuses and makes true accountability possible."[72]

Openness with Facts to Create Engagement and Accountability

Openness about the facts of performance is essential to the health of ethical pathways. Specifically, the cultural discipline of voice calls on employees to share their ethical concerns. For employees to be encouraged to do this, the leadership discipline of candor provides a crucial modeling by leaders of what they ask of employees. Openness about the facts of performance strengthens candor and encourages voice. Openness is essential to the discipline of accountability in both rewarding the ethically engaged and in eliminating the ethically unengaged. Sharing facts of the organization's performance strengthens all of these and other disciplines of ethical pathways.

One of the key shifts that signals to employees their leadership's sincerity about engaging their minds and hearts is when the leadership tells the truth about the condition of the organization and opens the books, warts and all. This openness elevates the relationship between executives, leaders, and staff to an adult partnership. The message in this openness is: we know we can trust you with the facts of our performance, and we need your partnership when we are falling short or need to reach new heights of performance. It is an invitation to every employee to engage in what are usually boardroom-level conversations regarding performance and needed action.

A critical shift in the transformation of Baptist Health Care was the creation of a "no secrets" culture.[73] In support of this culture, the communications team at Baptist fulfills its purpose to "gather and disseminate information to all staff, and establish and maintain guidelines for the posting of communications throughout the hospital."[74] For example, after attending a regular leadership retreat, leaders are given a "cascade kit" that provides them with the tools and information to share with their employees what was discussed and decided at the retreat. The impact of this "no secrets" culture has been dramatic:

> In stark contrast to our pre-transformation days, when we get bad news from one of our surveys or reports today, the word spreads more quickly than the good news does. While we always want to take time to enjoy and celebrate our successes, we want our employees to know as quickly as possible when a score has dropped so that we can have "all hands on deck" to bring it back up. How can employees throughout the hospital help a department that is suffering in silence? This public accountability is shocking and a little scary to many healthcare leaders, but when you think of it as a way to hold each other up when we're struggling, it makes sense. That's what a "no secrets" culture is all about.[75]

In Short

Ethical infrastructure leverages common management systems to embed ethical disciplines in the organization's processes to strengthen ethical health. The key disciplines to accomplish this embedding are ethical engagement, accountability, and management by facts. Ethical engagement creates and sustains a critical mass of employees that drives the organization's focus on ethical pathways, at the same time isolating and removing unethical influences. Accountability embeds the vision, mission, and values of an organization in common processes in order to nurture the organization's noble purpose, sustain the integrity of policies and procedures, ensure the organizational fit of new employees, and tie the performance appraisal system to standards of ethical behavior. Management by facts supports engagement and accountability by measuring and freely sharing facts of performance so that successes can be celebrated, shortcomings can be addressed, ethical vulnerabilities can be monitored, and the aspirations of the organization can be assessed against current reality.

Chapter 12 provides a diagnostic you can use to measure the vital signs of the health of your ethical pathway of infrastructure.

References

1. [No author cited.] 1969. *The Random House Dictionary*. New York: Random House, p. 275.
2. [No author cited.] 2005. How employees view ethics in their organizations 1994–2005 [National Business Ethics Survey]. Washington: Ethics Resource Center.
3. *Random House Dictionary*, p. 53.
4. Alexander, J. [Dean, Montfort College of Business, University of Northern Colorado] 2005. Presentation to Executive Forum on Governance and Ethics, California Council for Excellence.
5. Sardone, F. [President and CEO, Bronson Healthcare Group] 2006. Interview with author, Kalamazoo, MI, July 21.
6. Corporate Executive Board. 2004. *Engaging the Workforce, Focusing on Critical Leverage Points to Drive Employee Engagement*. Washington: Corporate Executive Board, p. 98.
7. Stubblefield, A. 2005. *The Baptist Health Care Journey to Excellence*. Hoboken, NJ: John Wiley & Sons, p. 5.
8. Butts, D. [ex-Vice President, Illinova] 2006. Interview with author, Decatur, IL, October 31.
9. Bronson Healthcare Group. 2006. LEADERship [from a PowerPoint presentation].
10. Potgeisser, M. [Director of Human Resources, Bronson Healthcare Group] 2006. Interview with author, Kalamazoo, MI, November 9.
11. Bronson Healthcare Group, LEADERship.
12. Siegel, B. [Coordinator, Baptist Health Care Leadership Institute] 2006. Interview with author, Pensacola, FL, November 9.

13. Potgiesser, M. [Director of Human Resources, Bronson Healthcare Group] 2006. E-mail to author, November 10.
14. Slater, R. 1999. *The GE Way Fieldbook*. New York: McGraw-Hill.
15. Stubblefield, *Baptist Health Care Journey to Excellence*, pp. 100–107.
16. Baptist Health Care. 2003. Legends of Baptist Health Care [from an internal document].
17. Payne, L. [Linen Department, Baptist Hospital] 2006. Interview with author, Pensacola, FL, July 14.
18. McGee-Cooper, A., and Loper, G. 2001. *The Essentials of Servant-Leadership*. Waltham, MA: Pegasus Communications, p. 5.
19. Schaffer, G. [President, Johns Hopkins Bayview Medical Center] 2006. E-mail to author, December 21.
20. Ridge, G. [President and CEO, WD40] 2004. Interview with author, San Diego, December 7.
21. Stubblefield, *Baptist Health Care Journey to Excellence*, p. 42.
22. Stubblefield, *Baptist Health Care Journey to Excellence*, p. 43.
23. Stubblefield, *Baptist Health Care Journey to Excellence*, p. 43.
24. Illinova. 1997. Vision workshops for leaders, May.
25. O'Toole, B. [Vice President, Mission and Ethics, Sisters of Mercy Health System] 2006. Interview with author, St. Louis, November 20.
26. Sardone, interview with author.
27. Stubblefield, *Baptist Health Care Journey to Excellence*, p. 25.
28. Foster, L. 1999. *Robert Wood Johnson: The Gentleman Rebel*. State College, PA: Lillian Press, p. 615.
29. Foster, *Robert Wood Johnson*, p. 615.
30. Corace, C. [Director, Credo Survey and Organizational Analysis, Johnson & Johnson] 2006. Interview with author, New Brunswick, NJ, June 9.
31. Corace, interview with author.
32. Corace, interview with author.
33. Corace, interview with author.
34. Confidential respondent. 2003. Interview with author for dissertation research.
35. Esgil Corporation. 1980. Policy on acceptance of gifts. San Diego: Esgil Corporation.
36. Esgate, R. [President, Esgil Corporation] 2006. Interview with author, San Diego, October 10.
37. Corace, interview with author.
38. Whitney, J. 2006. Pharmaceutical sales 101: me-too drugs. *Gurnica* [www.guernicamag.com], February.
39. Vesely, R. 2005. Kaiser doctors conflict of interest policy tightened. *Oakland Tribune*, April 27.
40. Pollack, A. 2006. Stanford to ban drug makers' gifts to doctors, even pens. *New York Times* [www.nytimes.com], September 12.

41. Brennan, T., Rothman, D., Blank, L., and others. 2006. Health industry practices that create conflicts of interest. *Journal of the American Medical Association*, January 25, p. 429.
42. Brennan and others, Health industry practices that create conflicts of interest, p. 430.
43. Lin II, R., and Engel, M. 2006. Stanford bans taking freebies from drug companies. *Los Angeles Times*, September 13.
44. Hofmann, P. 2006. Responding to critical errors. *Healthcare Executive*, September/October, p. 32.
45. Buzachero, V. [Senior Vice President, Human Resources, Scripps Health] 2006. Interview with author, San Diego, November 11.
46. Potgeisser, interview with author.
47. Tom's of Maine. 2006. www.tomsofmaine.com.
48. O'Toole, interview with author.
49. Baptist Health Care. 2006. Nursing peer interview guide.
50. Potgeisser, interview with author.
51. Stubblefield, *Baptist Health Care Journey to Excellence*, p. 78.
52. Siegel, interview with author.
53. Millemann, M. [President, Millemann and Associates] 2006. Interview with author, Portland, OR, November 20.
54. Employees, Bronson Hospital. 2006. Interviews with author, Kalamazoo, MI, July 11.
55. Employees, Baptist Hospital. 2006. Interviews with author, Pensacola, FL, July 14.
56. Kerr, S. 1975. On the folly of rewarding A, while hoping for B. *Academy of Management Journal*, December, p. 769.
57. Frost, C. 1978. MSU Business Topics [Michigan State University], Winter.
58. Foster, C., and Godkin, L. 2000. Gainsharing and patient satisfaction. *Health Progress*, July/August.
59. Bronson Healthcare Group. 2006. Gainshare program personnel policy.
60. Bronson Healthcare Group. 2007. Leadership commitment statement.
61. Potgeisser, interview with author.
62. Baldrige National Quality Program. 2006. *Health Care Criteria for Performance Excellence*. Gaithersburg, MD: Baldrige National Quality Program.
63. Baldrige National Quality Program, p. 4.
64. Collins, J. 2001. *Good to Great*. New York: HarperBusiness, p. 69.
65. Toffler, B.L. 2003. *Final Accounting*. New York: Broadway Books.
66. Toffler, *Final Accounting*.
67. Sandrick, K. 2006. Defining and measuring community benefit. *Trustee*, October, p. 1.
68. Institute of Medicine. 2000. *To Err Is Human: Building a Safer Health System*. Washington: National Academy Press.

69. Berwick, D., Calkins, D., C. McCannon, C.J., and Hackbarth, A. 2006. The 100,000 Lives Campaign. *Journal of the American Medical Association*, January, p. 326.
70. Berwick and others, The 100,000 Lives Campaign, p. 326.
71. Stubblefield, *Baptist Health Care Journey to Excellence*, p. 189.
72. Stubblefield, *Baptist Health Care Journey to Excellence*, p. 191.
73. Stubblefield, *Baptist Health Care Journey to Excellence*, p. 44.
74. Stubblefield, *Baptist Health Care Journey to Excellence*, p. 121.
75. Stubblefield, *Baptist Health Care Journey to Excellence*, pp. 45–46.

12

A Diagnostic for the Ethical Pathway of Infrastructure

Perfect happiness I believe was never intended by the deity to be the lot of any one of his creatures in this world; but that he has very much put in our power the nearness of approaches to it, is what I as steadfastly believe.

—Thomas Jefferson

THIS CHAPTER provides a "vital signs" diagnostic to help you assess at a high level the health of the ethical pathway of infrastructure for your organization. After you score the diagnostic, you can use the results to choose a discipline for your focus of action. Read more on this choice in "Interpreting the Diagnostic" below.

The following are some broad guidelines for conducting the diagnostic:

1. Be sure to introduce the use of the questionnaire by sharing why you think completing and discussing the results will be a valuable use of time. Also share its purpose, which is about gaining understanding and making improvements, and is not about blame.
2. Assure those taking the diagnostic that it is safe to respond. Generally, the smaller the group completing the diagnostic, the more difficult it is to maintain anonymity, and the more important it is that those taking the diagnostic trust your good intent. If different departments or teams are being assessed, be clear how confidentiality will be maintained and how differences between areas will be managed. Be sure the diagnostic will not be used to place blame on the leader of a comparatively low scoring area, but will be used to expose opportunities for improvement.
3. If you are conducting the diagnostic across different parts of your organization or with different groups within an area, consider using a trusted facilitator to administer, tally, and present the findings. As mentioned later in this chapter, that facilitator could also be used to manage discussions and to help build action plans.
4. Use the diagnostic and what you learn from it with caution. You would not make a diagnosis from a patient's vital signs, but you would use them as one input. This diagnostic and others in this book are best used in the same way, provoking questions, not answers, and opening up discussion and thinking, not closing them off.

Appendix 1 presents a comprehensive diagnostic survey to assess the health of all four ethical pathways. This is a better tool to gather a complete

picture of ethical health. Instructions on how to complete an on-line version of the questionnaire can also be found in appendix 1.

The "From-To's" of Ethical Infrastructure

The disciplines of ethical infrastructure exist to some degree in all organizations. They are not completely present or completely absent. Their condition can be thought to occur somewhere along a continuum. Figure 12-1 shows some of the "from-to's" of the disciplines and gives a sense of the condition we want to minimize and the one we want to instill. The infrastructure from-to's reflect the employee's view of the organization.

The Ethical Infrastructure Diagnostic

Any work group can take this diagnostic. Even though management systems are usually organizationwide in scope, the diagnostic may be used to test whether these systems are equally effective in different parts of the organization. Similar to other diagnostics in this book, the questions in this diagnostic are connected to a specific discipline.

A short description of the discipline precedes the questions to remind you what discipline is being considered in the questions. Figure 12-2 is a score sheet to use in producing a score for each discipline and a total score. There are three options for responding to each question:

- *Strongly Agree*—The behavior or point of view is a pervasive, common practice. **Score a 5.**
- *Sometimes Agree*—You see the behavior or point of view, but it is inconsistent, and you cannot count on its happening routinely. **Score a 3.**
- *Strongly Disagree*—The likelihood of the behavior or point of view occurring is much more unusual than usual. **Score a 1.**

Circle the number that applies for each question. Score the diagnostic as you go along.

Ethical engagement is the commitment to ethical pathways by means of structures and processes that strengthen and sustain engagement of employees, and evoke the commitment of their hearts and minds.

1. Our leaders engage employees' hearts and minds in building an ethical organization.
2. We celebrate our successes and have fun doing it.
3. I understand clearly how my job impacts the values and goals of the organization.
4. I know that senior leadership looks for ways to make it easier for us to do our jobs the right way.

Accountability builds on ethical engagement to create shared accountability for organizational and personal integrity in common management processes such as hiring, performance appraisal and incentive structures,

Figure 12-1. The "From-To's" of the Disciplines of Ethical Infrastructure

Discipline	From	To
Ethical Engagement	Generally, the leadership doesn't seek advice on ethical issues from the rank and file.	We are all partners here in creating an organization that lives its values everywhere in the organization.
	I do my job, but I couldn't really say it impacts the big picture. In fact, I'm not sure what "the big picture" is.	I know how what I do every day supports our values and goals.
	I wouldn't recognize most of the leadership team if I passed them in the hallway.	Our leaders are familiar to us; we consistently see them on our units and in our departments. They always ask what we need to do a better job.
Accountability	Around here you would have to commit a crime to get fired; we just can't afford to lose anyone, no matter if they lack some integrity.	We hire people who are a good fit for our values, and we let go of people who aren't, even those who have been here a long time, and even if we have to go short on staffing.
	Performance appraisal is a joke; everyone meets or exceeds performance standards, and everyone ends up with the same raise.	My performance appraisal and my raise are impacted by how well I demonstrate the organization's values.
	You can find our vision, mission, and values on the walls, but we don't talk about them at all.	I own this place, and I take responsibility for what happens where I work and in the entire organization.
Management by Facts	I have no way of knowing how ethical our organization is, other than our leaders say we are.	We know we have a strong ethical culture, leadership, and infrastructure, and strong personal integrity, because we measure for their strength and intervene when necessary to make them stronger.
	If we haven't been sued recently or gotten any bad press, we must be ethical.	We measure leading indicators so we are doing what is necessary to reduce our exposure to ethical lapses.
	Every employee has read and understands our code of conduct, and that is a key measure of how ethical we are.	We need to consistently measure whether we are living our vision, mission, and values.
	Our leadership spreads good news and hides bad news.	Our leadership shares the facts of our performance; we celebrate our successes, and own up to our failures and improve on them.

Figure 12-2. Ethical Infrastructure Diagnostic Score Sheet

	Strongly Agree	Sometimes Agree	Strongly Disagree	Discipline Total	÷ Number of Questions	= Average Score
Ethical Engagement						
Question 1	5	3	1			
Question 2	5	3	1			
Question 3	5	3	1			
Question 4	5	3	1			
Score					4	
Accountability						
Question 5	5	3	1			
Question 6	5	3	1			
Question 7	5	3	1			
Question 8	5	3	1			
Question 9	5	3	1			
Question 10	5	3	1			
Question 11	5	3	1			
Question 12	5	3	1			
Score					8	
Management by Facts						
Question 13	5	3	1			
Question 14	5	3	1			
Question 15	5	3	1			
Question 16	5	3	1			
Score					4	
		Total Score			16	

policies and procedures, and ethical decision making. Accountability breathes life into those processes so that employees are active contributors to the ethical health of the organization.

5. The vision, mission, and values of our organization are guiding lights for our actions.
6. Our policies and procedures help us do our jobs consistently in the right way.
7. We are very strict in making sure everyone adheres to our policies and procedures.
8. We assess the impact on our values of decisions we make.
9. We hire only those who are a good fit for our values.
10. New hires really understand how important it is to their future here to live our values every day.
11. When the organization meets its goals, we can count on being rewarded.
12. If you do not demonstrate the organization's values, your performance appraisal will suffer.

Management by facts seeks to convert informal ideas of what constitutes ethical health into formal performance metrics that are actively tracked and, good, bad, or indifferent, are freely shared with employees and other stakeholders to prompt recognition and performance interventions.

13. Facts about the organization's performance, good or bad, are freely shared with employees.
14. We use regular sets of facts about performance beyond financial measures to celebrate our successes.
15. We use regular sets of facts about performance beyond financial measures to create action where needed to improve performance.
16. How we compare to other health care organizations in our performance beyond financial measures is shared freely with employees.

Scoring the Diagnostic

The following are steps to score the diagnostic to produce an average score for the questions for each discipline and an average score for all 16 questions. Figure 12-3 shows an example of a completed score sheet.

1. Go down the columns vertically and add the scores for each set of questions for a discipline.
2. Add the scores for each discipline across to produce a discipline total.
3. Divide the discipline total for each discipline by 4 or 8 (the number of questions) to find the average score for each discipline.
4. Total all the discipline totals vertically to produce the total score.
5. Divide the total score by 16 (the total number of questions) to find the average score for all of the disciplines combined.

Figure 12-3. Example of a Completed Ethical Infrastructure Diagnostic Score Sheet

	Strongly Agree	Sometimes Agree	Strongly Disagree	Discipline Total	÷ Number of Questions	= Average Score
Ethical Engagement						
Question 1	(5)	3	1			
Question 2	5	(3)	1			
Question 3	5	(3)	1			
Question 4	(5)	3	1			
Score	*10*	*6*		*16*	4	*4.00*
Accountability						
Question 5	5	(3)	1			
Question 6	5	(3)	1			
Question 7	5	(3)	1			
Question 8	5	(3)	1			
Question 9	5	(3)	1			
Question 10	5	3	(1)			
Question 11	5	3	1			
Question 12	5	(3)	(1)			
Score		*18*	*2*	*20*	8	*2.50*
Management by Facts						
Question 13	5	3	(1)			
Question 14	5	(3)	1			
Question 15	5	(3)	1			
Question 16	5	3	(1)			
Score		*6*	*2*	*8*	4	*2.00*
		Total Score		*44*	16	*2.75*

Interpreting the Diagnostic

You will decide your own approach in interpreting the results, but consider the following questions and approaches in your interpretation.

Questions and Approaches to Interpretation

1. What is the total score average?
   Obviously, if the average score for an individual discipline or the total of all disciplines is 3 or below, it is a red flag. "Sometimes" may be an acceptable average for some surveys; but in the case of an ethical pathway, any lack of consistency in living values is an invitation to ethical erosion. In fact, any score is a basis for a conversation about how to improve. You may well see scores of 5 for individual questions; however, an average score of 5 is both an opportunity to acknowledge success and also to explore whether this perfect ethical condition holds up under scrutiny.
2. On what one discipline would you focus for discussion and change?
   You can select a discipline on which to focus in at least three ways:
   - It can be the discipline with the lowest average score.
   - It can be the discipline with the most 1 scores.
   - It can be the discipline that, if paid attention to, you decide will produce the best opportunity for change (this may or may not be the lowest scoring discipline).

   Whatever discipline you choose to focus on, do not be surprised if discussion about it leads to discussion about one or more other disciplines. This is because the disciplines are related to each other.
3. To enrich a conversation about these results, you can choose the discipline with the best score and compare it to a weak-performing discipline. This comparison provides an opportunity to not only ask what is not working about a weak-performing discipline, but also to ask what we can learn from what we are doing right with a high-performing discipline.
4. Remember that this is a high-level diagnostic and, as such, should not be used to provide answers but to provoke focused questions and open discussion.

Thoughts for Each Discipline

Each discipline has its own characteristics. Ways to explore the implications of responses to the questions within each of the disciplines follow.

Ethical Engagement

The underlying questions being probed are: (1) whether employees are ethically engaged by a leadership that evokes and appreciates their ethical wisdom and celebrates their contributions; (2) whether employees can connect their work to the organization's intentions; and (3) whether employees feel supported by their leaders in getting their work done. If the answers to these questions are less than positive, it is first worth looking at what is missing, given that each question examines a different aspect of ethical engagement. Are the responses weak across the board? If so, the question is whether we as leaders believe we can create and sustain ethical health without engaging employees and without establishing processes to sustain that engagement. If the leadership believes in engagement, but has not fully established it, the question becomes: what immediate plans can be put in place to plan and build momentum for ethical engagement? If the leadership does not believe in the value of engagement, then it would be better not to take action pretending that it does. If the response to selected questions is weak, then it makes sense to explore more deeply what is missing for employees and what processes might be needed.

Accountability

The questions in the diagnostic for this discipline seek to identify the degree of animation of common processes discussed in chapter 11, including the vitality of the vision, mission, and values, whether policies and procedures are seen as providing ethical wisdom and the rigor with which they are followed, the role of values in decision making, the hiring and orientation of new employees for fit, the rewards connected to important organizational values and intentions, and the role of ethical behavior in performance appraisals.

For each low score the key question is: what does the organization need to do to successfully embed actions and measures for ethical health into its common systems, given that there is a likely disconnect between what the organization says it values and what these processes reflect? In other words, to what extent is the leadership rewarding "A" while hoping for "B," and how can it close important gaps where it is doing so?

Management by Facts

One issue being probed here is the extent to which the organization relies on informal measures to assess ethical health or on factual and important lagging and leading indicators organized in ways that show trends, comparative performance, and successes and failures. The clearer the facts, the better the possibility of taking action, as opposed to inconclusive debating of opinions based on anecdotes. The second issue is how widely the facts are shared. This diagnostic is to be completed by employees whose responses will indicate the degree to which they have knowledge and access to facts of performance. If scores are low on sharing facts, the question for leadership is: if these facts do not exist, why not? And more likely, if they do exist, what is the thought process that has leadership not share data freely with employees? This inquiry can lead to underlying assumptions about whether employees can handle bad news or whether leadership believes (incorrectly) its ability to lead is strengthened by holding information closely.

Approaches to Action

As a general principle, the results of this diagnostic should be shared and discussed with the leadership and employees in the areas for which the diagnostic was completed. Obviously, the discussion needs to be orchestrated and may need to include, for example, skilled facilitators from the training and development department. This facilitation support is also useful to relieve you of the burden of both leading and participating in the discussion.

Be sure to allow sufficient time for the discussion. Participants need to be able to explore and absorb the implications of the findings and to reach a productive course of action. The resources about dialogue listed in endnote number 19 in chapter 4 may be useful in providing the tools to create a productive set of discussions.

Finally, this discussion provides the opportunity to strengthen and model the disciplines of ethical infrastructure, especially the discipline of ethical engagement, in those you include in the conversation and by your openness to the ethical wisdom they have to share. This may require your courage in moving beyond the comfortable and the familiar. But as an act of personal integrity, it is an invaluable contribution to your colleagues and the organization.

V

The Ethical Pathway of Personal Integrity

13

The Three Disciplines of Personal Integrity

The antidote to exhaustion is not necessarily rest. . . .
[T]he antidote to exhaustion is wholeheartedness.
—David Whyte

IN CHAPTER 1 we defined personal integrity as:

> **A state of wholeness and peace experienced when our goals, actions, and decisions are consistent with our most cherished values**

Like other ethical pathways, personal integrity is supported by disciplines. The three disciplines that support this pathway are personal legacy, mindfulness, and choice (figure 13-1). We also discussed in chapter 1 the need for a partnership of goodwill between the organization and those who work within it (figure 13-2). The ethical pathway of personal integrity shifts the focus from the organization to individuals who work within it and their

Figure 13-1. The Three Disciplines of Personal Integrity

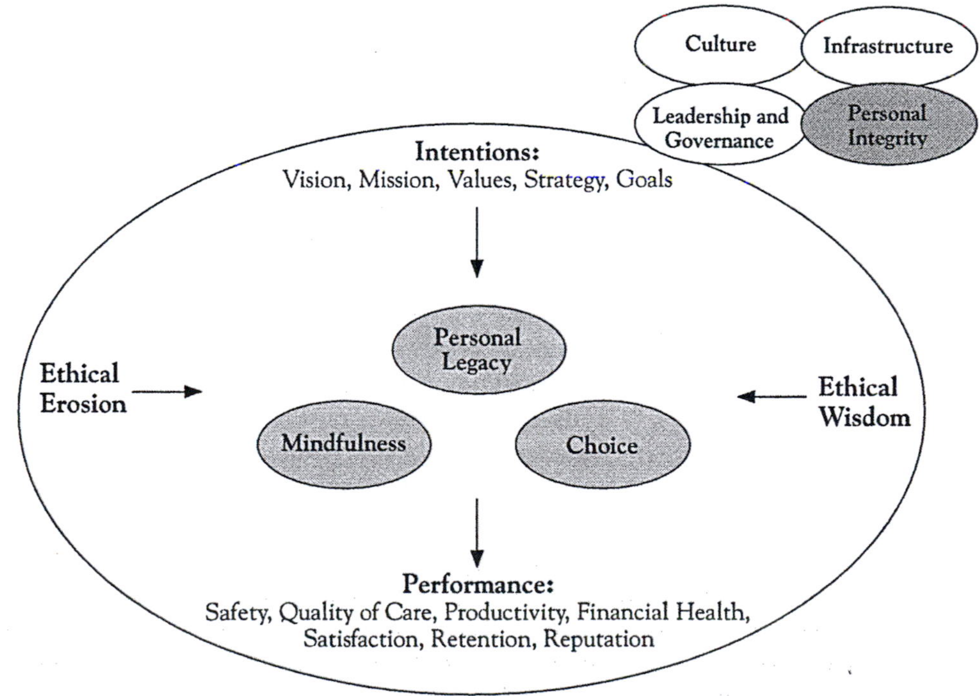

Figure 13-2. A Partnership of Goodwill

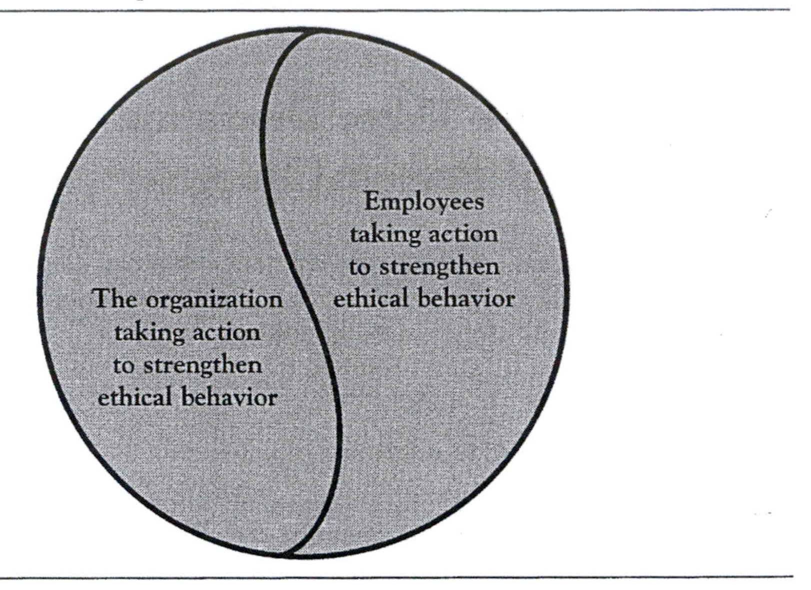

personal role in strengthening and sustaining ethical pathways. There is an implicit value embedded throughout this discussion: that is, your personal legacy, choices, goals, and cherished values do not include any that would cause harm to others; they include only those that would enrich others.

The Three Disciplines: An Overview

Like disciplines in any ethical pathway, the disciplines of personal integrity—personal legacy, mindfulness, and choice—are interdependent. We need to be mindful if we are to make the choices that shape our personal legacy. It is our personal legacy that drives our choices and decides about what we need to be most mindful. And our choices shape our personal legacy.

Personal legacy is what we build for others during and after our lives through our actions at work and elsewhere, and through our values. It is the highest expression of the goals mentioned in the definition of personal integrity.

Mindfulness, first discussed in part II, "The Ethical Pathway of Culture," is the private voice of ethical wisdom. It brings ethical dilemmas and issues to our awareness, such as a sense of calm or comfort with a decision, a gut reaction or discomfort, or a nagging doubt that something may be "off" with a decision at odds with our goals and cherished values. Mindfulness signals the presence or absence of wholeness and peace that is a part of personal integrity.

Choice is the freedom we exercise both in moment-to-moment ethical decisions and in larger decisions such as where we choose to work, the attitude we bring to work, whether we withhold or offer discretionary efforts, and what we choose to say and do to shape our work environment.

The Discipline of Personal Legacy

Legacy as a discipline was first introduced in part II, "The Ethical Pathway of Culture." In that context, legacy is defined as the discipline of making decisions driven by their long-term impact on the vision, mission, and values of the organization rather than by short-term expediency, which will produce immediate results but at the expense of vision, mission, and values. In this discussion we take a personal view of legacy—what it is, what it takes to build an ethical legacy in our lives, including at work, and what gets in the way of building our legacy.

The dictionary defines *legacy* as "a gift" and "something handed down by a predecessor."[1] Our personal legacy is what we build for others through the way we live our values in every part of our life, including work. It is the highest expression of the goals mentioned in the definition of personal integrity. It is not about the benefit we experience for ourselves, but about what we pass on for the benefit of others.

Creating a Personal Legacy

Every one of us is creating a personal legacy, whether we consciously choose to or not. We are all influential, whether we mean to be or not. Parents may feel like they are beating their head against a brick wall when trying to have their child eat well, until one day, shocked, they overhear their child tell another child to eat those vegetables because "they are good for you." Or parents hear their child scream angrily at someone, only for the parents to realize that the words the child uses are the same they use when they fly into a rage. One person in a work area with a negative attitude can sour a department and make the work experience unpleasant. On the other hand, one person can lift the mood of a work area by his or her contagious enthusiasm. Our mood, our words, even our silence toward those we know and with strangers, can leave a legacy of pleasure and value or one of displeasure or distress.

For some people their personal legacy is a well-fed family with a roof over their heads, who are shielded from harm and encouraged to live a life of strong values and healthy aspirations. The legacy of good parents is found in the opportunities and values of their children. For others it is the same legacy but with an extended view of whom they include in their "family." For some their legacy is to infuse their personal faith in every aspect of their lives, wanting to look back knowing that they have lived their life as the best possible expression of that faith. For some it is to impact social issues important to them in a positive way and, in that way, leave behind a better world. For some it is to care for and to heal the sick so that others may have the opportunity to lead a healthy and fulfilling life. For some it may be a combination of these or other aspirations. When we are unaware of our intended legacy, we may be effective, but we may also lose opportunities to make the difference we intuitively seek. The clues to whether we are creating our personal legacy are found in the resonance or dissonance we experience between our goals and cherished values and our everyday thoughts and actions. The diagnostic in chapter 14 contains questions to help you in clarifying your legacy.

Personal Legacy at Work: Careers of Significance

In my experience the people who are happiest at work and who make the greatest positive difference are those for whom work is an opportunity to create a part of their personal legacy. They see work as much more than a necessary evil to be endured. They look to work as an important opportunity to live their values and goals every day.

Sam Odle, past chairman of the American College of Health Care Executives (ACHE), in his inaugural speech at ACHE's 2005 Congress, encouraged his audience to lead careers of significance. He said, "Certainly what we obtain for ourselves and for the welfare of our families and others in our private lives are of great importance and signify success. . . . [T]he daily issues that press on us can leave us overwhelmed and fatigued from constantly fighting to stem the tide of pressures that surround us: budgetary, regulatory and political. We can so easily get wrapped up in personnel issues, in operational problems, in chasing technology, in asset management, and in measuring clinical outcomes. . . . But we who have chosen leadership roles in health care have chosen more. We have chosen what is at its heart a career committed to health, to healing, and to compassion. It is the legacy we leave in support of these great purposes that will mark us as having led careers of significance."[2] A career of significance contains the following three elements: (1) it is an expression of personal legacy; (2) it demonstrates that legacy through the example we set; and (3) it keeps faith with the future we seek to create, even in difficult circumstances. Let us look more closely at setting an example and keeping faith with the future.

Setting an Example

Sometimes modeling personal integrity and our legacy can feel natural and easy. It is an experience that is at once pleasing and fulfilling, such as when we take care of a patient and his or her family and feel the wholeness that comes from a job well done in a full spirit of caring. At other times modeling personal integrity can be uncomfortable. It may be an experience of giving voice to our values in a difficult situation in which we feel at risk and face an uncertain outcome, such as when we have to confront someone about behavior at odds with the values of the organization, especially when that person is intimidating to us. What we do at those times when our own integrity is challenged is a personal act of leadership observed by others who are looking beyond our words to our actions. By going beyond our comfort zone in service of a life of integrity, we encourage others to do the same. Our impact on others by "walking our talk" can be profound.

One person who exemplified walking his own talk was Mahatma Gandhi. His grandson told the story of a family living in Gandhi's community who came to the Mahatma asking him to speak with their child who was having health problems because of his addiction to sugar. As told by Gandhi's grandson,[3] the child was so addicted that when he could not obtain prepared desserts, he would resort to eating sugar by the spoonfuls. Although the parents forbade their child to eat sugar, they themselves continued to do so and kept sweets in the house. When the family, including the boy, met with Gandhi, he listened to their story and did no more than ask them to bring the boy back to him in 18 days. When Gandhi met the boy again, he spoke briefly and privately with him before sending the child on his way. The boy never ate forbidden sweets again. When his parents asked what Gandhi had said to the child, which could create such a change, Gandhi explained that he had requested they bring the child back in 18 days so he could have time to give up sweets himself. He told the child he would not eat sweets again until the boy was well and asked the boy to stop abusing sugar so he, Gandhi, could enjoy sweets again as soon as possible. Gandhi is famous, not only for saying, but for living the maxim, "Be the change you want to bring about."

Keeping Faith with the Future

This author holds a vision for a society in which ethical organizations are commonplace and unethical organizations are a rarity. Nevertheless, I sometimes doubt that this vision can become reality. I question whether what I do, or what anyone does, can stem the tide of unethical behavior in organizations. As a seemingly endless succession of corrupt executives and other public figures are convicted and sentenced or surprisingly are acquitted, as lawsuit after lawsuit is filed or settled, as entire industries, including health care, are exposed for fraud and are subject to record fines, I wonder if my optimism about the possibility of an ethical world at work is misplaced. At times it is hard to keep faith with the positive legacy of ethical organizations I am committed to help make happen.

You too may hear and read this bad news and get discouraged. Sometimes we may become discouraged by what we experience in our own lives at work or elsewhere and feel powerless to change the course of events. It may even seem that unethical acts and criminal behavior are part of the very DNA of organizations. In such times I consciously embrace a different point of view: that, in Jonas Salk's words, life is "continuous creation,"[4] ever changing and ever evolving, and that dramatic positive change is possible.

Salk's polio vaccine has saved countless lives, but what if he and many other physicians and healers had accepted the conventional wisdom expressed by Jean-Jacques Rousseau, a philosopher and the writer of a popular child-rearing manual of his time, when he wrote in 1762: "One half of the children born die before their eighth year. This is nature's law; why try to contradict it?"[5] What if a hundred years later, Florence Nightingale had succumbed to the same conventional wisdom that she described as the accepted truth: "The circumstances which govern our children's health are beyond our control. What can we do with the winds?"[6] Because of Salk's vaccine, we now live in a world in which the infant mortality rate, as unacceptable as it still may be, is greatly improved. A global study published by the World Health Organization in 2000 traces the dramatic decline of almost 60 percent in child mortality (death before the fifth birthday) during the second half of the 20th century. About 10.5 million children under age five died in 2000, 2.2 million less than in 1990. Today, the probability of a newborn dying before the age of five is about 7 percent globally, compared with 10 percent in 1990, 12 percent in 1980, and 25 percent in 1950.[7] In no country in the world does the death rate of children younger than five come close to Rousseau's "natural law."[8] Again, I am not saying that these numbers are acceptable. I am saying that change is possible and conventional truths are not always to be believed.

Imagine sitting in a room with some friends in 1907. That would be more than 10 years before women would be permitted to vote, 30 years before labor laws would limit employer work abuses, including the use of child labor, and 50 years before Rosa Parks, a tired seamstress, refused to give up her seat on a Montgomery, Alabama, bus, which helped to ignite the Civil Rights Movement. Imagine telling your friends that in the lifetimes of people born in 1907, the United States would appoint a black secretary of state to be succeeded by a black female secretary of state, and that parents would be complaining about children not knowing the meaning of hard work. Your friends would accuse you of delusional thinking. And given the truths of the time, they would be sensible in their judgment. Who is to say that 100 years from now high ethical standards at work will not be the naturally accepted norm?

However, there is a more subtle point to be made about keeping faith with the future. We are not just observers of life; we are always participating. When we lose faith in the future of an ethical society, we not only acknowledge the hopelessness of creating that future, but we also perpetuate the opposite future. In the words of university professor and consultant Robert Quinn: "When we accept the world as it is . . . we deny our innate ability to see something better, and hence our ability to *be* something better. We become what we behold. . . . When we accept the social order as 'reality,' as something that cannot change, then we are complicit in our own enslavement. By the same token, the better world we seek is within us, if only we change our vision."[9] So, keeping faith with our personal legacy changes what is possible for others as well as for ourselves.

Personal Legacy: Playing Our Part

Even when we believe in a future that reflects our legacy, other challenges occur. One challenge is that when the gap between the current reality we face and what we want to accomplish seems insurmountable, we can become more overwhelmed than inspired. One of the difficulties in seeking to create ethical organizations or an ethical society is that we can easily become frustrated when it seems we are not making fast enough progress to get the job done. Building organizational and personal integrity is a challenge that has occupied many generations with numerous ebbs and flows, much like the ups and downs that occur in our own lives as we strive for our goals. Impatience with the speed of change can hinder rather than enable progress when our energy is diverted into frustration, anger, and disappointment, and away from constructive action.

The Lesson of Notre Dame Cathedral

The history of Notre Dame Cathedral in Paris is a lesson in change, patience, and personal legacy. When I speak before groups I often ask if anyone in the audience has visited Notre Dame Cathedral. Invariably, a surprising number have. I then ask what one word describes their experience of the cathedral. Usually the responses include "magnificent," "inspiring," and "moving." The story of Notre Dame Cathedral is a profound example of the power in playing one's part and, in doing so, creating a positive personal legacy.

A basilica, later to be replaced by a church, was built about 528 on the site that is now Notre Dame Cathedral. Maurice de Sully, newly appointed as bishop of Paris in 1160, considered the church unworthy for its role; it had become known as the parish church of kings. He ordered the demolition of the existing structure that year, and construction of the Notre Dame Cathedral that we know today began in 1163. That construction was largely accomplished 87 years later in 1250, although the cathedral was not fully completed until 1300, 137 years after construction began. The cathedral has undergone many ups and downs but still stands today, more than 800 years after its construction began.[10]

Given the limited life expectancy of the time, generation upon generation of workers who played their part according to their capability in building the cathedral never saw its completion. Bishop de Sully was among them. He died in 1196, having committed most of his energy and his personal wealth to the edifice. Today, many hundreds of years later, we enjoy and are inspired by the fruits of their labor—their legacy. Even though the builders of Notre Dame are mostly anonymous to us, it is through their efforts that today we can stand in the cathedral and be inspired and awed in the presence of magnificence.

This is the way we will build an ethical society and organizations with high ethical standards: by playing our personal part to the best of our ability, whatever our position and whatever our role, large or small. We do not have to be perfect to play this role. I have worked for more than 40 years and, by my reckoning, during that time I've "stolen"—there really is no more accurate way to describe it—from my employers enough paper clips, paper pads, pens, pencils, tape, elastic bands, and other office supplies to stock an aisle at Staples. And these are not my only ethical lapses. For example, at times I have lost my way as a consultant, becoming more focused on chasing revenue than on providing the value to the client to which I committed. Imperfect as I am, I talk, write, and consult about ethics. What works for me is to be committed to act ethically in my own life, one decision at a time, and to play my part. I believe in a future when ethical decision making at work and elsewhere is so commonplace as to be unremarkable. I hold to this even though I do not expect it to occur in my lifetime. I believe it will come about through my modest efforts, along with those of countless others I will never know.

My Favorite Joke

Growing up in England, I heard about a man who, trying to find his way to London by car, becomes hopelessly lost on some unidentifiable back road about 200 miles from his destination. To his relief he spots someone on the road, pulls up alongside him, explains that he is lost, and asks, "Can you tell me how to get to London?" The other man puts his head down deep in thought, shakes his head slowly, looks up at the driver, and replies, "Well, if I were you I wouldn't start from here."

Whatever the distance we have to travel, and some parts of society, organizations, and individuals may make slower progress along the road than others, we can only start by facing and acknowledging the current reality (although without accepting it as unchangeable) and begin to take action from that point, one conversation and one action at a time. This patient way of building our legacy is beautifully encapsulated in a story told by the novelist Anne Lamott: "Thirty years ago my older brother, who was ten years old at the time, was trying to get a report on birds written that he'd had three months to write. It was due the next day. We were out at our family cabin at Bolinas, and he was at the kitchen table close to tears, surrounded by binder paper and pencils and unopened books on birds, immobilized by the hugeness of the task ahead. Then my father sat down beside him, put his arm around my brother's shoulder and said, 'Bird by bird, buddy. Just take it bird by bird.'"[11]

The Discipline of Mindfulness

In chapter 4, mindfulness was discussed at length as a discipline of an ethical culture and as the private voice of ethical wisdom. It is the self-awareness that brings ethical dilemmas and issues to our thoughts, such as a faint signal or sense of calm or comfort with a decision, a gut reaction, a discomfort, or a nagging doubt, that something could be "off" with a decision. Our ethical wisdom can also alert us when we act inconsistent with our intended personal legacy, our goals, and our cherished values. Michael Neill, a leading life coach in Los Angeles, tells a story about a teacher who posed his favorite student with a particularly difficult and frightening dilemma.[12]

> "Imagine you are dreaming the most incredibly vivid dream of your life," began the teacher. "In the dream, you seem to be some sort of an adventurer, and each adventure brings with it new challenges and creative solutions. You experience many wonderful things, and some not so wonderful.
>
> "You come to realize that in your dream, anything is possible. On one of your adventures, you encounter a very high wall so you imagine yourself a rope and climb to the top. In another, you are falling off a cliff but before you reach the ground you begin to fly. Eventually, you begin to look forward to each new adventure. Until one time, for no apparent reason, everything seems to go wrong.

> "It is dark, so dark that you cannot see your hand before your face. Even before you can hear or see anything, you sense danger. Strange and uncomfortable sounds begin crawling out from the depths of your imagination and coming closer. Cautiously, you strike a match. Everywhere you look, you are surrounded by the most hideous creatures you have ever seen.
>
> "You try to run, but your legs will not move. You try to scream, but no sound will come out. Everything you've learned up to this point seems to abandon you, and the likelihood of a hideous death surrounds you. What would you do?"
>
> The student seemed lost in thought for many moments, and the teacher could see a range of fearful emotions play across her face as she lived the scenario fully in her mind. Suddenly and without warning, the student opened her eyes and began to laugh. "I know what I would do," the student said. "I would wake up."

The above story illustrates essentially what mindfulness is—waking up all the time, that is, waking up to our ethical wisdom; waking up to what nags us as a spur to greater personal integrity; waking up to the possibility that what we have held as the limits of possibility for ourselves, for others, and for the organization may be limits of our own creation; waking up to others we may have written off or pigeonholed long ago for reasons lost over time or reasons kept alive by repetition; waking up to our own hypocrisy when we demand of others a level of honesty and integrity we do not first model. This is all mindfulness.

Recognizing Ethical Wisdom

Ethical wisdom is very different from being "right" or self-righteous. I can be disturbed because I am not getting something I want, but that is different from being disturbed because my ethical wisdom urges me to act in a way consistent with my personal integrity. Ethical wisdom will always draw us toward our personal legacy and our values. Being "right" or self-righteous will have the opposite effect.

This author had his own epiphany (my comeuppance, to be more precise) about being "right" and self-righteous when I was consulting at a hospital in Baltimore. Every effort I made to meet with the vice president of nursing was blocked by her assistant, who not only repelled my efforts, but also did so in a brusque and dismissive manner. I labeled her to my colleagues in unflattering terms. One day I criticized her to someone who worked at the hospital, and she told me that the assistant had changed after the death of her young son in a car accident about six months earlier. In the blink of an eye my feelings for the assistant changed from being upset to being compassionate and mingled with shame for the way I had spoken about her. From that moment on, I related to her with a kind attitude, no matter what her mood. In speaking with her, I offered the very small amount of caring I could. Whereas before I experienced frustration around her, now I experienced an opportunity to live my values. I never did get to meet the vice president of nursing, and it never again upset me that I did not. In this case I did not listen to the quiet voice of mindfulness. More precisely, I was awakened by someone else. That is also of great value.

Mindfulness in Ethical Decision Making

It is important to be mindful of the personal preferences and biases we and others bring to ethical decision making. By increasing our awareness of how we think about and seek resolution of ethical issues, we can manage our own preferences and biases in a conversation. By appreciating the preferences and biases of others involved in an ethical issue, we can listen better and be heard more effectively. And by having everyone involved in conversations be mindful of the different approaches to solving an ethical issue, conversations are more likely to be productive. Chapter 15 provides a diagnostic developed by Brian O'Toole, vice president of mission and ethics at Sisters of Mercy Health System. It is included in this book with his permission. Based on four approaches to ethical decision making, the diagnostic is designed to heighten mindfulness and to create appreciation for our own preferences and those of others in support of effective ethical decision making.

The four approaches are: (1) the principle approach; (2) the consequence approach; (3) the virtue/character approach; and (4) the morals sentiment approach. The principle approach is based on the belief that actions are ethically right or wrong in all places, all situations, at all times. In other words, they are absolutes and part of a morality shared by all. The Golden Rule is a good example. The consequence approach is driven not by absolute principles, but by a focus on the outcome of an ethical decision when decision makers weigh several possible results and arrive at the decision likely to produce the best result. The virtue/character approach resembles the principle approach except that the moral "oughts" here apply to a particular person, role, or group, and not to everyone. This approach examines intentions and motives to assess the ethical character of a person, a role, or a group. The moral sentiment approach bases ethical decisions on feelings. People using this approach need to feel at peace with their decisions; if they do not, then something is wrong. Each of those approaches is discussed more fully along with the diagnostic in chapter 15.

The Discipline of Choice

Mindfulness supports choice because it opens up different ways of thinking about a situation, our organization, others, and ourselves. Choice is the freedom we exercise both in moment-by-moment ethical decisions we make and in larger decisions, such as where we choose to work, the attitude we bring to work, whether we withhold or offer our discretionary effort, and what we choose to say and do to shape our work environment. When we choose behaviors and actions consistent with our values, our personal integrity is enriched. When we make a conscious choice about where we work and the conditions under which we work, although we may experience a dissonance between our values and those of the organization, we are at least at peace because we understand that we are choosing the circumstances in which we work, and we can also choose to leave. On the other hand, when we believe that we have no choice about how we behave at work or in what we are required to do, even if it is unethical or at worse illegal, or that we have no choice about where we work, then we feel trapped in a situation that erodes our personal integrity.

Exercising choice even when there seems to be none is critical to personal integrity. Viktor Frankl, psychiatrist and famous World War II concentration camp survivor, writing about life and death in the most extreme of human circumstances, said, "Everything can be taken from a man but one thing: the last of the human freedoms—to choose one's attitude in any given set of circumstances, to choose one's own way."[13]

Choice in the Moment

Viktor Frankl also wrote that "what matters . . . is not the meaning of life in general but rather the specific meaning of a person's life at a given moment."[14] There are many moments in life when we are challenged to live our values. Sometimes we make decisions that disappoint us; sometimes we make decisions that evoke pride. In his book *The Heart Aroused,* David Whyte tells a story about Joel Henning, a self-employed consultant and a teacher. Joel was a successful consultant to a large company at the vice-president level for some time. He was summoned on short notice to the company CEO's office. He had never met the CEO before and he was excited, thinking he had finally broken into the top level of the client. As it turned out, when Joel met the CEO, he found out quickly that the CEO wanted Joel to persuade a vice president Joel had been coaching to take a position the vice president was so far refusing. Joel suggested it might be better if the CEO spoke to the vice president directly (a sound piece of coaching). To which the CEO replied, "I don't find that remark helpful for my purposes, or for your future with this company."[15] Faced with the choice of standing his ground (being true to his values) and potentially losing a major source of income, or doing the CEO's bidding and surviving the threat, Joel, a good person and a good consultant, folded and agreed to meet with the vice president that very day.

The pressure to make a snap ethical decision can force us away from mindfulness to a more primal reaction driven by fear and threat rather than by personal integrity. Did Joel do the right thing? Well, he protected a stream of income, but at the cost of his integrity. He would later tell the story to his students as a warning about the challenges we all face and sometimes do not succeed in meeting well. To the extent we can buy time in similar circumstances, we can give ourselves an opportunity to reflect on a more mindful course of action. Sometimes we may react in unsatisfactory ways and then reclaim our values after reflection.

In another story, Richard Howells, a consultant and friend, reflects on a pivotal moment in his life regarding his personal integrity: "The first time I was pulled up short I was working on a U.S. Senate campaign in the '60s for a Republican. The campaign manager, an older authority figure, asked me to go to a local college campus to recruit college kids, dress them like hippies, give them some of the Democratic candidate's campaign material, and send them down to a Republican fundraiser to harass and upset the attendees. This would result in strengthening their opposition to the Democratic candidate and possibly produce larger donations for the Republican candidate. I knew it wasn't right, but I was 21 and this was a guy in authority. Before taking action, I talked to my girlfriend and she said, 'You can't do that!' I was embarrassed that I had to be told what I should have known myself. I went back and told the campaign manager that this was something I couldn't do. I remember feeling nervous and apologetic, and my voice was shaking. He was, after all, a powerful figure running a U.S. Senate campaign. He was disappointed and angry but accepted my decision. It was hard to be asked to do that, it was hard to know that I considered doing it, and it was hard to be reminded that it was wrong. But after I spoke up I felt a sense of pride and much more at peace with myself."[16]

There are lessons from these stories. The first is that we are all susceptible at any moment to fall short—to have our personal integrity fly out the window. We may acquiesce to an unethical decision. It may be in a casual conversation when we choose to criticize someone at work because we do not want to deal with the consequences of speaking up on behalf of that person. It may be that we choose to complain about the inaction of others rather than act ourselves to improve a situation. Knowing that we will fall short, it is important that we do not become discouraged or deterred.

The second lesson is that it is never too late to restore our personal integrity by acknowledging our failures, becoming more aware of our susceptibilities, and deciding what we will choose to say and do in a similar situation in the future. This is critical to our own welfare and our legacy. Viktor Frankl said: "Psychological observations of the prisoners have shown that only the men who allowed their inner hold on their moral and spiritual selves to subside eventually fell victim to the [concentration] camp's degenerating influence."[17] It is only by losing all heart when we fail ethically and succumbing to pressures that take us away from our legacy and cherished values that we lose focus on our personal integrity and weaken its guiding influence in our lives.

Choice in the Big Picture

Albert Hirschman, an economist, wrote a book about consumer and citizen choices whose title helps frame this discussion of choice in the big picture: *Exit, Voice, and Loyalty*.[18] To which I would add, "Retiring in Place."

Exit and Retiring in Place

There are two ways we can withdraw from an employer: by moving on or by retiring in place. The responsible way is to move on, to take our talents and contributions elsewhere. It is responsible because we are exercising our power of choice and integrity when we act constructively to seek a match between our values and our work. Sometimes the motivator for leaving is financial benefit. Often it is to find a place where our values and gifts can be better expressed—where we can be happier.

The irresponsible way to exit is to retire in place—to show up every day in body but not in mind or spirit. To withdraw like this, we damage our integrity because behaving in this way is not normally accompanied by satisfaction and a positive attitude, but by dissatisfaction reflected in constant complaints and blame of someone or something in the organization. It is irresponsible because, when we act by withholding our best effort, then justify it by blaming our circumstances, powerlessness, and lack of choice, we make others responsible for our welfare and our choices. It is a disservice to ourselves, to our co-workers, and to those the organization serves.

We do not have to work for any one organization. There are always alternatives. We may be unhappy in our work, but when we judge the alternatives to be less desirable or irresponsible, then we stay in spite of our unhappiness. Choosing to stay in an unsatisfying job situation happens for sensible reasons. Among them is a commitment to a reliable level of income and benefits that provide for our needs and for the needs of those who rely on us, such as members of our family. Or we may have a stake in retirement benefits after long-term employment, which we cannot duplicate through a job change, or which require only a few more years of service to maximize. Or we may be comfortable with the known, however unsatisfactory, believing every employer has its flaws and better the "devil you know." But we can make such choices and still bring our heart and minds to our work. There is too much at stake in health care today for retiring in place to be tolerated. Those who do so need to become aware of the choices they make, take responsibility for them, and change or expect to be told to leave.

Even when we continue to work with a good heart in an unsatisfactory situation, we can forget that we are responsible for whatever choices we make. When that happens we can feel trapped, become victims of circumstance, and lose sight of our personal goals and values. Sometimes this is easer than we think. This danger is encapsulated in a poignant part of a poem written by an AT&T manager:

> Ten years ago . . .
> I turned my face for a moment
> And it became my life.[19]

These few words speak to how easy it is to lose sight of our personal priorities, choices, and goals. The antidote is to keep scanning for and making conscious choices about where we work. The Ethical Choice Alarm Clock process in chapter 14 is designed to sustain awareness about the choices we have made and those we will make in the future.

Voice and Loyalty

Having chosen to stay in an organization that does not fully reflect our values, not retiring in place but choosing to participate in improving the organization in ways consistent with our values, we are now faced with our personal relationship to the discipline of voice, first discussed in chapter 4. For Albert Hirschman, voice "is a far more 'messy' concept [than exit] because it can be graduated, all the way from faint grumbling to violent protest; it implies articulation of one's critical opinions rather than a private, 'secret' vote in . . . anonymity . . . and finally it is direct and straightforward rather than roundabout."[20] Our will to exercise our voice increases with our degree of loyalty [or allegiance] to the organization. And here is the paradox of this dynamic. The freer we are to leave, the freer we are to use our voice fully. For example, you will hear people explain that they are free to speak their minds at work because they have, to use a polite term, "to heck with you" money set aside that frees them from the financial need to keep their current job. As Albert Hirschman put it, "The likelihood of [choosing] voice increases with the degree of loyalty. . . . [W]hile loyalty postpones exit, its very existence is predicated on the possibility of exit. That even the most loyal member can exit is often an important part of his bargaining power vis-à-vis the organization."[21] So if we are to express ourselves fully and to claim our voice, we need to care enough about our organization's improvement and be free enough to choose to stay and act wholeheartedly, even while knowing we could choose to leave. For this to happen, we cannot be victims of circumstance or be driven by our fears and anxieties.

Exit, Voice, and Loyalty at Kaiser: The Story of Tom Jensen

Tom Jensen is a board-certified child, adolescent, and adult psychiatrist. He received the California Medical Association's Profiles in Courage Award in 2000 and a Special Commendation from the American Psychiatric Association in 2001. This is what happened that merited such recognition.

In 1999 Jensen returned from Maine to San Diego with his wife and took a position with the San Diego medical group of Kaiser Permanente. He was immediately asked to participate in a policy that he believed was not only contrary to his training, but was also not legal or ethical. Specifically, as a psychiatrist he was expected to prescribe medications for patients he had not seen or examined, based solely on the recommendation of mental health professionals such as social workers and family therapists, including social worker trainees. He tried to raise the issue according to the internal procedures set out by Kaiser. Kaiser's response was to terminate him for failing to adhere to the policy.[22] Determined to do all he could to change the policy, and even though fired, Tom Jensen brought a lawsuit against Kaiser seeking an injunction to stop the policy. The American Psychiatric Association's president-elect, Daniel Borenstein, condemned the policy, but Kaiser at first defended it.[23] However, in May of 2000, the Southern California Kaiser Permanente medical group declared an end to the policy.[24] Wanting to make sure the policy change would be permanent, Tom Jensen continued his lawsuit, which was settled in August of that year and led to a permanent change in the policy that was negotiated as part of the settlement.[25]

In all this Tom Jensen was experiencing his own crisis. "Some people I knew were no longer speaking to me. I thought I would be black-balled and prevented from practicing due to my violating the unspoken maxim that physicians don't tell on other physicians. I thought I would never be able to practice either for another employer or in a profitable independent practice." In spite of these fears, he persisted. "What kept me going was that I knew this was the right thing. Prior to filing the suit my wife asked me 'why are you doing this?' My answer was 'because I don't want to wake up, turn on the news, and find out that someone who was prescribed the wrong medication shot up a school or did something else awful.' From that point on, I had her total support."[26]

Looking back he takes pride in protecting the interests of Kaiser's patients and is grateful that he continues his work in private practice. As for his feelings towards Kaiser, "I have great respect for the attorneys from the Kaiser Foundation who, I believe, put an end to the practice. I have received many encouraging calls from physicians inside Kaiser, although from outside the psychiatry department, who thanked me for what I did. However, I am still troubled that physicians would choose to follow a policy that is illegal in California and places patients at risk, and then not rise to support a change when someone, me in this case, informed them."[27]

When asked what counsel he would give others in a similar situation of conflict with an unethical policy, he says, "Try to work from within the system by following their policies, but be prepared for the worst if you are fired and carefully consider a strategic plan to change the policy from the outside if it comes to that. Make sure your spouse is supportive of this and that you have a plan for supporting your family during this process."[28]

Looking at these events through the framework of exit, voice, and loyalty, Tom Jensen's first actions were ones of exercising voice and demonstrating loyalty both to Kaiser and to its patients. Once fired, he sustained his voice and his loyalty to patients but abandoned any loyalty to Kaiser just as they had abandoned their loyalty to him. His actions continued to be driven by his loyalty to patients, and he did not still his voice until the issue was settled.

Tom Jensen was faced with many choices in this example in which common practice did not equate to ethical practice: to protest or not, to continue to fight for change or not, to risk his professional life or not, to settle for anything less than a permanent change in policy, to be willing to lose friendships and professional affiliations, and to suffer financially among them. His courage was fueled by a concern both for patients and for his personal integrity. We may or may not be faced with such choices in our own lives, but his experience is something we can all learn from.

In Short

Personal legacy is what we leave for others, when all is said and done, by leading a career of significance consistent with our personal integrity. Mindfulness, staying awake to our ethical wisdom, is a critical discipline to keep both our personal legacy and choices in the forefront of our behaviors and decisions at work. Being conscious to have choice and to the choices we make in the moment and in the big picture are essential if we are to be responsible for expressing our personal integrity in all parts of our life, including work. The following chapter provides a diagnostic to measure the vital signs of the health of your ethical pathway of personal integrity.

Let me conclude this part of the book with the following quote from Bear Heart, a Native American shaman. It sums up this discussion of personal integrity. And let me wish you well on your own journey to strengthen organizational and personal integrity.

> The word *memorial* does not indicate that someone has died. It symbolizes that someone has lived. What is going to be that living memorial that you're going to leave behind? That I am going to leave behind? Why are we here? We are here to add something, to construct, to preserve. To leave something good for the little ones who are going to come into our world. Let that motivation be firmly established in your heart and mind that you can say "I will stand for this. I will live for this."[29]

References

1. [No author cited.] 2003. *Oxford English Reference Dictionary*, 2d rev. ed. Oxford, England: Oxford University Press, p. 817.
2. Odle, S. [Past Chairman, ACHE] 2005. Inaugural Speech at ACHE Congress, March 14.
3. Eklof, T. 2004. Highlights from Arun Gandhi's lecture concerning his grandfather. Cathedral Heritage Foundation, January 25.
4. Salk, J. 1992. Are we being good ancestors? *World Affairs*, December, p. 16.
5. Cerf, C., and Navasky, V. 1984. *The Experts Speak*. New York: Pantheon, p. 31.
6. Nightingale, F. 1860. *Notes on Nursing*. London: Harrison, p. 7.
7. World Health Organization. 2000. Drop in world child mortality reaches target, new study shows, but many countries lagging. Press release, October 12.
8. UNICEF. 2004. *Child Mortality Statistics for 2002*. New York: UNICEF.
9. Quinn, R. 2004. *Building the Bridge As You Walk It*. San Francisco: Jossey-Bass, p. 36.
10. [No author cited.] 2006. Historic overview, Gothic architecture: Notre Dame de Paris. www.elore.com [Earthlore Web site].
11. Lamott, A. 1994. *Bird by Bird*. New York: Anchor Books, p. 18.
12. Neill, M. 2006. MNCT [Michael Neill's daily coaching tip]. www.geniuscatalyst.com. Used with permission.
13. Frankl, V. 1959. *Man's Search for Meaning*. New York: Washington Square Press, p. 86.
14. Frankl, *Man's Search for Meaning*, p. 131.
15. Whyte, D. 1994. *The Heart Aroused*. New York: Doubleday, p. 45.
16. Howells, R. [President, Howells Consulting] 2005. Interview with author, Portland, OR, August 22.
17. Frankl, *Man's Search for Meaning*, p. 90.

18. Hirschman, A. 1970. *Exit, Voice, and Loyalty*. Cambridge, MA: Harvard University Press.
19. Whyte, *The Heart Aroused*, p. 231.
20. Hirschman, *Exit, Voice, and Loyalty*, p. 16.
21. Hirschman, *Exit, Voice, and Loyalty*, p. 82.
22. [No author cited.] 2000. Kaiser's prescribing policy leads to lawsuit, ethics concerns. *Psychiatric News* [www.psych.org], May 5.
23. Kaiser's prescribing policy leads to lawsuit, ethics concerns.
24. [No author cited.] 2000. Controversy leads Kaiser to end prescribing policy. *Psychiatric News* [www.psych.org], May 19.
25. [No author cited.] 2000. San Diego psychiatrist settles lawsuit with Kaiser. *Psychiatric News* [www.psych.org], October 6.
26. Tom Jensen [Psychiatrist in private practice]. 2006. Interview with author, San Diego, June 19.
27. Tom Jensen, interview with author.
28. Tom Jensen, interview with author.
29. Bear Heart. 1996. *The Wind Is My Mother*. New York: Clarkson Potter, p. 259.

14

A Diagnostic for the Ethical Pathway of Personal Integrity

I always wanted to be somebody
but now I see I should have been more specific.
—Lily Tomlin

THIS CHAPTER provides the first of two diagnostics on personal integrity, each of which is useful in a distinct way. The second diagnostic on approaches to ethical decision making can be found in chapter 15. The diagnostic to measure the "vital signs" of personal integrity in this chapter is similar to diagnostics in other parts of the book. It is intended to help you reflect on the health of your personal integrity, which you can share with others.

The following are broad guidelines for conducting the diagnostic:

1. Be sure to introduce the use of the questionnaire by sharing why you think completing and discussing the results will be a valuable use of time. Also share its purpose, which is about gaining understanding and making improvements, and is not about blame and not for performance appraisal.
2. Assure those taking the diagnostic that it is safe to respond if you ask them to share their findings within a group. Different from the previous diagnostics in this book, the personal integrity diagnostic is a very personal questionnaire.
3. If you are conducting the diagnostic across different areas of your organization or with different groups within an area, and you expect individuals to share their results with others in a work group different from their own, make sure that a safe environment is created to support individual development. As mentioned later in this chapter, a trusted facilitator could also be used to manage the discussions and to help build action plans.
4. Use the diagnostic and what you learn from it with caution. You would not make a diagnosis from a patient's vital signs, but you would use them as one input. This diagnostic and others in this book are best used in the same way, provoking questions, not answers, and opening up discussion and thinking, not closing them off.

Appendix 1 presents a comprehensive diagnostic survey to assess the health of all four ethical pathways. This is a better tool to gather a complete

picture of ethical health. Instructions on how to complete an on-line version of this questionnaire can also be found in appendix 1.

The "From-To's" of Personal Integrity

The disciplines of personal integrity exist to some degree in all persons. But unlike the light from an on-off switch, they are not completely present or completely absent. Their condition can be thought to occur somewhere on a continuum. Figure 14-1 shows some of the "from-to's" of the disciplines and gives a sense of what we want to minimize and what we want to instill. You will notice that some of the elements of mindfulness are repeated from the diagnostic on the ethical pathway of culture in chapter 5.

The Personal Integrity Diagnostic

The questions in the following diagnostic are connected to a specific discipline. A short description of the discipline precedes the questions to remind you what discipline is being considered by the questions. Figure 14-2 provides a score sheet to use in producing a score for each discipline and a total score. There are three options for responding to each question:

- *Strongly Agree*—The behavior or point of view is common practice for you. **Score a 5.**
- *Sometimes Agree*—You demonstrate the behavior or point of view, but it is inconsistent, and you cannot count on its happening routinely. **Score a 3.**
- *Strongly Disagree*—The likelihood of the behavior or point of view occurring is much more unusual than usual. **Score a 1.**

Circle the number that applies for each question. Score the diagnostic as you go along.

Personal legacy is what we build for others during and after our lives through our work and our values. It is the highest expression of the goals mentioned in the definition of personal integrity.

1. I am clear about what I want my personal legacy to be.
2. I feel that if I do my part along with others, I am creating a better ethical future for those who follow.
3. I think about the example I will leave for others after I stop working.
4. I know that I am a role model for my co-workers.

Mindfulness is the private voice of ethical wisdom. It is the self-awareness that brings ethical dilemmas and issues to our awareness. It is a faint signal, such as a sense of calm or comfort with a decision, a gut reaction, discomfort, nagging doubt, or a feeling that something could be "off" with a decision or at odds with our goals and cherished values.

Figure 14-1. The "From-To's" of the Disciplines of Personal Integrity

Discipline	From	To
Personal Legacy	What I do doesn't matter in the long run.	What I choose to do and not to do has everything to do with the impact I have.
	My words and actions have little impact on the future of where I work.	I make a difference in everything I say and in every action I take.
	Efforts to build a fully ethical environment at work are bound to fail; it's just the way it is.	As long as we each play our part, we will succeed eventually in building an ethical work environment, or at least pass on an improved situation for those who follow to build on.
	I don't have time to think about a personal legacy.	I am clear about the legacy I want to leave for others and think about it frequently.
Mindfulness	I don't think about the ethics of what I am being asked to do or about decisions that are being made.	I am sensitive to my emotional, mental, or physical reactions that signal to me something may be "off" ethically.
	I assume my superiors are fully aware of the consequences of their decisions.	My reactions to situations are important, and I have a lot to say about what is right and what is wrong.
	There is too much wrong ethically to be able to do much about it.	I acknowledge what we all could do better ethically, and I also take time to encourage myself and others by seeking to do what is right.
Choice	I don't have choices; I pretty much take what life gives me and survive it the best I can.	I always have a choice, even if it is to choose my attitude and actions in difficult life circumstances.
	My life at work is pretty much about avoiding conflict and going with the flow so that I do not get hurt.	I consistently try to act with personal integrity. When I am faced with ethical issues, I am always willing to bring up my concerns.
	Work is what I have to do to provide money for my real life.	Work is an important place to live my values and to grow in my personal integrity.

Figure 14-2. Personal Integrity Diagnostic Score Sheet

	Strongly Agree	Sometimes Agree	Strongly Disagree	Discipline Total	÷ Number of Questions	= Average Score
Personal Legacy						
Question 1	5	3	1			
Question 2	5	3	1			
Question 3	5	3	1			
Question 4	5	3	1			
Score					4	
Mindfulness						
Question 5	5	3	1			
Question 6	5	3	1			
Question 7	5	3	1			
Question 8	5	3	1			
Score					4	
Choice						
Question 9	5	3	1			
Question 10	5	3	1			
Question 11	5	3	1			
Question 12	5	3	1			
Score					4	
		Total Score			12	

5. I think about whether I am expressing my personal values at work.
6. I reflect on ethical decisions to be sure they are consistent with my personal values.
7. I trust my instincts when a decision may be at odds with my personal values.
8. I am conscious of when my actions are driven by fear and when they are driven by ethical wisdom.

Choice is the freedom we exercise both in moment-by-moment decisions and in larger decisions about where we choose to work, the attitude we bring to work, whether we withhold or offer our discretionary effort, and what we choose to say and do that shapes our work environment.

9. I have the freedom to stand up for my personal values at work.
10. I choose to speak up about ethical concerns I have at work.
11. I know I have choices about where I work.
12. I regularly evaluate whether I am working in the best place for me.

Scoring the Diagnostic

The following are steps to score the diagnostic to produce an average score for the questions for each discipline and an average score for all 12 questions. Figure 14-3 shows an example of a completed score sheet.

1. Go down the columns vertically and add the scores for each set of questions for a discipline.
2. Add the scores for each discipline across to produce a discipline total.
3. Divide the discipline total for each discipline by 4 (the number of questions) to find the average score for each discipline.
4. Total all the discipline totals vertically to produce the total score.
5. Divide the total score by 12 (the total number of questions) to find the average score for all of the disciplines combined.

Interpreting the Diagnostic

You can decide your own approach in interpreting the survey results, but consider the following questions in your interpretation.

Questions and Approaches to Interpretation

1. What is the total score average?
   Obviously, if the average score for a discipline is 3 or below, it is a red flag. "Sometimes" may be an acceptable average for some surveys; but in the case of a personal integrity, any lack of consistency in living our values is an invitation to ethical erosion. You may well see scores of 5 for individual questions; however, an average score of 5 is both an opportunity to acknowledge yourself and also to explore whether this perfect personal integrity holds up under scrutiny.

Figure 14-3. Example of a Completed Personal Integrity Diagnostic Score Sheet

	Strongly Agree	Sometimes Agree	Strongly Disagree	Discipline Total	÷ Number of Questions	= Average Score
Personal Legacy						
Question 1	(5)	3	1			
Question 2	5	(3)	1			
Question 3	5	(3)	1			
Question 4	(5)	3	1			
Score	*10*	*6*		*16*	4	*4.0*
Mindfulness						
Question 5	5	(3)	1			
Question 6	5	(3)	1			
Question 7	5	(3)	1			
Question 8	5	(3)	1			
Score		*12*		*12*	4	*3.0*
Choice						
Question 9	5	3	(1)			
Question 10	5	(3)	1			
Question 11	5	(3)	1			
Question 12	5	3	(1)			
Score		*6*	*2*	*8*	4	*2.0*
		Total Score		*36*	12	*3.0*

2. On what one discipline would you focus for discussion and change? You can select a discipline on which to focus in at least three ways:
   - It can be the discipline with the lowest average score.
   - It can be the disciple with the most 1 scores.
   - It can be the discipline that you decide will produce the best opportunity for change (this may or may not be the lowest scoring discipline).

   Whatever discipline you choose to focus on, do not be surprised if discussion about it leads to discussion about one or more other disciplines. This is because the disciplines are related to each other.
3. To enrich a conversation about these results, you can choose the discipline with the best score and compare it to a weak-performing discipline. This comparison provides an opportunity to not only ask what is not working about a weak-performing discipline, but also to ask what you can learn from what you are doing well with a high-performing discipline.
4. Remember that this is a high-level diagnostic and, as such, should not be used to provide answers but to provoke focused questions and open discussion. Although the diagnostic is a personal reflection, exploring its implications is best done in conversation with others, especially those you trust and who are willing to challenge you in a spirit of support and encouragement.

Thoughts for Each Discipline

Each discipline has its own characteristics. Ways to explore the implications of responses to the questions within each of the disciplines follow.

Personal Legacy

Question 1 focuses on the clarity of your personal legacy—whether you can articulate it for yourself and for others. Whatever your score, consider the following question as a way to clarify your personal legacy further. What "gifts" to others make me the most joyful at having given? You might choose to answer this for different areas of your life, that is, family, friends, community, work, and society.

Question 2 probes your patience and belief that modest individual actions will lead to the ethical environment you seek. If you score low for this question, experiment at work with the point of view that doing your part is enough and see what changes occur in your own attitude and in what you see around you. You may experience more peace of mind and a greater sense of collaboration in building an ethical future.

Questions 3 and 4 are about modeling. If you score low, observe and listen at work for how even casual comments and taken-for-granted behaviors shape the future as well as the present, and reflect on whether you have a bigger impact than you have imagined.

Mindfulness

All four questions probe self-awareness about your values and the degree of consistency between those values and the values you live at work.

Questions 5 and 6 probe mindfulness with a more cerebral approach. You may choose to list your values (this is especially valuable if you are unclear when articulating them) and then, for each value, assess the degree to which you express that value at work and, if not, what gets in your way. Examples will help. You will learn about what you can change in your own behaviors and how to live your values more fully.

Questions 7 and 8 probe mindfulness with a more visceral approach, assessing the degree to which you are sensitive to what drives your reactions. Is it a fearful, self-protective reaction? Or is it an expression of your ethical wisdom? It is best to use specific examples to reflect on where you believe you succeeded or fell short. You can ask three questions if you fell short: Have I been more committed to being "right" than building a solution? What can I do now to impact the situation? What will I do differently when a similar situation occurs, so I better leverage my ethical wisdom? In looking at examples of when you were successful in expressing your ethical wisdom, you can ask: What steps can I take to further strengthen my access to ethical wisdom in future discussions and decisions? What steps can I take to strengthen the ability of others to leverage their ethical wisdom?

Choice

Questions 9 and 10 focus on choice in the moment. Scoring low on either or both of those questions invites the following questions: To what degree are my choices about living my values at work driven by the circumstances that I face or by the personal choices I make? Am I willing to challenge my assumptions about my lack of freedom to make choices in expressing my values where I work? If yes, what specific assumptions am I willing to challenge and how will I do it? If no, what choices still remain for me?

Questions 11 and 12 focus on choice in the big picture. Scoring low on either or both invites the following questions: Have I given up on making my own decisions about where I work? What have I decided about my ability to choose where I work? Am I willing to challenge my assumptions about my lack of freedom to make choices about where I work? If yes, what specific assumptions am I willing to challenge, and how will I do it? If no, what choices still remain for me?

Whether you are living your values at work or not, consider using the "Ethical Choice Alarm Clock" that follows.

The Ethical Choice Alarm Clock

What does it take to stay awake to our choices? Sometimes we get jolted by a change in circumstance—whether welcome or unwelcome. We may get a job offer out of the blue that gives us an opportunity to exit our current situation when we were not even thinking about choices. Sometimes an exit may be forced on us when we are laid off and have no alternative but to engage with new choices. It may be an epiphany of some sort that wakes us up. However, waiting for circumstances to change or for a sudden realization takes our fate and our choice out of our hands. The Ethical Choice Alarm

Clock is a proactive approach to affirm or change our current choices. Here is how it works:

1. Set your alarm clock. Mark on your calendar when you will next take stock of your work situation. The time frame you select (three months, six months, or a year) will depend on how frequently you want to reassess your situation.
2. Take stock of your situation when the alarm goes off. Ask yourself the following questions: What is my experience of work? Do I dread going to work or look forward to it? Is there an unbridgeable gap between what I value and what the organization values? Do I need more and more private time to recover my energy after work, or am I tired but mostly satisfied after working? Do I take my frustrations at work out on my family or others, or does my experience of work enhance my relationships and life outside of work? If I were looking for a job, is this the one I would choose as a place to fulfill my needs, including my need to express my values in my work?
3. Reflect. Examine these questions closely and take your time. Talk to people who know you well and who care for your welfare. They will have insights and perspectives to help you get a complete picture. And take time to be still and listen to your own wisdom to guide you.
4. Make your choice. Take the sum of what you notice, hear, and feel, and then choose. You may choose to exit, in which case it is time to put a set of actions in place, together with a time line. Although you are not happy, you may choose to stay, either for what you see as lack of immediate choice or because you hope you can make a positive difference in the values of the organization. If you are unhappy and feel you lack choice, then at least commit to not spreading your unhappiness at work. If you are hopeful, decide specific ways to impact the current situation before your alarm clock goes off again. If you choose to stay and are happy, decide specific ways in which you will exercise your voice even more fully at work.
5. Reset your alarm clock and relax. Set a date when you will next take stock. Make it a shorter time if you feel you are in a fluid situation, and longer if you are in a stable situation (but no more than a year). Then relax knowing you have made your choice and, by doing so, claimed your personal power—a power you can only lose by forgetting that you are a chooser, not a victim, of your situation.

Approaches to Action

The following steps will help you in gaining value from the results of this diagnostic:

1. Block out a quiet time away from work to write down your responses to the questions you choose to explore.

2. Share your responses, thoughts, and feelings with others you respect and know have your best interests at heart. Seek their input in answering some of the questions posed in the diagnostic and its interpretation. Do not choose to share with others who merely commiserate with you in a complaint session. Only choose those who are willing to challenge your assumptions and beliefs, especially about your strengths and limitations.
3. Decide that you are willing to be coached. For example, I was in a conversation with my coach, and about 20 minutes into the conversation—after I had responded to her observation with "I know that"—she told me that I often said that and that it gave her no room to make a difference with me. She woke me up, and I listened to her more intently and generously. You get the idea.
4. Appreciate what is and is not working well in your own ethical behaviors and actions, and respect yourself. You would not be reading these words if you did not care about living a life of personal integrity.

15

The Approaches to Ethical Decision Making Diagnostic

I have often thought that the best way to define a man's character would be to seek out the particular mental or moral attitude in which, when it came to him, he felt himself most deeply and intensely active and alive. At such moments, there is a voice inside which speaks and says, "This is the real me."

—William James

THIS CHAPTER provides the second of the two personal integrity diagnostics. This diagnostic was developed by Brian O'Toole, vice president of mission and ethics at Sisters of Mercy Health System, and is included in this book with his permission. The diagnostic is designed with the following four benefits in mind: (1) to increase your own awareness of how you think about and seek resolution of ethical issues; (2) to increase the shared awareness among members of a decision-making team or work group to increase communication and the group's effectiveness in decision making, (3) to enable you to work and communicate more effectively with anyone with whom you are engaged in discussing ethical issues; and (4) to appreciate that different views on how to solve an ethical issue may be more a function of difference in approach rather than difference in the commitment to resolve the issue.

Use this diagnostic and what you learn from it with caution. This diagnostic and others in this book are best used in the same way, provoking questions, not answers, and opening up discussion and thinking, not closing them off.

The Four Approaches to Ethical Decision Making

There are four distinctly different ways in which people make ethical decisions. Almost everyone uses all four of these ways. We utilize different approaches in different roles, in different situations, and in different times in our life. But we normally do so without an awareness that we are choosing from a number of options available to us. Some people use one way predominantly. Others vary their approach according to a variety of factors. Regardless, we often hold to our approach unmindfully, unimpressed by arguments we hear about other approaches and often trapped in a frustrating, inconclusive, and win-lose conversation.

The four ways to make ethical decisions are: (1) the principle approach; (2) the consequence approach; (3) the virtue/character approach; and (4) the moral sentiment approach. Each of these approaches are based on well-established ethical theory; but for our purposes, it is important to recognize that ethical theory actually explains and elaborates on how people make decisions naturally. People utilize these approaches even if they have never learned any of the ethical theories. Each approach has its upside and downside.

The Principle Approach

The principle approach is based on the belief that there are actions that are ethically right or wrong in all places, all situations, and at all times. In other words, they are absolutes and part of a morality shared by all. The Golden Rule is a good example. You do unto others as you would have them do unto you, not just when it is convenient or easy. You follow the Golden Rule all the time because it is a universal principle. People who speak from a belief in the principle approach often use words such as *must*, *ought*, *duty*, *obligation*, *always*, and *never*.

The upside of this approach is that thinking and decisions rest on a firm and immutable set of values and ethical solutions that apply to everyone without exception. The downside is that principles may not be universally agreed upon; and because these principles are seen as absolutes, it is difficult to reconcile them in decision making. One pharmacist may make a personally principled decision to fill a prescription for a "day-after" abortion pill. Another may refuse to do so based on a different principle.

The Consequence Approach

The consequence approach is driven not by absolute principles, but by a focus on the outcome of an ethical decision when decision makers weigh several possible results and arrive at the decision likely to produce the best result. People who use this approach often ask questions such as, "What's the bottom line?" "What effect will this have?" "What good will this bring about?" and "Will this help in the long run?"

The upside of this approach is that a concern for outcomes is an important factor in making ethical decisions, and the approach respects that concern. The downside is that it may lead to a calculating approach that pays insufficient attention to the principles involved and may be susceptible to what outcomes are decided to be important. A physician whose business is important to the welfare of the organization, but who receives a "slap on the wrist" for behavior for which other less influential physicians have had privileges suspended, is the subject of an action driven by a financial outcome, not by an outcome concerned with employee morale.

The Virtue/Character Approach

The virtue/character approach resembles the principle approach except that the "moral oughts" apply to a particular person, role, or group, and not to everyone. This approach examines intentions and motives to assess the ethical character of a person, a role, or a group. People using the virtue/character approach often use the words *good* or *bad*, rather than *right* or *wrong*. They say: "She's a good friend," "He's a good leader," or "They walk the talk." On the other hand they say, "He's a bad leader." Judgments made in this approach do not address the morality or the consequences of an action. They address the character of the person performing the act. Their own personal integrity is very important to people who use the virtue/character approach.

The upside of this approach is that it encourages a focus on our own moral character and personal responsibility as well as that of others. It also gives others a clear understanding of who you are and what you stand for, and invites them to do the same. The downside of this approach is that, taken to excess, the sense of personal responsibility may result in an individual's taking too much responsibility on their own shoulders, thereby easing the need for others to exercise their personal responsibility in decisions and actions to resolve an ethical issue. In addition, prejudging others as "good" or 'bad" characters will shape the point of view we take and hinder new ways of thinking about an ethical issue.

The Moral Sentiment Approach

The moral sentiment approach bases ethical decisions on feelings. People using this approach need to feel at peace with their decision; if they do not, then something is wrong. People who use the moral sentiment approach say, for example, "I don't feel good about this," "This feels good to me," "This just does not seem right," "Is everyone comfortable with this?" and "Can everybody live with this?" For a person using this approach, the strength of his or her concern is measured by the strength of his or her feelings. As discussed in chapter 4, those who respond from feelings are often at a disadvantage when asked to explain or defend their position by colleagues who use the principle or consequence approach and who will ask for objective reasons to support a feeling. The person using the moral sentiment approach may try to convince others by using stories that evoke similar feelings in listeners.

The upside of this approach is that it taps into ethical wisdom and encourages acknowledgment of faint signals when a decision may feel "off," regardless of whether the feelings experienced are slight or strong. The downside of this approach is that, while it is extremely valuable for getting an issue on the table, it needs to be complemented by other approaches that blend feeling and thinking on the issue.

Scoring the Diagnostic

The diagnostic in this chapter is composed of 15 scenarios. Each scenario has four possible responses. Select the response most natural to you. You may be attracted to more than one response; nevertheless, choose only one. There is no right answer. The key to your answers can be found in appendix 2. The key will tell you which approach you selected for each scenario. Use the score sheet (figure 15-1) to write your chosen response for each scenario (a, b, c, or d). After doing this for all 15 scenarios, go to appendix 2 to see what approach (principle, consequence, moral sentiment, or virtue/character) you selected and then circle it on the score sheet. You will quickly see that most of us use more than one decision approach, but it is also true that each of us has a preferred approach or approaches.

Figure 15-1. A Diagnostic Score Sheet for Four Approaches to Ethical Decision Making

	Your Response (a, b, c, or d)	**Consequence (C)**	**Moral Sentiment (MS)**	**Principle (P)**	**Virtue/ Character (V/C)**
Scenario 1		C	MS	P	V/C
Scenario 2		C	MS	P	V/C
Scenario 3		C	MS	P	V/C
Scenario 4		C	MS	P	V/C
Scenario 5		C	MS	P	V/C
Scenario 6		C	MS	P	V/C
Scenario 7		C	MS	P	V/C
Scenario 8		C	MS	P	V/C
Scenario 9		C	MS	P	V/C
Scenario 10		C	MS	P	V/C
Scenario 11		C	MS	P	V/C
Scenario 12		C	MS	P	V/C
Scenario 13		C	MS	P	V/C
Scenario 14		C	MS	P	V/C
Scenario 15		C	MS	P	V/C
	Total Times Selected				

The Ethical Decision Making Diagnostic

There are no right answers to the following questions or scenarios. Answer each item with the response that seems most natural to you and to your way of making ethical decisions.

1. A violent storm devastates a nearby area in your state, leaving many injured and homeless. Places of worship and local charities want to take up a special collection to address the needs of those victims. You generously donate $50 because:
   a. You feel sorry for the tragic victims of the storm, are moved to help, and personally feel better giving a generous donation.
   b. You figure that if everyone donates a reasonable amount, then such contributions won't hurt as much if spread among many individuals, and, overall, there will be a great benefit to the storm victims.
   c. You believe that as you were spared from the storm, you have an obligation to share your resources with the less fortunate.
   d. It would seem selfish and insensitive of you not to make some donation.

2. What, for you, is the most convincing argument why our country should not allow capital punishment?
   a. Capital punishment has not been shown to be a deterrent to crime and may in fact contribute to violence in society.
   b. Capital punishment is a barbaric and abhorrent practice and unfairly affects poor minorities.
   c. Life is sacred and no one has the right to take another life.
   d. Capital punishment dehumanizes us as a society, and it is practiced out of a spirit of revenge, which is a demeaning human quality.

3. A close friend of yours confides that he is having an adulterous affair. You disapprove of this because:
   a. Cheating on one's spouse is sneaky, dishonest, and a betrayal of trust. These are not qualities you want to see in your friend.
   b. It is wrong to be unfaithful in marriage. Adultery is a violation of marriage vows.
   c. You want the marriage to work, and it saddens you to think that the marriage of your close friends, which you valued and took for granted, has now deteriorated to this.
   d. You fear that in the end, your friend, his spouse, and their children will be severely hurt by this experience, and you see no good coming out of it.

4. You are a member of your hospital's ethics committee. A case is presented regarding an elderly patient with end-stage cancer that has metastasized into the bones. The patient is now in your ICU in

multiple organ failure and is ventilator-dependent. He lacks decision-making capacity and has no advance directives. His prognosis is poor and he is expected to die. His elderly wife insists, however, that "everything be done" to keep him alive. The attending physician wishes to try to wean the patient off the ventilator and "let nature take its course." You believe the ethics committee should support the physician's decision because:

a. The patient is dying. Cardiopulmonary arrest is inevitable, and efforts to resuscitate him in this condition will, in all likelihood, fail.
b. Families do not have a right to hold doctors and hospitals hostage by demanding medically futile treatments.
c. Conducting CPR would anguish caregivers if they break this man's bones in a useless attempt to revive him, which, at best, will only prolong his dying.
d. Physicians and caregivers should not be forced to violate their professional obligation to provide medical treatments that, in their judgment, will cause significant harm to a patient with little likelihood of any corresponding benefit.

5. You make a New Year's resolution to be less critical and more supportive of your spouse, children, or friends because:
   a. It's the right thing to do. All people should make a resolution at the start of a new year to improve themselves and to be better in their relationships.
   b. You don't feel good about how you've been acting lately, and you feel a need to rejuvenate your relationships.
   c. You've been disappointed in yourself in how you've been acting lately, and you want to become a better spouse/parent/person or friend.
   d. There has been a lot of bickering and misunderstanding lately, and your New Year's resolution, it is hoped, will help everyone get along better, which will lead to a more pleasant home environment or a better overall outlook on life.

6. You believe the management style of your administrative team has been too hierarchical. You would like to improve dialogue and team decision making. You argue for this with your CEO by saying:
   a. Better dialogue and team decision making are essential ways to show respect for and promote dignity and self-respect.
   b. We feel frustrated by our inability to impact key decisions. Low morale is indicative of a problem here.
   c. Pooling of ideas can lead to better results and better decision making.
   d. Part of being a good leader is to be able to dialogue with one another and to make decisions by consensus.

7. You are promoting budgeting for a special multidisciplinary approach to the needs of the dying and their families in your institution. Even though all the costs of providing this service will not be reimbursed, you nonetheless argue for this approach, saying:
   a. This is a good way to make sure that our caregivers do not over-treat or undertreat the terminally ill, which is a chronic problem in our American health care system.
   b. If these needs are not addressed, it contributes to interest in assisted suicide, which is morally wrong.
   c. Part of our professional responsibility as caregivers is to address the special needs of the terminally ill in our community.
   d. We often feel helpless in dealing with the dying and their loved ones; this service will provide us with an excellent way to respond compassionately to those most deserving of our care.

8. Your elderly mother suffers a massive stroke and is now largely unresponsive, with a poor prognosis for improvement. Years ago she gave you her power of attorney with only one directive: "I trust you to do whatever is best for me." Her physician asks you about the insertion of a feeding tube into her stomach. You are reluctant to do so because:
   a. You don't think living in your mother's condition is good. As her son or daughter, you'd be letting your mother down if you didn't live up to your promise to do what you thought was best for her.
   b. It tears you up inside to see your mother like this. You can't believe she'd want to have her life prolonged under these conditions.
   c. You don't see any good reason to provide anyone, but especially your mother, a treatment that would keep only the body alive, but not the mind.
   d. You can see how a feeding tube would be necessary to keep your mother alive; but if she ends up in a nursing home, bed-bound, and "out of it," then it seems this is only going to prolong her suffering as well as your own grief.

9. A seriously ill patient in your hospital dies suddenly. Although his death is not entirely unexpected, it is quickly learned that a medical error contributed directly to the patient's death. When someone suggests altering the medical record to conceal the error, you argue against this, saying:
   a. It is unlikely that you can keep this error a secret, and when the truth comes out, the penalty will be even greater for trying to conceal the error.
   b. It is wrong to alter a medical record.
   c. Not only "a" and "b," but more important, you'll be setting a bad example and teaching your staff that it's acceptable to lie.
   d. Not only "a" and "b," but you would feel dishonest and sneaky trying to be deceptive.

10. You were "let go" from your former health care position and given a relatively meager severance packet. You harbor some ill feelings about this. At your new health care position you are occasionally given the opportunity, and are often tempted, to "bad mouth" the corporate leadership of your former health care employer. Normally, you refrain from this, however, because:
    a. You know you wouldn't feel right publicly expressing your negative feelings merely to keep "grinding the axe" against your former employer.
    b. You may create a negative impression about yourself at your new position.
    c. You've never been the kind of person to "bad mouth" others.
    d. In today's health care environment, it is not wise to "burn your bridges."

11. A member of your management team uses profanity at meetings. In private, you ask him to stop because:
    a. Personally, you find this offensive and very inappropriate.
    b. You are concerned that the use of profanity detracts from the effectiveness of the member's contributing remarks.
    c. The use of profanity casts his character in a bad light, especially in a meeting with fellow health care professionals.
    d. It is wrong to use profanity, and its use is demeaning to everyone in the room.

12. A downsizing at your institution is planned. You argue that all those affected, even lower-level employees, should be offered benefits and training or outplacement help. The costs of your proposal greatly concern your CEO. You still argue for your position, however, saying:
    a. We should consider the Golden Rule—we would all want to be treated this way if we were to be laid off.
    b. This approach is consistent with the mission and values of our health care organization.
    c. This approach would minimize the negative effect, not only on those laid off, but also on the survivors, and on the future of the organization.
    d. A layoff is devastating, and we owe it to employees as human beings to try to minimize the suffering this layoff will cause them.

13. Your widowed mother passes away. Your siblings begin to disagree over how to claim mementos from her house. You propose that everyone take turns selecting one item, because:
    a. We're a family. Mom wouldn't want her children fighting over her possessions.

b. It is fair; it is the most just and equitable way of dispensing mementos.
c. This will minimize bickering and ensure that everyone has some special remembrances.
d. This is hard enough to do as it is—why make it harder? When we are all dealing with our own grief, we should at least be considerate of one another.

14. You hold a position of influence in your physician-hospital organization (PHO), and are involved in contract negotiations. Your PHO is competing with a health care facility in another city for a particular managed care contract. You are contacted by a discontented, high-level employee from the other health care facility and offered critical information—for a price—which would allow your PHO to be successful in obtaining the contract. Although you are sorely tempted to meet with this person to acquire this information, in the end you decide against doing so because:
    a. This would be wrong; it would violate the business rules of fair play and forthright negotiations.
    b. You would feel dishonest doing this, and would be greatly offended if your competitor engaged in this practice.
    c. You are not the kind of person to make deals "under the table," and you refuse to compromise your own values and integrity.
    d. There is always the possibility that your action would be discovered, which could not only potentially ruin the deal, but would also cause you embarrassment and quite likely limit your effectiveness in any future business negotiations.

15. Your hospital completes a merger with another smaller hospital. Your board encourages the CEO to supplant their top management quickly with your own leadership team to absorb the smaller hospital into your own mission, philosophy, values, and culture. However, you are uncomfortable with this approach, and instead argue that your hospital should work with the smaller hospital's leadership and preserve much of their own management style and culture, while trying to ease them into the way your system works, because:
    a. You have already sensed the anxiety and uncertainty gripping the management and employees at the smaller hospital resulting from the merger, and it wouldn't seem right to increase their insecurity and concern by quickly and drastically changing what is familiar to them.
    b. It would be wrong to eliminate competent leadership and disrespectful to the smaller hospital's ingrained culture.
    c. Following your board's advice may create "bad blood" between the two hospitals and delay working together effectively.

d. You wouldn't like yourself very much or feel very proud of your hospital if you agree to "boxing" the top management and "running roughshod" over a culture that had been in place for so long at the smaller hospital.

Go to appendix 2 to find out what approach you chose for each scenario.

Using the Results

The following are important points to remember. First, all four approaches to ethical decision making are valid, and each is supported by extensive literature in ethics. Second, almost every one of us uses all four ways of ethical decision making. We utilize different approaches in different roles and at different times in our life. Some of us use one way predominantly, a second way less often, and so forth. Others vary their approach to ethical decision making depending on a variety of factors. Again, this occurs naturally or subconsciously, and normally, it is not deliberate or with specific intent.

For Yourself

The diagnostic in this chapter is a tool to promote mindfulness. Use the insights you gain to recognize how you approach ethical decisions and, just as important, the approach or approaches that you use the least. When you are not mindful of these varied approaches, you will tend to respond in discussion to those who reflect your way of thinking and to discount those who express an approach you do not prefer.

When you present your opinion on an ethical issue, consider supporting your point of view with three arguments: a principled argument, a consequence argument, and a virtue/character argument. (It may be difficult to articulate a moral sentiment argument.) In this way, you are responding to different approaches that may be shared by your audience.

For a Team

Take time to build shared mindfulness about the different approaches that are preferred by individuals within the team to build awareness and respect for those different approaches.

One source of potentially irresolvable moral conflict occurs when two parties argue or negotiate their positions from different approaches. Agreement or consensus often may occur only when discussion is shaped by the same approach. In working to resolve a particular issue, you may choose to discuss it from different points of view, but not at the same time. For example, the entire team may agree to discuss the issue using a principle approach and then use other approaches in succession. Or the team may agree to choose an approach that is best suited to resolve the issue.

Appendixes

Appendix 1

The Ethical Health Vital Signs Diagnostic

To take the on-line version of this diagnostic, please go to www.newpageconsulting.com or contact Jack Gilbert at jack@newpageconsulting.com.

The "Ethical Health Vital Signs Diagnostic" brings together all of the diagnostics for individual ethical pathways first presented in chapters 5 (culture), 8 and 10 (leadership and governance), 12 (infrastructure), and 14 (personal integrity). This diagnostic provides a complete overview of the ethical health of the organization. For more assistance in analyzing the diagnostic and courses of action, turn to the appropriate chapter from the above list for the pathway in question.

The following are broad guidelines you should follow in conducting the diagnostic:

1. Be sure to introduce the use of the questionnaire by sharing why you think completing and discussing the results will be a valuable use of time. Also share its purpose, which is about gaining understanding and making improvements, and is not about blame.
2. Assure those taking the diagnostic that it is safe to respond. Generally, the smaller the group completing the diagnostic, the more difficult it is to maintain anonymity, and the more important it is that those taking the diagnostic trust your good intent. If different departments or teams are being assessed, be clear how confidentiality will be maintained and how differences between areas will be managed. Be sure the diagnostic will not be used to place blame on a comparatively low scoring area but to expose opportunities for improvement.
3. If you are conducting the diagnostic across different areas of your organization or with different groups within an area, consider using a trusted facilitator to administer, tally, and present the findings. The facilitator could also be used to manage the discussions and to help build action plans.
4. Use the diagnostic and what you learn from it with caution. You would not make a diagnosis from a patient's vital signs, but you would use them as one input. This diagnostic is best used in the same way,

provoking questions, not answers, and opening up discussion and thinking, not closing them off.

Scoring the Diagnostic

The questions in this diagnostic are connected to individual ethical pathways and the disciplines within each pathway. A short description of the discipline precedes the questions to inform you what discipline is being considered by the questions. Figures A-2 (culture), A-3 (leadership), A-4 (governance), A-5 (infrastructure), and A-6 (personal integrity) are score sheets for producing scores for each pathway. There are three options for responding to each question:

- *Strongly Agree*—The behavior or point of view being asked about is pervasive, common practice. **Score a 5.**
- *Sometimes Agree*—You see the behavior or point of view, but it is inconsistent, and you cannot count on its happening routinely. **Score a 3.**
- *Strongly Disagree*—The likelihood of the behavior or point of view occurring is more unusual than usual. **Score a 1.**

Circle the number that applies for each question.

The following are steps to score the diagnostic to produce an average score for the questions for each discipline. You will repeat these steps for every ethical pathway diagnostic. Figure A-1 shows an example of a completed score sheet.

1. Go down the columns vertically and add the scores for each set of questions for a discipline.
2. Add the scores for each discipline across to produce a discipline total.
3. Divide the discipline total for each discipline by the number of questions to find the average score for each discipline.
4. Total all the discipline totals vertically to produce the total score.
5. Divide the total score by the total number of questions to find the average score for all of the disciplines combined.

The Ethical Health Vital Signs Diagnostic

The diagnostic is segmented into the four pathways (the diagnostic for the pathway of leadership and for governance is in two parts), each of which can be scored separately. Suggestions for interpreting the diagnostic can be found after you have completed the entire diagnostic.

The Ethical Pathway of Culture Diagnostic

The ethical pathway of culture diagnostic follows. Score the diagnostic as you go along.

Mindfulness is the private voice of ethical wisdom. It is the self-awareness that brings ethical dilemmas and issues to top of mind. It is an early signal, such as a sense of calm or comfort with a decision, a gut reaction, discomfort, nagging doubt, or a feeling that something could be "off" with a decision.

Figure A-1. Example of a Completed Diagnostic Score Sheet

	Strongly Agree	Sometimes Agree	Strongly Disagree	Discipline Total	÷ Number of Questions	= Average Score
Mindfulness						
Question 1	(5)	3	1			
Question 2	5	(3)	1			
Question 3	5	(3)	1			
Question 4	(5)	3	1			
Score	10	6		16	4	4.0
Voice						
Question 5	5	(3)	1			
Question 6	5	(3)	1			
Question 7	5	(3)	1			
Question 8	5	(3)	1			
Score		12		12	4	3.0
Respect						
Question 9	5	3	(1)			
Question 10	5	(3)	1			
Question 11	5	(3)	1			
Question 12	5	3	(1)			
Score		6	2	8	4	2.0
Tenacity						
Question 13	(5)	3	1			
Question 14	(5)	3	1			
Question 15	5	(3)	1			
Question 16	5	(3)	1			
Score	10	6		16	4	4.0
Legacy						
Question 17	(5)	3	1			
Question 18	5	(3)	1			
Question 19	5	(3)	1			
Question 20	5	(3)	1			
Score	5	9		14	4	3.5
		Total Score		66	20	3.3

Figure A-2. Ethical Pathway of Culture Diagnostic Score Sheet

	Strongly Agree	Sometimes Agree	Strongly Disagree	Discipline Total	÷ Number of Questions	= Average Score
Mindfulness						
Question 1	5	3	1			
Question 2	5	3	1			
Question 3	5	3	1			
Question 4	5	3	1			
Score					4	
Voice						
Question 5	5	3	1			
Question 6	5	3	1			
Question 7	5	3	1			
Question 8	5	3	1			
Score					4	
Respect						
Question 9	5	3	1			
Question 10	5	3	1			
Question 11	5	3	1			
Question 12	5	3	1			
Score					4	
Tenacity						
Question 13	5	3	1			
Question 14	5	3	1			
Question 15	5	3	1			
Question 16	5	3	1			
Score					4	
Legacy						
Question 17	5	3	1			
Question 18	5	3	1			
Question 19	5	3	1			
Question 20	5	3	1			
Score					4	
		Total Score			20	

1. Leadership* is passionate about employees living the organization's values every day.
2. Where I work we take the time to talk about our ethics and values when making decisions.
3. I take the time to reflect on whether the decisions we make on a daily basis are consistent with the vision, mission, and values of the organization.
4. I think about whether or not my core values are consistent with the organization's values.

Voice is the public voice of ethical wisdom. It brings mindfulness into open conversation and enables ethical issues to be revealed and explored in a constructive spirit in many forums, such as meetings, informal conversations, employee surveys, or other forms of communication. Voice is shared mindfulness that leverages collective ethical wisdom.

5. Our organization is a safe place to express differing points of view about the ethics of a decision.
6. It is safe to speak up about an ethical concern without having a full set of facts.
7. I speak up when I think the organization's values are being ignored or discounted.
8. The organization encourages employees to express their opinions when they have something to say about our ethics.

Respect is listening to others with generosity rather than suspicion and with a commitment to understand and value different views. Respect strengthens the ability to work on ethical issues as colleagues, not critics, irrespective of differences.

9. I can speak freely and directly about my ethical concerns with my boss.
10. I can speak freely and directly about my ethical concerns with my peers.
11. I can speak freely and directly about my ethical concerns with other departments or disciplines.
12. The organization values different points of view among its employees.

Tenacity is being unstoppable in the quest for ethical behavior and ethical decision making. It is the shared commitment to see difficult

---

*Whom *leadership* refers to will vary depending on the scope of the diagnostic. For example, if it is for the organization, then leadership will refer to the executive team. If it is for a work team, then leadership will refer to the team leader.

conversations through to their resolution no matter what. Tenacity is harnessing—not avoiding—problems, addressing fundamental issues, and grappling with ambiguous situations.

13. In this organization we don't hide our ethical concerns.
14. We deal with ethical concerns until they are resolved, even when it requires having uncomfortable conversations.
15. We will delay a decision when there are unresolved ethical issues connected with that decision.
16. When our values clash with pressures to cut corners, we don't give up on our values.

Legacy is making ethical decisions in a spirit of stewardship and understanding the implications and the consequences of our behaviors and decisions for those who will follow, including fellow employees, patients, their families, and our own families. Legacy is acting in keeping with the long view, personally and organizationally, consistent with vision, mission, and values.

17. My actions and decisions are building a future here I will be proud of.
18. I am happy to recommend my organization to other people as a place to build a satisfying career.
19. Our vision and our values drive our decisions, both small and large.
20. Our organization will let go of valuable staff who don't respect our values rather than compromise values for greater efficiency or greater revenue.

The Ethical Pathway of Leadership Diagnostic

The ethical pathway of leadership diagnostic follows. Score the diagnostic as you go along.

Noble purpose is the calling of health care expressed in the vision, mission, and values of an organization and those who work in it, including its leaders.

1. Our leader strongly believes in the vision, mission, and values of our organization.
2. Our leader reminds us that we are here to increase the health and welfare of the communities we serve.
3. Our leader focuses us on the vision, mission, and values of our organization.
4. Our leader will do the right thing for our patients and their families, even if it hurts the organization financially.

Figure A-3. Ethical Pathway of Leadership Diagnostic Score Sheet

	Strongly Agree	Sometimes Agree	Strongly Disagree	Discipline Total	÷ Number of Questions	= Average Score
Noble Purpose						
Question 1	5	3	1			
Question 2	5	3	1			
Question 3	5	3	1			
Question 4	5	3	1			
Score					4	
Ceaseless Ambition						
Question 5	5	3	1			
Question 6	5	3	1			
Question 7	5	3	1			
Question 8	5	3	1			
Score					4	
Candor						
Question 9	5	3	1			
Question 10	5	3	1			
Question 11	5	3	1			
Question 12	5	3	1			
Score					4	
Passion						
Question 13	5	3	1			
Question 14	5	3	1			
Question 15	5	3	1			
Question 16	5	3	1			
Score					4	
		Total Score			16	

Ceaseless ambition is a leader's high and consistent level of ambition for performance, critical to stopping ethical erosion and evoke and leverage ethical wisdom.

5. Stretching us to take big positive steps in the way we do things is a major priority of our leader.
6. Our leader insists that we are innovative in our work.
7. Our leader trusts us to do the right thing when we try to improve how we work.
8. Our leader does not micro-manage us.

Candor is a leader's authenticity, self-awareness, humility, and self-mastery in all his or her dealings and in the uncompromising demand for the use of ethical pathways to produce results.

9. When our leader tells us how we are doing, good or bad, we can trust what he or she tells us.
10. Our leader's values are clear to us.
11. Our leader is trying to improve the way he or she leads.
12. Our leader is "rock solid" in acting consistent with our values.

Passion is a leader's infectious enthusiasm and commitment for the calling of health care and the vision, mission, and values of the organizations he or she leads.

13. Our leader shows enthusiasm for the work we do.
14. We get fired up by our leader's enthusiasm for what we do.
15. Our leader visits our work area.
16. When we suffer, our leader suffers.

The Ethical Pathway of Governance Diagnostic

The ethical pathway of governance diagnostic follows. Score the diagnostic as you go along.

Noble purpose is the calling of health care expressed in the vision, mission, and values of an organization and those who work in it, including its leaders.

1. The vision, mission, and values of the organization are always at the forefront of our thinking when the board makes decisions.
2. When stakeholders in the community ask me as a board member what are the organization's priorities, I tell them it is realizing our vision, mission, and values.
3. The board takes time to reflect on how its work is contributing to the vision, mission, and values of the organization.
4. We actively seek means and forums to speak about the noble purpose of our organization with stakeholders in the community.

Figure A-4. Ethical Pathway of Governance Diagnostic Score Sheet

	Strongly Agree	Sometimes Agree	Strongly Disagree	Discipline Total	÷ Number of Questions	= Average Score
Noble Purpose						
Question 1	5	3	1			
Question 2	5	3	1			
Question 3	5	3	1			
Question 4	5	3	1			
Score					4	
Independent Engagement						
Question 5	5	3	1			
Question 6	5	3	1			
Question 7	5	3	1			
Question 8	5	3	1			
Score					4	
Ethical Culture						
Question 9	5	3	1			
Question 10	5	3	1			
Question 11	5	3	1			
Question 12	5	3	1			
Score					4	
Ethical Succession						
Question 13	5	3	1			
Question 14	5	3	1			
Question 15	5	3	1			
Question 16	5	3	1			
Score					4	
		Total Score			16	

Independent engagement is the board setting its own priorities and agenda, becoming informed on the issues before it, and partnering with the CEO with its own point of view.

5. The board, not the CEO, sets board priorities.
6. We have regular educational sessions that help us understand current issues and trends impacting our organization, including ethical issues.
7. The board's exchanges with the CEO are conversations between equal partners in decision making.
8. The board has a firm grip on the ethical health of the organization.

Ethical culture is modeling by the board of the disciplines of an ethical culture.

9. I am sensitive to personal discomfort with a decision signaling something may be "off" ethically.
10. I can speak freely and directly about any concerns I have about our integrity as a board and as an organization.
11. The board encourages and respects different points of view on issues and decisions we face.
12. The board deals effectively with conflicts and disagreements among board members or with the CEO.

Ethical succession is the consistent inclusion of criteria for integrity in CEO and board succession planning.

13. The board's review of CEO and executive performance regarding ethical leadership is regular and rigorous.
14. A validated incident of unethical behavior results in the removal of a board or executive candidate from succession consideration.
15. The board uses a rigorous process to screen prospective executive candidates, which includes a thorough assessment of their track record as persons of integrity.
16. The board uses a rigorous process to screen prospective board members that includes a thorough assessment of their track record as persons of integrity.

The Ethical Pathway of Infrastructure Diagnostic

The ethical pathway of infrastructure diagnostic follows. Score the diagnostic as you go along.

Ethical engagement is a commitment to ethical pathways by means of structures and processes that strengthen and sustain the engagement of employees and evoke the commitment of their hearts and minds.

Figure A-5. Ethical Pathway of Infrastructure Diagnostic Score Sheet

	Strongly Agree	Sometimes Agree	Strongly Disagree	Discipline Total	÷ Number of Questions	= Average Score
Ethical Engagement						
Question 1	5	3	1			
Question 2	5	3	1			
Question 3	5	3	1			
Question 4	5	3	1			
Score					4	
Accountability						
Question 5	5	3	1			
Question 6	5	3	1			
Question 7	5	3	1			
Question 8	5	3	1			
Question 9	5	3	1			
Question 10	5	3	1			
Question 11	5	3	1			
Question 12	5	3	1			
Score					8	
Management by Facts						
Question 13	5	3	1			
Question 14	5	3	1			
Question 15	5	3	1			
Question 16	5	3	1			
Score					4	
		Total Score			16	

1. Our leaders engage employees' hearts and minds in building an ethical organization.
2. We celebrate our successes and have fun doing it.
3. I understand clearly how what I do in my job impacts the values and goals of the organization.
4. I know that senior leadership looks for ways to make it easier for us to do our jobs the right way.

Accountability builds on ethical engagement to create shared accountability for organizational and personal integrity in common management processes, such as hiring, performance appraisal and incentive structures, policies and procedures, and ethical decision making. Accountability breathes life into those processes to enable employees to be active contributors to the ethical health of the organization.

5. The vision, mission, and values of our organization are guiding lights for our actions.
6. Our policies and procedures help us do our jobs consistently in the right way.
7. We are very strict in making sure everyone adheres to our policies and procedures.
8. We assess the impact on our values of decisions we make.
9. We hire only those who are a good fit for our values.
10. New hires really understand how important it is to their future to live our values every day.
11. When the organization meets its goals, we can count on being rewarded.
12. If you do not demonstrate the organization's values, your performance appraisal will suffer.

Management by facts seeks to convert informal ideas of what constitutes ethical health into formal performance metrics that are actively tracked and, good, bad, or indifferent, are freely shared with employees and other stakeholders to prompt recognition and performance interventions.

13. Facts of the organization's performance, good or bad, are freely shared with employees.
14. We use regular sets of facts about performance beyond financial measures to celebrate our successes.
15. We use regular sets of facts about performance beyond financial measures to create action where needed to improve performance.
16. How we compare to other health care organizations in our performance beyond financial measures is shared freely with employees.

Ethical Pathway of Personal Integrity Diagnostic

The ethical pathway of personal integrity diagnostic follows. Score the diagnostic as you go along.

Figure A-6. Ethical Pathway of Personal Integrity Diagnostic Score Sheet

	Strongly Agree	Sometimes Agree	Strongly Disagree	Discipline Total	÷ Number of Questions	= Average Score
Personal Legacy						
Question 1	5	3	1			
Question 2	5	3	1			
Question 3	5	3	1			
Question 4	5	3	1			
Score					4	
Mindfulness						
Question 5	5	3	1			
Question 6	5	3	1			
Question 7	5	3	1			
Question 8	5	3	1			
Score					4	
Choice						
Question 9	5	3	1			
Question 10	5	3	1			
Question 11	5	3	1			
Question 12	5	3	1			
Score					4	
		Total Score			12	

Personal legacy is what we build for others during and after our lives through our work and our values. It is the highest expression of the goals mentioned in the definition of personal integrity.

1. I am clear about what I want my personal legacy to be.
2. I feel that if I do my part along with others, I am creating a better ethical future for those who follow.
3. I think about the example I will leave for others after I stop working.
4. I know that I am a role model for my co-workers.

Mindfulness is the private voice of ethical wisdom. It is the self-awareness that brings ethical dilemmas and issues to our awareness. It is a faint signal, such as a sense of calm or comfort with a decision, a gut reaction, discomfort, nagging doubt, or a feeling that something could be "off" with a decision or at odds with our goals and cherished values.

5. I think about whether I am expressing my personal values at work.
6. I reflect on ethical decisions to be sure they are consistent with my personal values.
7. I trust my instincts when a decision may be at odds with my personal values.
8. I am conscious of when my actions are driven by fear and when they are driven by ethical wisdom.

Choice is the freedom we exercise both in moment-by-moment decisions and in larger decisions about where we choose to work, the attitude we bring to work, whether we withhold or offer our discretionary effort, and what we choose to say and do that shapes our work environment.

9. I have the freedom to stand up for my personal values at work.
10. I choose to speak up about ethical concerns I have at work.
11. I know I have choices about where I work.
12. I regularly evaluate whether I am working in the best job and place for me.

Interpreting the Diagnostic

You can decide your own approach in interpreting the survey results, but consider the following questions and approaches in your interpretation.

Questions and Approaches to Interpretation

1. What is the total score average?
   Obviously, if the average score is 3 or below, it is a red flag. "Sometimes Agree" may be an acceptable average for some surveys; but in the case of an ethical pathway, any lack of consistency in living

values is an invitation to ethical erosion. In fact, any score is a basis for a conversation about how to improve. You may well see scores of 5 for individual questions; however, an average score of 5 is both an opportunity for acknowledgment and to explore whether this perfect ethical condition holds up under scrutiny.

2. On what one pathway would you focus for discussion and change?
   You can select a pathway on which to focus in at least three ways:
   - It can be the pathway with the lowest average score.
   - It can be the pathway with the most 1 scores.
   - It can be the pathway that, if paid attention to, you decide will produce the best opportunity for change (this may or may not be the lowest scoring pathway).

   Whatever pathway on which you choose to focus, do not be surprised if discussion about it and its disciplines leads to discussion about one or more other pathways and their disciplines. This is because the pathways and disciplines are related to each other.
3. On what discipline(s) would you focus for discussion and change?
   You may choose to focus on one discipline or a small number of disciplines from more than one pathway, or you may choose more than one discipline from within a single pathway.
   You can select a discipline on which to focus in at least three ways:
   - It can be the discipline with the lowest average score.
   - It can be the discipline with the most 1 scores.
   - It can be the discipline that, if paid attention to, you decide will produce the best opportunity for change (this may or may not be the lowest scoring discipline).

   Whatever the discipline on which you choose to focus, do not be surprised if discussion about it leads to discussion about one or more other disciplines. This is because the disciplines are related to each other.
4. To enrich a conversation about these results, you can choose the discipline with the best score and compare it to a weak-performing discipline. This comparison provides an opportunity to not only ask what is not working about a weak-performing pathway or discipline, but also to ask what we can learn from what we are doing right with a high-performing discipline.
5. Remember that this is a high-level diagnostic and, as such, should not be used to provide answers but to provoke focused questions and open discussion.

Thoughts for Each Discipline

To deepen understanding of the pathways and disciplines and of the implications of the responses, turn to the appropriate part in the book. The ethical pathway of culture is discussed in part II, leadership and governance in part III, infrastructure in part IV, and personal integrity in part V.

Approaches to Action

As a general principle, the results of this diagnostic should be shared and discussed with those who completed it, whether it was you and a few colleagues, a work team, a department, a discipline, or an organization. Obviously, the larger and the more diverse the group, the more the sharing and discussion need to be orchestrated and may need to include, for example, skilled and trusted facilitators from the training and development department. This facilitation support is also useful to relieve you of the burden of both leading and participating in a discussion. This support will allow you to participate freely in the discussion.

Appendix 2

Answer Key to "The Approaches to Ethical Decision Making Diagnostic" in Chapter 15

THE DIAGNOSTIC in chapter 15 is composed of 15 scenarios. Each scenario has 4 possible responses. This key will tell which approach you selected for each scenario. Use the score sheet (figure 15-1) to write your chosen response for each scenario (a, b, c, or, d). After doing this for all 15 scenarios, you will use the information here to find out what approach (principle, consequence, moral sentiment, or virtue/character) you selected so you can circle it on the score sheet.

The four approaches are coded as follows. Chapter 15 includes full descriptions of these approaches.

C = Consequence
MS = Moral sentiment
P = Principle
V/C = Virtue/character

Here are the responses for each scenario and the approach for that response. For example, if you selected response *b* for scenario 1, then you chose the consequence approach (C). If you selected response *d* for scenario 2, then you chose the virtue/character approach (V/C)

Scenario 1

a. MS
b. C
c. P
d. V/C

Scenario 2

a. C
b. MS
c. P
d. V/C

Scenario 3

a. V/C
b. P
c. MS
d. C

Scenario 4

a. C
b. P
c. MS
d. V/C

Scenario 5
a. P
b. MS
c. V/C
d. C

Scenario 6
a. P
b. MS
c. C
d. V/C

Scenario 7
a. C
b. P
c. V/C
d. MS

Scenario 8
a. V/C
b. MS
c. P
d. C

Scenario 9
a. C
b. P
c. V/C
d. MS

Scenario 10
a. MS
b. C
c. V/C
d. P

Scenario 11
a. MS
b. C
c. V/C
d. P

Scenario 12
a. P
b. V/C
c. C
d. MS

Scenario 13
a. V/C
b. P
c. C
d. MS

Scenario 14
a. P
b. MS
c. V/C
d. C

Scenario 15
a. MS
b. P
c. C
d. V/C

Index